Populist Authoritarianism

Populist Authoritarianism

Chinese Political Culture and Regime Sustainability

Wenfang Tang

University of Iowa

OXFORD
UNIVERSITY PRESS

OXFORD

UNIVERSITY PRESS

Oxford University Press is a department of the University of Oxford.
It furthers the University's objective of excellence in research, scholarship,
and education by publishing worldwide. Oxford is a registered trade mark
of Oxford University Press in the UK and in certain other countries

Published in the United States of America by
Oxford University Press
198 Madison Avenue, New York, NY 10016,
United States of America

Library of Congress Cataloging-in-Publication Data
Names: Tang, Wenfang, 1955– author.
Title: Populist authoritarianism : Chinese political culture and regime
sustainability / Wenfang Tang, University of Iowa.
Description: New York, NY : Oxford University Press, 2016. |
Includes bibliographical references and index.
Identifiers: LCCN 2015025430| ISBN 9780190205782 (hardcover : alk. paper) |
ISBN 9780190205799 (pbk. : alk. paper) | ISBN 9780190205805 (ebook)
Subjects: LCSH: Political culture—China. | Populism—China. |
Authoritarianism—China. | China—Politics and government.
Classification: LCC JQ1516 .T353 2016 | DDC 306.20951—dc23
LC record available at http://lccn.loc.gov/2015025430

1 3 5 7 9 8 6 4 2

Printed in Canada

To my parents

CONTENTS

The PA Model and the BA State   162
The PA Model and the Existing Studies of Mass Politics   163
The PA Model and the Study of Comparative Politics   165

ACKNOWLEDGMENTS

In 1986 I took a course with professor Tang Tsou on the Chinese Communist movement as a graduate student at the University of Chicago. I wrote a paper about the Mass Line ideology and forgot about it. At the time, I thought that China was moving away from the radical revolutionary policy and toward a modern, rational, and rule-based stable bureaucratic society. Nearly 30 years later, amid the tremendous changes on the surface in Chinese politics and society, I kept seeing the continuity from China's recent political past. I found my Mass Line paper and reread the literature, which formed the foundation of chapter 1. I want to thank the late professor Tang Tsou, whose broad vision and comprehensive understanding of the nature of Chinese politics encouraged me to study contemporary Chinese politics with a historical perspective.

In the process of writing this book, I benefited from the comments and suggestions of many people. John Kennedy, Jie Chen, and the two anonymous reviewers at Oxford University Press read the entire manuscript and made numerous suggestions and corrections. They also urged me to include much relevant literature that I missed in the early drafts.

I want to express my respect and condolence for my friend and college classmate Tianjian Shi, who passed away unexpectedly in 2009 and created an unfillable hole in the study of Chinese politics. Tianjian's interest in traditional Chinese culture and its role in contemporary Chinese politics inspired me to think about the role of the Chinese Communist Party's governance style in formulating China's political culture, together with Tianjian's study on traditional values and beliefs.

My colleagues in Taiwan strongly disagreed with me on my comparisons of political trust in China and Taiwan and prompted me to revise chapter 5 and add chapter 8 on survey reliability in China.

William Parish read chapter 5 on political trust in China and Taiwan and challenged my empirical findings. His comments made me strengthen the methodological discussion of the causal relationship between government responsiveness and regime support.

Melanie Manion and her students at the Comparative Politics Seminar at the University of Wisconsin at Madison read chapter 2 and grilled me on political support. Their comments made me go beyond the ad hoc findings and think about the theoretical significance of political trust.

Susan Shirk introduced me to the most recent literature on authoritarian politics. Her study on public opinion and foreign policy in China motivated me to write chapter 3 on the role of popular nationalism in domestic politics.

In writing chapter 6 on protest, I benefited from comments made by Mary Gallagher, Elizabeth Perry, and Steven Angle. They urged me to trace the origin of contentious politics beyond the Communist movement and in traditional Chinese cultural values and beliefs.

Professor Cai He and his colleagues at Sun Yat-Sen University challenged my findings in labor dispute. Their criticism made me realize the difference between perceived and real disputes.

Ronald Inglehart made generous comments on chapter 4 on interpersonal trust, even though the findings challenged his own work on democracy and civic culture.

My colleague William Reisinger at the University of Iowa read the first and last chapters. He cautioned me in applying the civic culture literature to China, provided me with additional literature on ethnosymbolism in chapter 1, and forced me to think about the relationship between the CCP's intra-party democracy and the concept of populist authoritarianism in chapter 9.

The graduate students in my Chinese Politics Seminar and the undergraduate students in my Honor's Comparative Politics Seminar at the University of Iowa read the manuscript and made helpful comments and suggestions. Sometimes their spontaneous and intuitive reaction to certain findings and conclusions provided refreshing perceptions that led me to look at the subject matters differently.

The East Asian Institute at the National University of Singapore granted me a visiting position in the summers of 2013 and 2014. These visits provided me with the time and the ideal intellectual environment in which to complete the manuscript. I presented the findings on protest (chapter 6), labor dispute resolution (chapter 7), and survey reliability (chapter 8) and received very helpful comments from my colleagues at the East Asian Institute, particularly from Drs. Zheng Yongnian, Sarah Tong, and Qian Jiwei.

I wish also to thank the following individuals and organizations for their generosity in sharing the data and supporting my own effort at collecting data for this book. Professor Cai He and Sun Yat-Sen University's Center for Social Survey shared the 2012 China Labor Dynamic Survey.

Professor Robert Harmel and the China Archive at Texas A&M University made available the 2008 China Survey. Professor Yun-han Zhu and the Academic Sinica in Taiwan granted me permission to use the Asian Barometer Survey II. Professor Wang Weidong and the National Survey Research Center at Renmin University generously shared the data from the Chinese General Social Surveys.

The Chiang Ching-Kuo Foundation, the Stanley Hua Hsia Endowment, and the University of Iowa provided me with generous financial support to cover the 6th Wave World Values Survey China from 2012 to 2013. The Institute of Public Policy at the South China University of Technology provided a grant that allowed me to conduct four telephone surveys on public policy satisfaction from 2013 to 2015.

David McBride, the Editor-in-Chief in Social Sciences at Oxford University Press was patient and supportive during the review process of the manuscript. His comments made me rewrite the opening paragraphs of chapter 1 in order to capture the readers' attention by highlighting the theoretical framework and the key empirical findings.

Finally, I wish to express my deep appreciation for the Stanley Hua Hsia Endowment for allowing me to take many research trips, to hire graduate research assistants, and to receive a reduced teaching load that provided me with much needed time to write.

CHAPTER 1

Chinese Political Culture
and Regime Sustainability

In 2013, the residents of a community in the city of Xiamen protested and demanded additional compensation from a land transfer legal agreement that was signed 24 years prior between the community and a golf club owned by overseas investors. The protesters released their anger against local authorities by injuring several police. They also decided to publicly humiliate a female district government official by stripping her topless and making her stand on her knees and apologize to the public for not serving their needs. As a result, the district government allegedly agreed to build new roads and bridges, as well as a garbage processing center for the community. None of the protesters was arrested.[1]

Such a scene is almost a daily occurrence in today's China, leading many observers to believe that such events indicate the increasing possibility of democratization and the declining popularity of the Chinese authoritarian government. These observers seem to forget another, equally well-known fact in the post-Mao Chinese political life—the strong public support for the Communist Party by the majority of people in all walks of Chinese society. Why and how these two seemingly contradictory trends coexist and interact with each other in contemporary Chinese politics require further theoretical and empirical analysis.

The event in Xiamen exemplifies several important features that are characteristic of Chinese political life. It shows a regime operating in the ideological tradition of Mass Line that directly connects the state with the public, often bypassing administrative regulations and the legal procedure, resulting in weak institutions and civic organizations. The state often encourages the public to participate in local politics in an effort to correct unpopular policies and purge incompetent officials. Consequently, the mass public demonstrates a high level of political activism and is eager to confront local authorities and engage in contentious political behavior. Such high-risk behavior, which may be subject to local government retribution, is reinforced by a high degree of interpersonal trust, which is a product of community solidarity nourished under socialist central planning. In an authoritarian political system where competitive elections are missing, the government struggles to maintain its political legitimacy by responding to public demand more quickly than in an electoral cycle. All of these phenomena explain the high degree of regime support at the Center.

In the remaining chapters, I develop a preliminary theory of populist authoritarianism, which includes the following elements: the Mass Line ideology, strong interpersonal trust and rich social capital, individual political activism and political contention, weak political institutions and an underdeveloped civic society, an often paranoid and highly responsive government, and strong regime support. While such a theory of Chinese political culture can explain how and why the seemingly conflicting components are holding together for the time being, it cautions that such a process is highly unstable due to the lack of institutional guarantee.

This chapter discusses the historical and institutional context of the evolving Chinese political culture. Any discussion of "Chinese culture" can easily go back to the dynastic history. The focus of this chapter, however, is the political culture that was formed during the Chinese Communist movement in the early 20th century and continued to evolve after the Chinese Communist Party (CCP) seized political power in 1949.

WHY DOES POLITICAL CULTURE MATTER?

The concept of culture can be defined as social and psychological orientations. It is a "data container" including symbols, ideas, beliefs, norms, customs, knowledge, values, and attitudes (Sabetti 2007). Almond and Verba defined political culture as "the psychological or subjective orientations toward politics" (Almond and Verba 1963). Before examining political culture in China, it is necessary to establish political culture as a worthy subject for research. Political culture needs to assert itself against at least three sources of competition: institutionalism, rationalism, and ethnosymbolism. First, institutionalism believes that political institutions, not individual attitudes and values, determine political outcome (Jackman 1987; Jackman and Miller 1996a, 1996b; Tsebelis 2002; Rhodes, Binder, and Rockman 2008). While an institutional environment sets important parameters and constraints for individual behavior, political actors' personal beliefs still lead to different outcomes. It is not difficult to find examples of different political leaders occupying the same institutional post but producing different policy outcomes.

Second, rationalism downplays the importance of individual beliefs, feelings, and emotions. It argues that people make political decisions based on information gathering and the calculation of benefit and cost (Rowgoski 1976; Ferejohn and Kuklinski 1990; Popkin 1991; Sniderman, Brody, and Tetlock 1991; Page and Shapiro 1992; Lupia, McCubbins, and Popkin 2000). The study of political culture shares two things in common with rationalism. First, both stress the importance of individual political actors, their motivation, and their behavior. Second, both believe that individual motivation and behavior can be measured objectively, either through surveys, focus group studies, or lab experiments.

One problem for the rationalist view is its assumption that people can process information and take actions that lead to the optimal ratio between cost and benefit. Yet some studies show that people are not really capable of making objective decisions by using newly gathered information. Instead, new information is selectively used to reinforce people's preconceived beliefs (Taber, Lodge, and Glatha 2001; Lodge and Taber 2005). Further, voters who are given all the necessary information may make worse decisions than those who don't have the information but use their intuition instead (Lau and Redlawsk 2006). There is simply too much information, and it is too complicated to process.

A number of rational choice scholars have recognized this problem of information flooding. They introduced the idea of "bounded rationality" in which people take shortcuts to make "low-information" decisions (Elster 1983; Simon 1991; Popkin 1991). They seem to think that people are rational as long as they make self-satisfying decisions based on stereotypes, political ideology, consensus, and so on. By emphasizing the importance of these subjective orientations, however, these rationalist scholars are also suggesting the necessity of studying political culture.

The third challenge to the study of political culture using public opinion survey data comes from ethnosymbolism. Ethnosymbolism is best articulated by Clifford Geertz in his anthropological study of cultures (Geertz 1973) and is also advocated by some political scientists (Eckstein 1988; Laitin and Wildavsky 1988). At the core of ethnosymbolism is the assertion that cultures are represented by their symbols, such as languages, religions, rituals, and historical narratives. Understanding these symbols through participant observation and ethnography is crucial in studying how culture influences political outcome (Laitin and Wildavsky 1988). Ethnosymbolists are highly suspicious that subjective cultural orientations can be detected by public opinion survey questions. For them, the same concept or action can mean different things in different cultural contexts (Geertz 1973). For example, a survey question about interpersonal trust cannot detect the meaning of trust in different cultures, which can vary from trusting family members, community members, to strangers. Neither do the ethnosymbolists think countries can or should be compared based on survey questions (Eckstein 1988). For them, comparing the percentages of people who trust other people in different societies simply misses the variation in interpersonal trust between different subcultures within a country.

While ethnosymbolism makes important contributions in showing that subjective cultural orientations are linked to political actions and in expressing its well-founded concerns about the accuracy of survey data, relying exclusively on the ethnosymbolist notion is likely to run into several problems. First, cultural symbols can be overly interpreted, and universal human experiences are often overlooked. In the Chinese context, for example, the concepts of *guanxi* (relationship or personal network) and *mianzi* (saving face or pride) have been described as cultural symbols that carry particular importance in Chinese culture (Yang 1994; Mann 2000). Yet it wouldn't be an exaggeration to say that the necessity of personal networks and the need to satisfy one's pride can be found in any society, not only in China. Dwelling on such cultural symbols like *guanxi* and *mianzi* makes China seem unique and difficult to compare with other societies, while the meanings of these symbols are universal and can be easily compared across countries.

Further, relying on cultural stereotypes can blind the researcher from recognizing the diversity and the changing reality in a society. For example, the concept of *guanxi* may no longer capture the reality in China when more formal rules are developed during rapid economic growth.

Another problem with the overemphasis on cultural symbols is to overlook the outcome. Sometimes people in different cultures do different things or use different symbols to achieve the same outcome. For example, people show their agreement by shaking their heads in India, and nodding in China. Focusing on the difference in this case is a waste of time if one's research interest is whether people agree or disagree, regardless of whether they do so by nodding or shaking their heads.

Finally, while the ethnosymbolists' early criticism of survey research methodology is valid, such methodology has made tremendous progress since the 1970s. Survey researchers are capable of drawing more representative national samples in a large number of countries, which makes it possible not only to compare countries but also to examine the variation between subgroups within a country. In addition, survey researchers have developed more detailed measures of concepts than before. For example, they now ask people not only whether they trust each other but also the specific type of people they trust, such as their family, community, or strangers. Further, the same surveys have been repeated over time, allowing the researchers to approach their topics from a historical perspective as well as at a cross-section of time. Finally, survey researchers have made exciting progress in tackling the difficult problems of respondent truthfulness and establishing causal links between survey questions by embedding experiments in representative surveys. In short, even though the survey method still has many problems, it has the undeniable advantage of drawing conclusions based on representative samples that enjoy a level of generalizability superior to the ethnographic method that relies on in-depth case studies.

Following the tradition of political socialization and psychology (Almond and Verba 1963; Dahl 1966; Almond 1989, 1990; Lane 1992; Jennings 2007; Shi 2015), this study takes a behaviorist approach and holds that beliefs, feelings, and values play important roles in shaping political behavior and political outcomes. These beliefs, feelings, and values are the results of political socialization, as well as social and economic changes in a society. A particular political culture is a specific configuration of these beliefs, feelings, and values.

Political culture can be concretely defined and measured by a set or "rubric" (Reisinger 1995) of concepts that should be able to travel across country borders. These concepts include one's identity to the country and/or to one's own community, the level of confidence in political institutions, the relative importance between individual interest and group interests, respect for authority and the law, relationships with other people (trust and tolerance), belief in the modes and consequences of conflict resolution and political participation, and so on. These concepts are widely measured in the cross-country public opinion surveys such as the World Values Surveys (WVSs), the surveys conducted by the International Social Science Programme, and the Chinese public opinion surveys used in this book (more on those later).

MASS LINE: THE ORIGIN OF THE POPULIST AUTHORITARIAN POLITICAL CULTURE

Contemporary Chinese political culture is shaped by the theory of the Mass Line. The term "Mass Line" (*qunzhong luxian*) was first used by Li Lisan, a Communist Party leader, in a speech in 1928 (Han and Ji 2013). It served as a powerful theoretical and organizational principle for political mobilization by the CCP during the Communist movement in the first half of the 20th century. The theory of the Mass Line was most clearly articulated by Mao in 1943. In the article "Some Questions Concerning Methods of Leadership," Mao writes:

In all the practical work of our Party, all correct leadership is necessarily "from the masses, to the masses." This means: take the ideas of the masses (scattered and unsystematic ideas) and concentrate them (through study turn them into concentrated and systematic ideas), then go to the masses and propagate and explain these ideas until the masses embrace them as their own, hold fast to them and translate them into action, and test the correctness of such ideas in action. (Mao 1967, 119)

The key phrase in Mao's statement is "from the masses, to the masses" which assumes a close and direct relationship between the Party and the masses, or between political power and society (Tsou 1986, 290). This direct relationship requires both accessible elites and available non-elites if it is to exhibit a high rate of mass behavior and elite–mass interaction.

The Mass Line bears certain similarities to the mass society described by Kornhauser in his study of social movement and state-building in the West. In a mass society, according to Kornhauser, elites are accessible and non-elites are available in that there is a lack of independent groups between the state and the family. In the absence of social autonomy at all levels of society, large numbers of people are pushed and pulled toward activist modes of intervention in vital centers of society; and mass-oriented leaders have the opportunity to mobilize this activism for the capture of power (Kornhauser 1959, 41).

In China, the Communist Party weakened and even destroyed the traditional intermediate groups such as the rural gentry class and landowners, and it relied on the Mass Line as a method of political mobilization to win over the popular support by the peasantry and eventually defeated the Nationalist government in 1949.

The CCP's populist orientation continued after 1949. It was so effective for the CCP to gain political power that it continued to rely on the Mass Line in state-building, government policy making, economic development, and social restructuring. From 1949 to 1976, Mao and his followers in the CCP launched a series of political campaigns in order to consolidate the communist regime and promote social and economic development. One such campaign was the People's Commune Movement, launched in 1958, in which agricultural production was collectivized and rural communities played important roles in social, economic, and political life, partially replacing the role of the traditional family. Another important campaign was the Great Leap Forward Movement in 1958. Mao and other radical leaders of the CCP believed that the Mass Line could be used to promote China's industrial development by mobilizing the public enthusiasm rather than relying on the educated elites.

The most extreme mass political campaign in the early years of the post-1949 Communist regime was the Great Proletariat Culture Revolution, which lasted from 1966 until Mao's death in 1976. The Cultural Revolution was a massive social and political movement. Mao and his followers bypassed and destroyed the intermediate bureaucratic institutions and professional organizations and attempted to reach and mobilize the very bottom of Chinese society in order to achieve economic growth and social and political egalitarianism.

Some observers see the totalitarian nature of the Mass Line. For example, Graham Young argues that Party leadership is central in the conception of the Mass Line, in which the Party must provide the policy guidance at all levels and over all areas of activity of state and society, and the Party's policy can be effected only through Party leadership (Young 1980). In his study of the Communist movement in eastern and central China from 1937 to 1945, Y. Chen (1986) contends that the Mass Line is merely the Party's "techniques of controlled polarization" between the peasant and landlord classes. By drawing a sharp line and by intensifying the tension between the two classes, the CCP was able to mobilize the peasant class and successfully destroy its potential rivalry—the traditional rural elites, and eventually rely on the support of the rural masses in defeating the Nationalist Party in the civil war. In short, the essence of the Mass Line is a relationship between the CCP as the manipulator and the masses as the manipulated.

Other scholars, however, see the empowerment of society under the Mass Line. For example, Meisner (1978) observed that under the socialist economic system, the Mass Line is ideally accompanied by the formation of more and more self-governing communities of producers. Politically, these "associations of producers" are capable of standing up against bureaucratic or political hierarchies, while at the same time recognizing their own interests that also tend to enhance the overall development of the society. Effective adaptation of the Mass Line may require political activism within grass-roots communities, which enhances solidarity, enthusiasm, and broadened awareness of social goals. It can also mobilize and strengthen community power in relation to higher political or bureaucratic authorities (Meisner 1978). Therefore, it is at the community level where the democratic nature of the Mass Line is realized.

Others describe the Mass Line as a democratic decision-making process (Blecher 1979). In the spirit of the Mass Line, statements on policy put forward by local leaders would not be regarded as final decisions or firm directives but as provisional formulations which the masses would be able to discuss, clarify, modify, or reject. Moreover, the masses could also influence the policy by their decisions about specification or implementation. A process of this sort could be described as the politics of consensus in which formal voting would be unnecessary (Blecher 1979, 109).

According to Blecher, the existence of this process of consensus politics can be proven by the facts that policy directives are generally clearer about the goals than the concrete forms; that new policies undergo considerable testing before promulgation; the frequency of "summing-up," "consolidation," and "rectification" campaigns at the mass level; and the frequent shifts of direction and emphasis in Chinese policy. These facts are all consistent with the Mass Line view that policy decisions are always somewhat provisional, subject to revision according to the masses' objections, suggestions, and interpretation (Blecher 1979, 108–109). Therefore, under the Mass Line, mass participation and influence are extensive and substantive. Angle compares democratic centralism—the guiding principle of the Mass Line, with Rawls' "decent society" (Rawls 1999, 64–66), in which people are rational, responsible, cooperative participants of social and political life (Angle 2005, 521).

While the Mass Line seems to resemble a democratic style of leadership, it is fundamentally different from liberal democracy. Liberal democracy consists of an elaborate set of institutions and game rules to implement the principle of "consent of the governed" and to compel rulers to take into account the interests, wants, preferences, and aspirations of the citizens more fully than under other forms of government (Tsou 1986, 271–272). On the other hand, the Mass Line is different from totalitarianism. Totalitarianism focuses on the total control of society by the state, while the Mass Line can be described as "totalist politics" which is built on the full-scale interaction between the state and society (Tsou 1986).

Another key difference between a mass society and a civil society is the role of social organizations. In a civil society, these organizations enjoy autonomy and the freedom from state control. In a mass society like China, social organizations such as trade unions, political parties, professional associations, and NGOs are co-opted under the same principle of democratic centralism (Salmenkari 2010).

Regardless the debate about whether the Mass Line embodies democratic or totalitarian nature of governance, it is undeniable that it profoundly shaped the political culture in contemporary Chinese society. Inherent in the Mass Line ideology are its three key components: (1) a direct link between the state and society with minimum interference of intermediate organizations and institutions, (2) a thorough mobilization of the masses in political participation, and (3) an implicit concept of social contract in which the elites serve the interest of the masses who in return grant political support for the state.[2] As is shown later in this chapter, the Mass Line continues to serve as a linkage between the state and society in the post-Mao Chinese political culture and a powerful instrument for political mobilization and regime legitimacy.

PRIMITIVE ACCUMULATION OF SOCIAL CAPITAL IN CHINA

While the Mass Line provided the political capital for the CCP's rule, the radical social and economic transformation in the early years of the socialist regime produced the social capital that became an important part of the Chinese political culture.

Marx (1867) used to describe the early stage of capitalism as a process of primitive accumulation of capital in which the capitalists acquired the means of production by force, such as the enclosure of land by capitalists in England. This process laid the foundation for the later development of the capitalist economic system. To use a similar metaphor, one can see the early stage of the communist regime in China as a process of the primitive accumulation of social capital which in turn laid the foundation for its political rule. After the Communists defeated the Nationalists in 1949, the new regime attempted to establish an egalitarian society under the dictatorship of the CCP. In their pioneer studies based on interviews with Chinese immigrants in the 1970s, William Parish and Martin Whyte detail the CCP's effort to build such an egalitarian society in rural and urban China. According to their studies (Parish and Whyte 1978; Whyte and Parish 1984), this equalitarianism is represented by public ownership of land, reduction of the role of the family, and the promotion of social equality.

The CCP first abolished private ownership of land, and collectivized both agricultural and industrial productions, in the 1950s. During the radical years of the Cultural Revolution in the 1960s and 1970s, the traditional role of family as the basic economic unit was weakened by the expansion of social services, such as public education, employment security, public health care, and pension programs. Social services drastically reduced parental influence and promoted equal access to education and employment, and greater equality in household income distribution. Although some traditional practices in gender discrimination persisted, the expansion of social services further promoted gender equality in education, female labor force participation, reduced fertility rates, improved health care, increased income, and a higher social and economic status among women.

The collectivization of land ownership, the weakened role of family, and the spread of social equality also changed the traditional way of social interaction. Family-centered social and economic life was replaced by rural farming communities based on collective land ownership, and urban residential communities based on the work unit. Although with considerable urban–rural gap and great regional variation, these new communities attempted to provide their members and their families with cradle-to-grave services, including guaranteed employment and income, child care, pension, health care, housing, rationed consumer goods, pension, and so on. Work unit-based housing and job security made these communities close-knit and stable. Public ownership and social equality further encouraged community sharing among their members. As a result, residents often developed strong identity and solidarity with their communities. Such a system of collective ownership had serious problems, such as economic inefficiency due to the lack of market incentives both at the group and individual levels. Yet it fundamentally changed the interpersonal relationship in Chinese society (see Parish and Whyte 1978; Whyte and Parish 1984; Womack 1991).

For many traditionally privileged social elites, such an egalitarian society was a pure nightmare. These social elites were downgraded to ordinary manual workers while those at the bottom of the social hierarchy were promoted to managerial and administrative positions. The talented students could not fulfill their potential by getting into schools through competitive exams because these schools had to provide room for those who would not have had the opportunity to receive formal education under the old system. The new system was sustained by political terror. Anyone who dared to oppose it was criticized, put in jail, and even tortured and beaten to death.

Yet this new system was a mass society in which the ordinary citizens were directly mobilized by and accessible to the leadership, as discussed in the previous section (Kornhauser 1959). The rank-and-file peasants and workers had the opportunity to participate in the destruction of the upper echelon, who would otherwise have enjoyed their privileges for the rest of their lives. Such unprecedented political participation by those at the bottom, though often extremely destructive and violent, nevertheless provided a sense of political efficacy among the poor. Further, the CCP seized political power in China under the slogan of national independence from the influence of Western powers. Hence a strong appeal of nationalism further strengthened the CCP's popularity among the Chinese people.

POLITICAL CULTURE IN POST-MAO CHINA

In the post-Mao era since the late 1970s, China experienced significant social and economic transformation. Economic planning was replaced by market competition, rural People's Communes were abolished, job security was replaced by performance-based labor contract, work units were stripped off many social functions, urban housing was privatized, meritocratic school entrance exams were restored, parental influence returned, and income inequality widened.

While many people focus on the explosive growth and transformation in post-Mao China, it is also important to point out some features of continuity. It is true that the CCP itself has gone through important organizational and personnel changes since the late 1970s, yet its political monopoly has persisted. It is still the only legitimate ruling party and it does not allow electoral challenges from other political forces. It still upholds Marxism–Leninism as its official ideology. It still uses nationalism to mobilize political support. Mao, whom many consider a tyrant and dictator, is still officially defined as a great leader whose tenure consisted of 70% contribution and only 30% mistake. While the CCP tightly controls the media and suppresses any political dissidents, it continues its tradition of populist authoritarianism by encouraging within-system direct popular political participation by using new technologies such as the online chat room dialogues between government officials and ordinary citizens.

While it is true that China has experienced four leadership changes since Mao Zedong (Hu Yaobang/Zhao Ziyang in the 1980s, Jiang Zemin in the 1990s, Hu Jintao in the 2000s, and Xi Jinping since 2012), and some describe the current leadership as the fifth generation (Li 2007), a closer look at the current leadership reveals that many of them are the sons and daughters of China's first-generation leaders. These new leaders completed their political socialization in the socialist era (1950s–1970s) before the post-Mao economic reforms in the 1980s, and they were strongly influenced by China's revolutionary tradition. In this sense, the current Chinese leaders are only the second generation.

One example of the political continuity in the post-Mao era is the renewal of the Mass Line. As mentioned previously, the Mass Line was widely adopted as an organizational principle and a tool for political mobilization before the CCP took power in 1949. It emphasizes the direct linkage between the CCP and the public with the slogan "from the mass, to the masses." It continued its popularity during the Cultural Revolution in the 1960s and 1970s when Mao relied on the same policy and mobilized the masses to overthrow the bureaucratic establishment. The post-Mao leaders all experienced their political socialization in this populist authoritarian political tradition and decided to devote an entire website to carry on the Mass Line after the 18th Party Congress in 2012 (*qunzhong luxian wang*).[3] One of the featured stories on the website was the CCP Secretary General Xi Jinping's two visits to Lankao County in Henan in 2014, where Jiao Yulu, a model party official, worked in the 1960s and was known for his populist work style.[4] Xi Jinping urged the Communist Party to continue to carry on the Mass Line because it is the "family treasure" (*chuan jia bao*) and the lifeline of the CCP (Xi 2014, 27).

Large-scale mass political campaigns also continued in the post-Mao era, including the national campaigns against prostitution and corruption (see chapter 9). Even though the leaders launched these campaigns in the name of "the rule of law," these campaigns represent a clear Mass Line style; they are large in scale with mass participation and swift punishment. Many victims were "presumed guilty" without proper trials (Jacobs and Buckley 2014). Even though the post-Mao leaders expressed their desire to strengthen the rule of law, they often referred to such policy as resembling the Confucian idea of group interest taking over individual rights (Buckley 2014).

Finally, China's demographic characteristics further suggest political continuity. As many as 52% of the population in the beginning of the 21st century were born in or before 1970,[5] who still had memories of the pre-reform egalitarian collective lifestyle (Bryant 2005). One only needs to visit one of the crowded Beijing restaurants featuring live performance of the Cultural Revolution songs and dances to see the nostalgia for some aspects of the revolutionary zeal from that era. These features of continuity will inevitably leave their mark in the political culture of today's China, mixed with the many recent changes.

THE PLAN OF THE BOOK

The remaining chapters of this book discuss several aspects of the Chinese political culture, including political support, national identity, interpersonal trust, political support in democratic and authoritarian societies, contentious politics, and labor dispute resolution.

Political Support: Local vs. Center

For a political culture to work smoothly with the political system, one of the most important elements of such political culture is political support. As discussed in chapter 2, when political support is measured by confidence in the key political institutions, such support in China was the highest among the selected countries in the 2005–2007 WVS. One common explanation of this strong political support is the Chinese government's successful performance in promoting economic growth and people's life satisfaction (Norris 2011). Yet public dissatisfaction with various issues in everyday life has grown steadily over the past two decades, in some cases reaching and in other cases surpassing the levels of public dissatisfaction that triggered massive urban protests in 1989. The answer to the seemingly contradictory trends of strong political support and high levels of life dissatisfaction may lie in the different levels of government. While people showed strong support of national government and political institutions, they may express much less satisfaction with the performance of lower levels governments, and such dissatisfaction may significantly increase people's collective political action, particularly against county-level governments.

Regime Stability and National Identity

While the number of collective political actions against the local governments may have increased rapidly in recent years, these actions are most likely ad hoc activities focusing on specific issues such as pay delays and disputes over real estate property development. Participants in these activities may not demand systematic changes in the political monopoly of the CCP. What the CCP is concerned about is the dissatisfaction with the central government. Such dissatisfaction, though relatively low at the moment, may be significantly related to people's desire to challenge the CCP's power monopoly and for their support for multi-party political competition. One tactic by the CCP to channel away people's attention to challenging its political monopoly is by mobilizing political support through nationalism. Chapter 3 compares national pride between Chinese survey respondents and the selected countries and analyzes how nationalism affects the demand for democratic change against the central government.

Social Capital

In addition to maintaining political support and national identity, the CCP also needs to utilize the social capital that it accumulated during the earlier years for social solidarity and political support. Chapter 4 compares social capital measured by interpersonal trust between China and other countries in different public opinion surveys. The chapter further dissects the meaning of interpersonal trust by using additional survey questions about the respondents' trust of 13 different groups of people and analyzes three types of interpersonal trust in China: family-based parochial trust, community-based trust, and societal trust (civic trust). Finally, the chapter examines how these three types of interpersonal trusts are related to regime support, national pride, and law-abiding behavior. The goal of the chapter is to find whether community-based social interaction that was created during the early years of socialism is still alive and functioning in promoting regime stability in the reform era.

Political Trust in China and Taiwan

Chapter 5 compares political trust in autocratic China and democratic Taiwan. The two societies share a similar cultural and political tradition but very different recent political experiences. Any difference between the two societies in political trust is likely the consequence of the different political systems, rather than cultural tradition (most similar systems design). The chapter compares political trust between China and Taiwan, which will be measured by institutional trust, national identity, leadership trust, and support for the political system. The chapter explores several competing theories of regime trust, including political mobilization, economic benefit, Confucian values, and political efficacy.

Protest and Regime Sustainability

Chapter 6 continues to tackle the seemingly contradictory trends of strong regime support and the growing public protests discussed in chapter 2. Through both case studies of several high-profile protests and analyzing large-N survey data, the chapter looks at how widespread public protests are and the specific targets of such protests, such as local versus central governments, economic and other social organizations, and the specific government officials and government policies. The goal of the chapter is to examine whether protests are purposefully used by the regime to promote regime support while allowing public anger to be released at the local level and on specific policies rather than on regime-challenging reforms.

Labor Dispute Resolution

Chapter 7 continues the discussion of contentious politics from chapter 6 but with a focus on the workplace. With more detailed survey data than in chapter 6, chapter 7 further examines the frequency and type of labor disputes. It compares what types of disputes are more likely to be resolved than others and the problem-solving rates among different types of economic organizations such as private and state-owned firms. Another focus of the chapter is to compare the effectiveness of different channels of problem solving. Specifically, it compares the effectiveness of institutional channels and non-institutional channels. The chapter tries to prove the hypothesis that non-institutional channels play a dominant role in problem solving if the Mass Line-based populist authoritarian political culture is still in action.

Political Trust: An Experimental Study

Chapter 8 revisits one of the key findings in this book, namely, political trust. In chapters 2 and 5, Chinese survey respondents consistently show a surprisingly high level of political trust in the central government and the CCP. Such findings have been frequently challenged by people who do not believe that it is even possible to conduct public opinion surveys in an autocratic state like China. With data drawn from carefully designed survey experiments, chapter 8 tests three hypotheses: (1) political fear is expected to play a minimum role in reducing political trust among Chinese survey respondents due to the recent loosening of the overall political environment, (2) these respondents, however, are expected to hide the truth if they sense that the answers are related to the socially undesirable behaviors, such as bribery and not returning money found on the street, and (3) people who are more integrated into the political system are more likely to hide their political distrust of the government, while the less integrated are more likely to be involved and hide their socially undesirable behavior.

Populist Authoritarianism: A Theoretical Discussion

In an inductive process, this book ends with a theoretical discussion of the concept of populist authoritarianism in chapter 9, including its necessary components and how they are related to each other. It discusses how such political culture interplays with governance and regime sustainability. The goal of the chapter is to develop a theoretical framework that can be used to explain other authoritarian regimes that carry similar populist traits.

USING SURVEY DATA TO STUDY POLITICAL CHANGE IN CHINA

Until the mid-1980s, studying political change in China was like writing a mystery novel about the Byzantine elite's political maneuvering behind the

Bamboo Curtain. Researchers were trained to read between the lines of the Communist Party newspaper *The People's Daily* and discern any subtle hints of possible policy change, and to scrutinize official photos of leader appearances to figure out the elite lineup in the power hierarchy and any potential personnel change. Field research was almost unheard of. Today, while elite politics remains an indispensable component in the study of Chinese political change, more and more researchers focus on individual attitudes, values, and behavior by using first-hand information collected in field research. The wide use of public opinion survey in the study of American politics has further inspired a new generation of American trained scholars to apply such methods to the study of Chinese politics.

The rise of the public opinion survey is also a close reflection of China's own political and economic change. For example, systematic information collection based on opinion surveys became an important part of decision-making when the post-Mao pragmatic and technocratic leaders came into power in the 1980s. The globalization of the Chinese economy promoted further international exchange, which created ample opportunities for foreign scholars to conduct public opinion surveys in China, and finally the implementation of competitive village elections in China led to a new wave of public opinion surveys which have traditionally been the principal method of electoral studies among political scientists in the West.

This study uses data from several Chinese national public opinion surveys based on representative samples, including the 2013–2014 Chinese Urban Surveys, the 2012 WVS China, the 2012 Chinese Labor Dynamics Survey, the 2010 Chinese General Social Survey, the 2008 China Survey, the 2008 Asian Barometer China, and the 2004 Institutionalization of Legal Reform Survey.

The Chinese data from the aforementioned surveys are compared with data from several cross-national surveys, including the 2005–2007 WVS conducted by the University of Michigan (http://www.worldvaluessurvey.org/, accessed 5/5/2013), the 2003 National Identity Survey conducted by International Social Survey Programme (ISSP, http://www.issp.org/, checked 5/5/2013), and the 2006 Asian Barometer Taiwan. These cross-national surveys put China in a comparative perspective. Cross-country comparisons are necessary because they allow researchers to examine the differences in individual political attitudes and values created by different political systems, while controlling for economic and cultural factors (most similar systems design). Alternatively, cross-country comparisons allow researchers to eliminate the effect of different political systems if these systems generate similar attitudes and values (most different systems design).

While cross-cultural surveys can provide insight in comparing the reasons and sources of political phenomenon within a country, they sometimes run into the typical problem of conceptual travel (Peters 1998). That is, the same concept may carry different meanings in different societies (Heath, Fisher, and Smith 2005). One example is the concept of democracy. While such a concept means individual rights and electoral competition in liberal democratic societies, it means guardianship or the responsibility of the state in taking care of its citizens in a Confucian society like China (Shi 2015; Lu and Shi 2015). This book tries to avoid this problem by not relying on support for democracy as a measure of regime legitimacy. Instead, public confidence in their respective political institutions is a more reliable measure of regime legitimacy and political support in different societies, regardless of whether they are liberal democracies or autocracies. When the term "democracy" is used in this book, it mostly likely means liberal democracy defined as individual rights, competitive elections, freedom of speech, rule of law, and so on.

In addition to cross-country comparisons, this book also compares the recent Chinese survey data with the data from eight Chinese urban surveys conducted by the Economic System Reform Institute of China from 1987 to 1992 (Tang and Parish 2000) and the 1999 Six-City Survey (Tang 2005). These earlier surveys provide a rare historical dimension for the examination of the change of Chinese public opinion over 25 years of rapid social and economic transformation. Appendix 1.1 provides further details of these surveys.

One problem with Chinese survey data is reliability. In an authoritarian country where the state closely monitors public opinion and mass political behavior, it is often doubtful that survey respondents would tell the truth. Many researchers have addressed this problem (Manion 1994; J. Chen 2004; Tang 2005; Wang 2006; Ren 2009; Shi 2009; J. Chen 2010). The general consensus among these authors is that the effect of political fear is weak due to the non-sensitive nature of most survey questions and the increasingly open political environment in China. Though they found the effect of social desirability among Chinese survey respondents, such an effect is also a problem in Western surveys where respondents attempt to find politically correct answers to controversial social issues (Ren 2009).

A simple but effective way to test the influence of political fear in China is to compare the answers to politically sensitive questions in China with those in other countries. The 2008 China Survey adopted a question from the 2003 ISSP Survey on National Identity: Would you support your government even if it is in the wrong? One would certainly expect a higher percentage of Chinese respondents giving affirmative answers due to political fear in one of the most authoritarian countries in the world.

Among the 35 countries and regions in the 2003 ISSP survey, an average of 48% would support their governments even if the governments were wrong. Somewhat surprisingly, only 46% of Chinese respondents in the 2008 China Survey would support the wrong government, not very different from the 35-country average. If political fear were present, one would certainly expect a higher percentage of Chinese respondents supporting their wrong government. As expected, those that scored below China were all democracies in various forms, including Australia, Taiwan, eastern Germany, New Zealand, the Philippines, Great Britain, Japan, Ireland, western Germany, France, Latvia, Finland, Norway, Canada, and Sweden, and the lowest was the Netherlands (33%). However, a total of 19 countries and regions scored the same or higher than China, many of which were democracies, including Austria, Slovak Republic, Denmark, Arab Israelis, the United States, Spain, Poland, South Africa, Uruguay, Czech Republic, Slovenia, Switzerland, Portugal, Russia, South Korea, Jewish Israelis, Chile, and Hungary, and the highest was Venezuela (69%). The Chinese respondents did not seem to be the most fearful, and many of them dared to oppose their government if it was wrong. This kind of comparison gives people more confidence in the reliability of Chinese survey responses, because the Chinese respondents did not seem to avoid politically sensitive questions more than the survey respondents in some democratic countries (figure 1.1).

As is discussed in various chapters in this book, some Chinese citizens often engage in confrontational and contentious action against local governments and their officials where the risk is higher due to the possibility of direct retribution. Such explicit action further suggests that Chinese survey respondents are not afraid of answering questions regarding their political opinion vis-à-vis their government (King et al. 2013).

Another problem is related to the "don't know" answers in Chinese surveys. It is suspected that Chinese respondents would say they don't know the answer when they are afraid to answer politically sensitive questions. Yet there is evidence that "don't know" answers are more likely related to the respondents' inability to understand the questions, rather than fear, as the lack of education is clearly related to the rise of "don't knows" in responding to democracy-related questions in both democratic and autocratic societies in the WVSs (Ren 2009). This book uses statistical techniques to estimate (impute) the "don't know answers" with the information on the respondents' answers to other questions in the surveys. In other cases where the number of "don't knows" is small, they are treated as random missing values.[6] The issue of data reliability is further addressed in various chapters, and more systematically in chapter 8.

In sum, this book intends to explain the formation of ordinary citizens' political attitudes and behavior and how they affect regime stability and

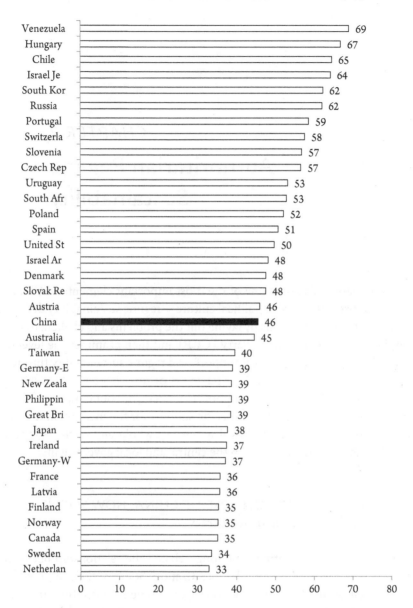

Figure 1.1:
"I would support the government even if it is in the wrong" (% yes, weighted)
Sources: 2003 Identity Survey II, International Social Survey Programme, and the 2008 China Survey.

governance in China. Public opinion is only one aspect of Chinese political life. It does not replace the need to study other components of the political process, such as bureaucratic politics, political institutional interaction, and elite politics. A better understanding of public opinion formation and its impact will compliment and refresh the existing studies on these topics.

CHAPTER 2

Authoritarian Regime Sustainability

This chapter discusses one of the most important elements of China's populist authoritarian political culture—regime sustainability defined as regime support. It begins by laying out the problems and challenges facing the Chinese Communist Party (CCP) and then examines the level of public life satisfaction, political support, and regime sustainability through public opinion survey data. Another focus of this chapter is to test two competing theories of political support in China: horizontal support focusing on the distinction between specific support for the incumbent leaders and diffuse support for the political system as a whole, and vertical support based on the distinction between the central and local governments.

THE COMING COLLAPSE OF CHINA: HOW SOON?
Modernization and Democracy

Scholars of democratization have long debated the relationship between economic modernization and democratization. Some of them do not see a clear relationship between modernization and democratization. Instead, they find that democracy can become more stable under modernization while democratization remains to be a top-down effort by elite manipulation (Przeworski and Limongi 1997).

Others believe that there is a positive relationship between modernization and democratization. They argue that economic modernization creates conditions for democracy regardless of social and cultural contexts (Welzel and Inglehard 2007; Dalton and Shin 2007). In addition to the fact that all advanced industrial countries are democratic, these scholars show that authoritarian regimes also tend to become democratic under sustained economic growth, such as in Latin America, East Asia, and Central and Eastern Europe (Inglehard and Welzel 2009).

One reason that economic development and modernization promote democracy is the irreconcilable conflict between authoritarianism and market capitalism, the latter being a necessary condition for economic growth (Friedman 1962). More importantly, modernization improves living standards, produces a well-educated, economically secure, and independent-thinking middle class, and encourages civic values and behavior that support human rights, self-expression, freedom of choice, social tolerance, and political engagement (Lipset 1960; Almond and Verba 1963; Inkeles 1974).

History has shown that when authoritarian regimes pass a certain threshold of per capita GDP, democracy emerges because the "enlightened" public demands more freedom and continued political control therefore becomes socially and economically too costly (Inglehard and Welzel 2009). Public opinion surveys conducted in the early 1990s showed that education played a significant role in promoting popular support for market reform and democratic change in Russia, Ukraine, and Lithuania (Reisinger, Miller, and Hesli 1994; Miller, Reisinger, and Hesli 1996).

After three waves of democratization throughout the world in the 19th century, in the post–World War II era, and since the 1970s (Huntington 1993b), China remains the largest and perhaps the most influential authoritarian state. Given its size and influence, the democratization of this single country would arguably symbolize the fourth wave and score a decisive victory for the world democratic movement. Democracy scholars have welcomed China's economic rise in the past three decades and have predicted that China was approaching that threshold of democratic transition (Rowen 1996; Diamond 2008; Inglehart and Welzel 2009).

Regime Crisis

Yet even when the conditions are ripe, such a transition still requires a crisis situation in order to materialize. Some believe that such a crisis is brewing in China. For example, Minxin Pei (2002, 2006) describes the crisis of governance in China as one which has evolved from multiple factors including widespread corruption, conniving local officials, political apathy, public dissatisfaction and its negative perception of the Chinese Communist Party (CCP), social inequality, personalized patronage in career advancement, the CCP's inability to gain support in the emerging private sector, a dysfunctional fiscal system in which "off-budget earnings exceeded budgeted tax revenue by two to one" (Pei 2002, p. 105), deteriorating education and health care, environmental pollution, increasing peasant riots and rural tax revolts, the large number of protests in recent years due to the lack of institutional channels for conflict resolution, and even rising traffic fatalities.

McFauquer (2006), while fully recognizing the CCP's economic achievements, warned of a "systemic erosion" due to the lack of charismatic leaders like Mao and Deng, the decline of all-encompassing ideology, rising social activism, corruption and the diminishing legitimacy of the CCP, and the unpopular image of the People's Liberation Army as a coercive force after its suppression of the 1989 student movement.

Chang (2001) predicted that the numerous problems facing the CCP would lead to the "coming collapse of China," including the bankruptcy of state-owned enterprises and massive unemployment, the mistreatment of immigrant workers, the loss of faith in Communism and its resulting ideological crisis, the rise of the Falun Gong religious sect and religious tension, and growing ethnic conflict. As a result, China would follow the Soviet Union and split into many separate states. "China is a lake of gasoline" and one only has to "throw a match" (p. 17).

Other seasoned China-watchers were also becoming pessimistic due to the seriousness of the problems China was facing. For example, David Shambaugh, who was a regular guest of the CCP's workshops, conferences and roundtables, lost his hope and predicted the "coming Chinese crackup." For Shambaugh, several signs indicated that the endgame of the communist rule in China had begun. These signs included economic slowdown, the lack of confidence of China's economic elites and their desire to leave the country, political repression, widespread corruption and the CCP's inability to cure it, and the loss of support by the party loyalists. Shambaugh saw this endgame as a protracted process with frequent political instability and possible coup d'états. He argued that the only way out of this political downturn was to remove the CCP's political monopoly and implement democratic reforms (Shambaugh 2015).

Public dissatisfaction with the widespread inequality in rural and urban areas, between rural and urban areas and between geographic regions, would further lead to demands for democratic multi-party elections or at least power sharing among factions within the CCP. Wei Jingsheng, China's founding father of the modern democratic movement who was jailed for 15 years after the failed "Democracy Wall" movement in 1979, predicted that "People know more about democracy and are more outspoken than before, they will push for democracy when dissatisfied with the government, just like in 1979 and 1989" (Schmetzer 1993).

Ironically, no one feels the sense of "total crisis" more urgently than the Chinese leadership itself (Tsou 1986). Official publications openly recognize many problems mentioned by China's critics, such as rising popular dissatisfaction with corruption, inequality, unemployment, deteriorating public services, environmental pollution, religious and ethnic tensions, increasing public protests and petitions, declining regime legitimacy, and failing ideological education (Research Group of the Organization Department of the Chinese Communist Party 2001; Hu 2006; Song 2011; Xi 2013). Gilley and Holbig's (2009) study of China's "opinion leaders" or official intellectuals based on 168 articles published between 2003 and 2007 revealed that 98% of them mentioned that these domestic problems both challenged and threatened the CCP's legitimacy.

Regime Durability

However, although civic values and political activism have been growing due to the many problems already mentioned, even within the CCP itself, democratic transition has proven to progress more slowly than expected. A number of scholars have shown that the Chinese Communist Party has demonstrated the ability to stay in power by adapting to modern conditions of economic growth and globalization (Nathan 2006). Gallagher (2002, 2005a) challenged the presumed spill-over effect of modernization and marketization on political change, and showed that the introduction of foreign direct investment to China reduced the tension between the state and labor by weakening the workers' ability for collective action and hence further strengthened state power. Manion (2004) showed that rather than being a result of authoritarian rule, corruption was purposely "designed" to promote local economic incentive, while keeping it under check at the center.

Kellee Tsai (2007), in her 2002–2003 survey of 1,525 registered private entrepreneurs in 10 provinces and in-depth interviews, showed how China's "adaptive informal institutions" could facilitate formal institutional change without regime change. In other words, informal institutions can promote policy change even though they cannot promote regime change. Similarly, in their 2006–2007 survey of 2,071 private enterprises in five coastal provinces, Chen and Dickson (2008, 2010) demonstrated how recruiting capitalists into the CCP served to promote the legitimacy of the party and reduce opposition. Drawing from field interviews and a 2001 survey of 316 villages in Shanxi, Hebei, Jiangxi, and Fujian, Lily Tsai (2007a, 2007b) found that local governments could be accountable and improve public services without institutional democracy, where local diffused religious activities and embedding and encompassing lineages overlap with local governments. Through informal institutional activities (religion and lineage), local governments could gain public support.

Drawing upon a random survey of 245 county officials in four Jiangsu counties conducted in the late 1990s, Landry (2008) focused on formal institutional change, rather than informal activities. He found that even under significant marketization, decentralization, and diminishing ideological control, the CCP showed its ability to stay in power by developing an elaborate personnel system which included, among other things, top-down appointments and term limits. Top-down appointments assured lower level officials' accountability to their superiors, and term limits prevented corruption and unchecked expansion of individual leaders' power that could be used to resist central policy. In addition, such a system was designed to promote young, educated, and capable cadres to the top, while keeping the less capable ones at lower levels.

Other researchers also noticed institutional changes in post-Mao China. For example, since 1998, 730,000 villages in China have implemented direct elections of village councils, which are the lowest administrative units in rural China. Currently, 600 million of 900 million eligible voters in China are involved. In some villages, the Communist Party dominates the elections through candidate nomination. In many other villages, non-party candidates compete with party-nominated candidates, and it is not uncommon that non-party candidates are elected (Liu 2002). Kennedy (2009) contends that village elections have reduced the local officials' political control and increased both regime legitimacy and public support for political institutions.

Writing before the 2002 16th Party Congress, Shirk (2002) correctly predicted Jiang's timely retirement. Nathan (2006) also accurately predicted the promotion of Xi Jinping and Li Keqiang to the Standing Committee of the CCP's Political Bureau in 2007. These successful predictions of leadership succession reflect these China scholars' knowledge and understanding of China's political system, and they further indicate that the CCP itself has become more predictable and transparent than in the Mao era.

Dali Yang (2006a, 2006b) studied the changing central–local relations during market reform and found that Beijing was able to maintain political stability under rapid economic modernization by strengthening its control over personnel appointment and fiscal policy, the regulatory institutions, and the provision of public services. Improved governing ability, combined with rising living standards, regional and social inequalities, and a relatively small middle class, has made it possible for the CCP to continue economic development without political reform.

Perhaps the strongest support for the regime stability argument comes from empirical evidence. Using the 2002 East Asia Barometer, Tianjian Shi (2009) found an average support of 90% for the central government, the CCP, and the National People's Congress in China. In his analysis of the 4th wave (2000–2001) of the World Values Survey (WVS) and the 2002 East Asia Barometer, Zhengxu Wang (2006) found that more than 95% of the Chinese respondents in both surveys had "a great deal" or "quite a lot" of confidence in the national government and the CCP, and he attributed such high levels of regime confidence to the strong performance of both institutions in improving the national economy and family living standards (also see Kennedy 2008). Manion (2006) analyzed the data from the 1990 and 1996 surveys of 2,300 villagers in Hebei, Hunan, Anhui, and Tianjin and found that competitive village elections significantly increased voter participation and the credibility of village leaders. Jie Chen conducted three Beijing surveys in 1995, 1997, and 1999, each with about 700 respondents. He constructed a regime support index, including institutional pride, confidence and respect, protection of citizens' basic rights, confidence in the legal system, and affirmation with regime values, and obtained a regime support score of 79 out of 100 (J. Chen 2004). In the 2006 Chicago Council on Global Affairs survey of global attitudes, Dali Yang (2007) found that 78% of Chinese respondents thought that it was advantageous for the Chinese government to manage the economy and the political system.

In a 1999 urban survey of 1,820 respondents in Shanghai, Chongqing, Guangzhou, Xian, Shenyang, and Wuhan, Tang (2005) found that Marxism–Leninism and Maoism continued to attract support from Communist Party members, females, the less educated, low income earners, older generations, and in regions under more revolutionary and socialist influence. Further, by using earlier urban surveys conducted by the Economic Reform Institute of China, Tang found that the 1989 Tiananmen protest was far from being pro-democratic when half of the urban residents in May 1989 wanted market reform to slow down and to return to the old socialist system, and when only about 20% of them wanted to speed up reform and expand it to political democratization (Tang 2005). These findings suggest that at least in its early stage, market capitalism may not go side by side with democracy (Przeworski and Limongi 1997).

The 2005–2008 5th wave of the WVS coordinated by the University of Michigan further indicated that Chinese respondents expressed the strongest support for political institutions including the military, the police, the legal system, the central government, the Communist Party, the national legislature, and the civil service. The combined factor index of political support based on the seven institutions ranged from 0 (no support) to 1 (maximum support). The average score for each country and region showed China at the top (0.60), followed by India (0.54), Malaysia and Turkey (0.49), Finland and South Africa (0.46), Switzerland (0.44),

Sweden (0.43), Indonesia (0.42), Japan (0.40), Australia, the United States, and Spain (0.39), western Germany and Thailand (0.38), Italy (0.37), South Korea (0.36), Brazil, Poland, and Chile (0.34), eastern Germany (0.33), Mexico (0.31), Slovenia (0.30), Taiwan and Serbia (0.29), and Argentina (0.25).

In post-Soviet Russia, even though competitive elections were implemented, democratization was far from being consolidated, and the legacy of authoritarianism showed lasting effects. For example, in a 1997 survey of 1,800 respondents in the Russian Federation, 59% thought that the Soviet system before perestroika was the best for Russia; 54% fully agreed and another 31% partially agreed that Russia needed strong leadership more than it needed democracy (Hesli 2007, tables 5.1 and 5.4).

Horizontal vs. Vertical Supports

Researchers who found regime durability were not blind to the problems described by the "coming collapse" view. For example, J. Chen (2004) suggested that political support was not always high in China. He borrowed Easton's distinction between diffuse regime support and specific regime support (Easton 1965, 1975) and constructed two indices. His diffuse support index contained the aforementioned six items related to people's support for China's political system (pride, confidence and respect of political institutions, protection of citizen's rights, confidence in the legal system, and affirmation with regime values), and his specific support index was measured by the respondents' satisfaction with nine policy items: inflation control, job security, reduction of income gap, housing improvement, social stability, medical care provision, welfare services, fighting corruption, and environmental protection. He found that while diffuse support was high (79 out of 100), specific support was only about 51 out of 100. In other words, the Chinese state enjoyed high support even as its policies and their outcomes were not popular (J. Chen 2004). Similarly, Shi (2009) separated trust in regime from trust in its agents. The former represented the central government, the CCP, and the National People's Congress, and the latter included local governments, individual government officials, and government officials in general. While regime trust scored over 90% on average, trust in its agents (or incumbent support) only averaged 60%.

The findings about the gap between the high system support and relatively low incumbent support provided important clues to understanding the seemingly contradictory trends between regime durability and political instability in China. However, these findings do not rule out the possibility that the lack of incumbent support can still lead to the collapse of the political system. Studies have shown that people would go on the streets and protest if they were dissatisfied, and indeed such protests have increased rapidly in recent years (Pei 2002, 2006). The distinction between system support and incumbent support is useful in describing democratic societies where governments and their agents can be replaced through elections. Such a distinction is less clear in China where there are no meaningful elections to replace the government and its officials; the political system *is* the incumbent government and the CCP. In addition, Chinese public opinion surveys rarely ask about the specific national leaders by name or position, making it difficult to separate incumbents from the system.

Further, earlier studies on the horizontal distinction between system and incumbent supports did not pay sufficient /attention to the vertical distinction of policy dissatisfaction at different levels of the government that some other researchers have noticed. For example, by using five rural surveys conducted between 1999 and 2005 and field interviews, O'Brien and Li (2005a, 2006) showed how rural residents exploited the vertical division within the Chinese state, and how villagers played the "rights promised" by the central government against the "rights delivered" by local governments, and how they successfully staged collective protests through such "rightful resistance." Landry (2008) found that more capable cadres enjoyed greater upward mobility, while the less educated and less capable ones stayed in local governments. Others also noticed that corruption and its popular dissatisfaction mostly existed at local levels, rather than at the center (Pei 2002; Manion 2004; Zheng 2004; Pei 2006; Jennings and Chen 2008). These findings suggest that the crisis of governance may be more of a problem at local levels than at the center.

While the studies on horizontal and vertical supports improve our understanding of regime stability in China, they both seem to suggest that Chinese political system at the national level is stable and that public dissatisfaction will not lead to popular demand for democratic reform at the system level. On the other hand, the theory of democratization and the evidence presented by the regime crisis view predict that the demand for systematic change would grow under strong public dissatisfaction with lower level governments and with incumbent leaders. If this claim is true, it may require additional explanation about the techniques used by the CCP to keep its political monopoly and stability.

The goal of this chapter is to take a step further in simultaneously exploring the vertical and horizontal divisions within the Chinese state. By doing so, I wish to test the hypothesis of regime crisis versus regime durability. Figure 2.1 shows the model of analysis.

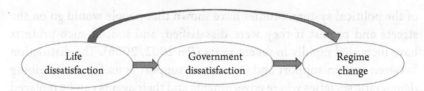

Figure 2.1:
An analytical model of authoritarian regime sustainability

As shown in figure 2.1, I first address the question of popular dissat-isfaction with policy outcomes related to everyday issues, the social and economic characteristics of such dissatisfaction, and how current levels of dissatisfaction compare with those during the 1989 Tiananmen pro-test. Second, I examine how dissatisfaction with policy outcomes causes regime dissatisfaction at different levels. Third, I examine the impact of regime dissatisfaction in promoting public demand for democratic change, while controlling for life dissatisfaction (see figure 2.1).

HOW SATISFIED AND HAPPY ARE THE CHINESE?

Following the regime crisis argument discussed earlier, China is experi-encing serious social and political problems, and one would expect strong public dissatisfaction and unhappiness. Yet the high levels of regime sup-port in China found in various surveys suggest a favorable evaluation of regime performance partly because of the rapid improvement of living standards in the past decades. Accordingly, one would expect less public unhappiness and more satisfaction with life.

The 2005–2008 WVS asked the following question in the selected countries and regions: "taking all things together, would you say you are very happy (coded 3), rather happy (coded 2), not very happy (coded 1), or not at all happy (coded 0)." I calculated the average score for each country or region based on the original 0–3 happiness scale and conver-ted these scores into a happiness index ranging from 0 to 100 (country or region average happiness score divided by 3 and multiplied by 100). As it turned out, among the 25 selected countries and regions, China ranked at the very bottom of this happiness index (65).[1] Above China were eastern Germany (65.5), Slovenia and South Korea (66), India (67), Taiwan and Spain (68), Italy and Chile (69), western Germany (70), Poland (71), Viet-nam and South Africa (72), Japan, Indonesia, Turkey, and Argentina (73), Finland (74), Brazil (75), Australia and the United States (76), Malaysia and Thailand (77), Switzerland (79), Sweden (80), and Mexico (83). So, at least in the 2005–2008 WVS, the Chinese were the most unhappy people among the 25 countries and regions. There seems to be a contradiction between the low level of happiness and the high level of regime support.

Next, I examine public satisfaction with several social issues related to everyday life, including experiences with corruption, consumer price, income level, social equality, and freedom of speech. These items were repeated in many Chinese surveys, including the seven urban surveys conducted by the Economic System Reform Institute of China (ESRIC) in May 1987, October 1987, May 1988, October 1988, May 1989, October 1989, and October 1991, the 1999 Six-City Survey, the 2008 China Survey, the 2012 WVS China, and the 2013 and 2014 Urban Surveys. The repeated questions in these surveys allow me to follow the change of public satisfaction over a period of 27 years, including the turbulent time during the 1989 Tiananmen protests. Although these surveys did not track the same respondents over time, they still provided some ideas about the average levels of public sentiment since they were based on random samples. Until longitudinal data become available, this is the only way to track the change of public opinion over time. Since the earlier ESRIC surveys were drawn from urban population, I use the urban subsamples in the 2008 China Survey and the 2012 WVS for more consistent comparisons.

In many ways, urban residents should have more clear memory of the socialist era than rural residents. Urban residents' lives were more subsidized by the state; they experienced more Mass Line–style political mobilization and campaigns; and they lived under more work unit-based community solidarity, as discussed in chapter 1. Consequently, they are more likely to see the contrast between the socialist era and market reform than rural residents.

In figure 2.2 (also appendix 2.2), public satisfaction seemed to be on the rise since the late 1980s. Satisfaction with clean government dropped from 33% in May of 1987 to its lowest point of 9% in May of 1989, and became one of the main reasons for the Tiananmen protests in the spring of 1989. In the post-Tiananmen era, satisfaction rose gradually and reached its historical high to 60% in May 2014, perhaps due to the official effort to crack down on corruption.[2] Another rising trend is satisfaction with consumer price. Dissatisfaction with inflation in the late 1980s was partially responsible for the 1989 urban protests (Tang and Parish 2000). Following an all-time low of only 4% in October 1988, satisfaction with consumer price climbed up to 41% in May 2014.

Satisfaction with freedom of speech recovered from its lowest point of 52% in May 1989 to 75% in May 2014, which was about the same level of its historical high of 76% in May 1987. Similarly, income satisfaction recovered from its lowest level of 28% in the eve of Tiananmen protests in

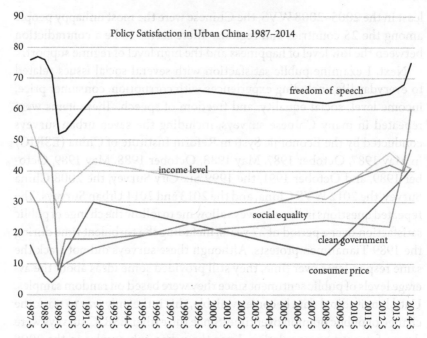

Figure 2.2:
Life satisfaction in urban China 1987–2014 (weighted %)
Sources: 1987–1991 ESRIC Urban Surveys, 1999 Six-City Survey, 2008 China Survey (urban subsample), 2012 WVS China (urban subsample), and 2013–2014 Urban Surveys.
Notes: See appendix 2.2 for further details.

May 1989 and rose to 41% in May 2014, though it was still 14% lower than the level of 55% in May 1987.

One other factor that triggered the Tiananmen protest was dissatisfaction with social inequality as satisfaction with equality dropped from 48% in May 1987 to only 8% in May 1989. Surprisingly, however, it climbed to 47% in 2014, which is about the same level as its historical high of 48% in May 1987. This relatively fast recovery was at odds with some researchers who insisted that social inequality was one of the most acute problems that could explode and cause serious political instability in Chinese society (Li, Chen, Zhang, and Li 2008). The un-alarming nature of perceived social inequality was nevertheless consistent with other studies. For example, in their 2004 National Survey on Social Inequality, Whyte and Han found that Chinese respondents were actually more accepting of social inequality than those in Western democracies (Han and Whyte 2009; Whyte 2010). This apparent contradiction was perhaps derived from the difference between real and perceived inequality. Real inequality had indeed risen drastically and made China one of the most unequal societies in the world, but the Chinese seemed to have become more accustomed to it.

In order to further examine the social and demographic characteristics, I converted the happiness index (happy) into a 0–1 scale (0 = least happiness and 1 = most happiness) and constructed a policy satisfaction factor index (0 = least satisfied and 1 = most satisfied) based on 13 items in the 2012 WVS China. These items included the respondents' expressed satisfaction with the following policy issues related to their daily life: environment, employment, social stability, social equality, democracy, health care, freedom of speech, clean government, effective governance, income level, crime control, housing, and pension/welfare.

Among the social and demographic factors, I focused on age, education, rural residents (compared to urbanites and migrants), gender (female vs. male), the respondents' self-assessed social status (low, lower middle, middle, upper middle, and upper), religiosity (ancestral worship by burning paper money), social group membership (groupmem) including the CCP and other officially sanctioned organizations such as the Communist Youth League, trade unions, business and professional associations, and the respondents' employment category (state and private sectors).

According to the view of social crisis caused by social inequality, rural–urban income gap, exploitation of farmers, mistreatment of migrant workers, rising unemployment, local corruption, and religious repression (Chang 2001; Pei 2002, 2006), one may expect less satisfaction and more unhappiness among the disadvantaged, such as the older generations, the less educated, lower social statuses, rural residents, private sector employees, religious practitioners, and females. Following the modernization school, economic growth and marketization would lead to more public dissatisfaction with authoritarian rule (Friedman 1962; Inglehart and Welzel 2009). Accordingly, the more educated and the private sector would show more dissatisfaction and less happiness. By contrast, in the regime stability view, the CCP has been able to co-opt various social, economic, and ethnic groups into party membership and other officially sanctioned organizations, to alleviate income inequality, to deliver social services, and to combat corruption (Read 2003; Mackerras 2004; Nathan 2006; Chen and Dickson 2008, 2010). As a result, one would not expect a significant amount of dissatisfaction and unhappiness in the private sector, among rural residents, and among those who hold membership in the officially sanctioned organizations.

The findings in table 2.1 only partially support the regime crisis view. The less satisfied include the younger, more educated, urban, lower classes, nonmembers of any official organizations, and private sector workers. Further, the dissatisfaction among the educated, urban residents and in the private sector provided also some support for the modernization school.

Table 2.1. LIFE SATISFACTION AND HAPPINESS BY SELECTED CHARACTERISTICS (OLS)

VARIABLES	(1) Policy satisfaction	(2) Happiness in life
Age	0.001**	0.000
Educ5	−0.018***	0.015***
Rural	0.053***	0.034***
Female	0.002	0.010
Myclass	0.045***	0.057***
Religiosity	0.007	0.048***
Groupmem	−0.002	0.036***
Statejob	0.002	0.014
Privatejob	−0.023**	−0.008
Constant	0.464***	0.463***
Observations	1,752	2,148
R^2	0.103	0.073

Source: 2012 World Values Survey China.
Notes: (1) "Political satisfaction" is a factor index (0–1) of the respondents' satisfaction with 13 policy items, including environment, employment, social stability, social equality, democracy, health care, clean government, effective governance, income level, crime control, housing, and pension/welfare. (2) "Life happiness" is the respondent's overall assessment of life satisfaction. It is converted into a 0–1 scale from the original 0–10 scale. (3) "Educ5" has five levels: 0 = no education, 1 = primary, 2 = junior high, 3 = senior high, and 4 = college and postgraduate. (4) "Myclass" is the respondent's self-assessed social status: 0 = low, 1 = lower middle, 2 = middle, 3 = upper middle, and 4 = upper. (5) "Religiosity" is measured by the respondent's practice of ancestral worship by burning paper money: 1 = yes, 0 = no. (6) "Groupmem" represents the respondents' organizational membership: 0 = nonmember, 1 = member, 2 = active member. (7) For all variables, missing values are excluded. (8) Appendix 2.1 shows further details of the variables in the equation.
**$p < 0.05$; ***$p < 0.01$.

Yet, except for the lower social classes who were both dissatisfied with policies and unhappy with their life, most other disadvantaged groups were not that consistent between policy satisfaction and happiness in life. For example, the younger generations were more dissatisfied with policies, but they were not significantly unhappier than the older age groups. Though the more educated were dissatisfied with policies, they were actually happier with life than the less educated. There was no significant group membership effect on policy satisfaction. Nonmembers were just as satisfied with policy issues as organizational members, but group membership made people happier. Though private sector employees were dissatisfied with policies, they were not significantly unhappier than others. For these groups, policy dissatisfaction does not necessarily lead to life unhappiness.

The other findings in table 2.1, however, seem to support regime durability. Some of the disadvantaged groups actually showed more satisfaction with policy issues, such as the less educated, suggesting the equalizing effect of welfare policies. Perhaps the most surprising finding was that rural residents were both more satisfied with policies and happier in life than urban residents, suggesting that the rural residents may not be a potential source of political instability as expected (Pei 2002, 2006). The fact that private sector workers were not noticeably unhappy does not support the prediction that the CCP had failed to co-opt the private sector (Chang 2001). Women were neither dissatisfied nor unhappy compared to men. Interestingly, religiosity, as measured by the practice of ancestral worship and by burning paper money, had a significant positive effect on happiness in life. This finding is consistent with other studies that show the stabilizing effect of religion because it makes people accept, rather than challenge, the status quo (Tang 2014).

In summary, the findings in this section suggest that although the Chinese were not very happy in comparison with people in other countries, the CCP's effort to reduce dissatisfaction showed some effect in increasing people's satisfaction with government policies. By 2014, the level of public satisfaction recovered significantly from the abyss during the 1989 Tiananmen protests. However, it is too early to conclude that the political crisis view is unfounded, since there was still a significant amount of dissatisfaction. It is necessary to further examine at whom the public dissatisfaction was directed and at what level. If the public anger is directly against the central rather than the local governments, the crisis view may prove true in predicting regime collapse in the near future.

GOVERNMENT DISSATISFACTION AND LIFE DISSATISFACTION

By separating systemic support from incumbent support (J. Chen 2004), earlier studies contributed to explaining the seemingly contradictory coexistence of strong institutional support and equally strong popular dissatisfaction in China. The implication of the system–incumbency argument was that the Chinese regime was durable even when people were angry with its officials. On the other hand, the view of vertical distinction saw the difference between different levels of the state as more important than the horizontal difference between system and incumbency (Li 2004; O'Brien and Li 2005a and 2005b, 2006). As a result, the Chinese regime was durable because people support the central government in Beijing but not local governments. In other words, the system–incumbency view separates the system from those who work in the system at each level of government, while the view of vertical distinction emphasizes the difference between various levels of the government but less the distinction between government offices and their officials at the same level.

The 2012 WVS China has two questions that address the vertical distinction within the state: (1) "How much do you trust central government officials, county or urban district officials, and village or urban sub-district officials?" (3 = trust a lot, 2 = trust, 1 = not trust, 0 = not trust at all); (2) "On a scale from 0 to 10, how satisfied are you with the central government, county or urban district government, and village or urban sub-district government?" I converted each question into a 0–100 scale (0 = no trust at all or not satisfied at all, 100 = max trust and max satisfaction) so that the two scales could be easily compared.[3]

Figure 2.3 shows that while the difference between trusting government officials and satisfaction with government performance was relatively small at each level, there were larger gaps between different levels of government, particularly between the central government and local governments. The satisfaction scores were 76 out of 100 for the central government, 62 for county and urban district government, and 54 for village and urban sub-district governments. Trusting officials at these levels followed a similar pattern: 83 for the central government, 60 for

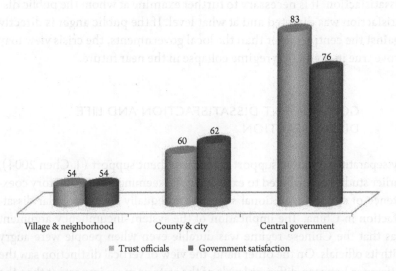

Figure 2.3:
Levels of government satisfaction and political trust (max = 100)
Source: 2012 World Values Survey China.
Notes: Political trust: "How much do you trust the following people: central government officials, county/city officials, village/neighborhood officials?" (3 = high trust, 2 = trust, 1 = distrust, 0 = high distrust). Government satisfaction: "How satisfied are you with the central government, county/city government, and village/neighborhood government?" (0–10 scale). Both are converted into 0–100 scales. Weighted by *wt_base*.

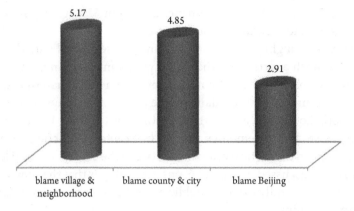

Figure 2.4:
Government dissatisfaction by policy dissatisfaction (OLS coefficients)
Source: 2012 World Values Survey China.
Notes: (1) Dissatisfaction with (a) village/neighborhood, (b) county/city, and (c) Beijing are dependent variables. They are the reversed 0–10 scales of the respondents' satisfaction with the central, county/city, and village/residential governments. (2) Policy dissatisfaction is the independent variable (dissatpolicy). It is a reversed 0–1 scale of a factor index of the respondents' satisfaction with 13 policy items, including environment, employment, social stability, social equality, democracy, health care, clean government, effective governance, income level, crime control, housing and pension/welfare. (3) If the policy dissatisfaction index only includes clean government and effective governance, the gap between the OLS regression coefficients for dissatbj, dissatcty, and dissatvil are even wider (1.174, 3.069, and 3.676). (4) Age, education, group membership, gender, social class, and urbanization are controlled in the OLS equations. See appendices 2.1 and 2.3 for further details. (5) The OLS coefficients can be interpreted as the increase of government dissatisfaction with the increase in policy dissatisfaction. For example, when policy dissatisfaction increases from minimum (0) to maximum (1), dissatisfaction with village/neighborhood, county/city, and Beijing governments increases by 51.7%, 48.5%, and 29.1%, respectively.

county and city governments, and 54 for village and urban neighborhood governments. In other words, horizontal distinction, or the difference between diffuse support and specific support at each level of government, to use Easton's distinction, was much smaller than the vertical distinction between the highest level of government and the local levels.

Yet satisfaction with the central government did not necessarily mean that the public wouldn't blame Beijing for their everyday problems and mismanagement of the country. It is necessary to test the specific impact of life dissatisfaction on government dissatisfaction.

In order to test how dissatisfaction with life affects dissatisfaction with government, I reversed the satisfaction factor index of 21 items in table 2.1 and examined how life *dissatisfaction* led to government dissatisfaction at the three levels. As shown in figure 2.4, when life dissatisfaction grew from 0 (minimum) to 1 (maximum), the probability for the respondents to blame the central government increased by about 29%. However, such tendency to blame the central government paled in comparison with blaming the local governments, which climbed to about 48% against county and urban district governments, and about 52% against the village governments and their urban counterparts.

Two points highlight the findings in this section. First, the Chinese were much angrier with their local governments than with Beijing. Second, they blame the local governments much more than they do the central government for their daily problems. These findings suggest that while both horizontal and vertical distinctions should be taken into consideration, the system–incumbency horizontal distinction seems to matter less than the vertical difference between the center and local levels. As is further discussed in chapter 6, one possibility is that the central government purposefully explores public anger in order to maintain public support for Beijing.

PUBLIC ANGER, POLITICAL ACTION, AND DEMOCRATIC CHANGE

The next question to address is whether government dissatisfaction encourages people to take political action and demand political democracy. Although the level of dissatisfaction with the central government was low, it would still threaten regime stability if such dissatisfaction led to radical political actions.

The 2008 China Survey asked the respondents whether they would participate in various political actions, including contacting media and social organizations, joining advocacy groups, petitioning, and protesting. Though China's media and social organizations are officially sanctioned, they have in recent years gained some freedom in voicing public discontent and negotiating on behalf of their members. The Chinese news media had played an active role in exposing problems related to corruption, police abuse, environmental pollution, and migrants' working conditions. Social organizations such as the local branches of the state-sanctioned Labor Union had represented the voice of the employees and had fought to improve wages, benefits, and work conditions (Chan 2001). Although contacting the official media and social organizations could be categorized as "autonomous" political participation (Jennings 1997), such moves posed limited challenges to the authorities and were mostly within-system activities. On the other hand, joining advocacy groups, petitioning, and protesting could force officials to pay more attention to public demands and created more serious challenges to regime legitimacy and stability.

Figure 2.5 shows a different picture of how central government dissatisfaction played out. In figure 2.5, dissatisfaction with Beijing did not lead

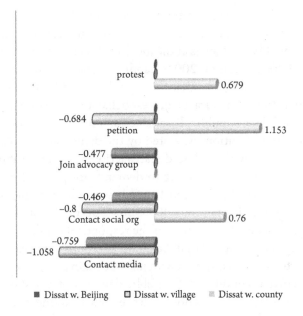

Figure 2.5:
Political action if dissatisfied with government (logit regression coefficients) in 2008
Source: 2008 China Survey.
Notes: (1) In the five logit regression equations (see appendix 2.4), the dependent variables are contact media, contact social organization, join advocacy group, petition, and protest, and the independent variables are dissatisfaction with Beijing, dissatisfaction with village, and dissatisfaction with county. Control variables include policy dissatisfaction, age, education, group membership, gender, 2007 family income, welfare benefits, urbanization, ethnicity, and occupation. (2) For dissatisfaction with village and dissatisfaction with county, coefficients for contact media, contact social organization, and petition are based on actions already taken; other coefficients are actions the respondents may take. See appendices 2.1 and 2.4 for further details.

to increased political actions. In contrast, it significantly reduced contacting the media and social organizations, and petitioning. The lack of political activism against the central government could be a result of public political apathy and the ability of the central government to suppress political actions (Jacobs 2009). Similarly, dissatisfaction with local governments at the village and urban sub-district levels also led to political inaction by reducing contacting the media and social organizations, and preventing one from joining advocacy groups. One possible explanation is that village authorities were able to reduce tensions in their communities through lineage and local traditional religious networks (Manion 2006; Lily Tsai 2007a, 2007b) or competitive village elections (Zweig and Fung 2007).

The most striking difference in figure 2.5 was the dissatisfaction with county and urban district governments. Such dissatisfaction encouraged political actions such as contacting social organizations and, more importantly, more aggressive actions including petitioning and protesting.

Clearly, political activism was the highest at this level. The explanation is likely rooted in the problems of corruption, ineffective management, and the low quality of officials at the local level, as mentioned by previous authors (Pei 2002; Manion 2004; Landry 2008). Another explanation, according to Li (2004), was that the high degree of trust in the central government actually encouraged protest behavior at the local level.

Finally, the effect of public dissatisfaction on popular demand for democracy requires attention. As stated by the democracy scholars, under rapid economic growth, public dissatisfaction with authoritarian governments would intensify, leading to demands for political change (Inglehard and Welzel 2009). I constructed two indices to measure such demand, using questions in the 2008 China Survey. The first was an imputed pro-democracy factor index of the respondents' disagreement with the following statements: (1) public demonstrations can easily turn into social disturbances; (2) a system with just one main party is most suitable to China's current conditions; (3) public demonstrations should be forbidden; (4) if everybody does not share the same thinking, society can be chaotic; (5) if a country has multiple parties, it can lead to political chaos. The second was an imputed civil disobedience factor index based on the respondents' disagreement with the following items: (1) never evading taxes; (2) always obeying laws and regulations; (3) willing to serve in the military. Both indices ranged from 0 (minimum) to 1 (maximum). These measures suggest that democracy here is defined by the Western liberal ideas of multi-party competition, freedom of speech, and individual rights to disagree with the government.

In figure 2.6, which was only based on the 2008 China Survey, as dissatisfaction with both life and public issues and with the central government grew from minimum (0) to maximum (1), the respondents' demands for democratization increased by 10.7% and 9.1%. Dissatisfaction with Beijing further encouraged civil disobedience by 17.8%. Nevertheless, dissatisfaction with local governments played no statistically significant role in promoting democratization and civil disobedience.

In short, two conclusions highlight the findings in this section. First, dissatisfaction with county-level governments resulted in the highest levels of radical political actions, while community governments and the central government were successful in neutralizing political actions directed against them. Second, public dissatisfaction, particularly dissatisfaction with the central government, proved to be a meaningful tool to promote the demand for liberal democracy such as competitive elections, media freedom, and ideological diversity, even if such dissatisfaction at the central government was weaker than at the local levels.

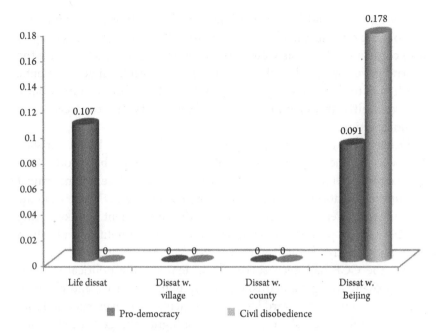

Figure 2.6:
Prodemocracy and civil disobedience by government dissatisfaction (OLS)
Source: 2008 China Survey.
Notes: The dependent variables are pro-democracy and civil disobedience. The independent variables in each OLS equation are central government dissatisfaction, county/city government dissatisfaction, village/neighborhood government dissatisfaction, and the overall life dissatisfaction factor index of 21 items. Controlled variables include age, age-squared, education in year, welfare benefits, Han ethnicity, female, rural, urban, migrant, group membership, imputed 2007 family income (log), and occupation. The effect of political fear is controlled by including whether there was any nonfamily-related adult present during the interview. PSU dummies are controlled. All shown non-zero coefficients are statistically significant at $p < 0.001$. See appendices 2.1 and 2.5 for further details.

CONCLUSIONS

This chapter has examined one of the key elements of regime sustainability—public political support. It began by discussing the opposing views between the coming collapse and regime stability in the existing literature. Second, it assessed the levels of life happiness and policy satisfaction among Chinese survey respondents and how these factors lead to public satisfaction with local and central governments. Finally, it analyzed how government satisfaction and economic modernization affect public demand for democratic change.

In some ways, the process of modernization-democratization had already begun in China when the survey data were collected. Education and urbanization had encouraged critical assessment of government policies, and critical evaluations of regime performance and policy outcome had led to increased political activism, demands for democratic reform, and civil disobedience. The findings in this chapter also confirmed the crisis view to some extent. Dissatisfaction with the central government, though not as intense as with local governments, was linked to the public support for civil society and democratic values, such as multi-party elections, ideological diversity, and the freedom of demonstration.

Other findings, however, suggest regime durability. Public satisfaction with income recovered noticeably since the 1989 urban protest, and satisfaction with freedom of speech peaked in 2014. Resentment against corruption, inflation, and social inequality had declined. Farmers and the private sector were relatively happy with the government. Unlike during the 1989 urban protests, most of people's anger and political radicalism were not directly against the central government. At least by the mid-2010s, the CCP had been successful in maintaining political stability by improving living standards, delivering public services, and channeling public complaint toward local governments. However, such stability rested on a delicate balance. China was a highly charged society filled with conflict and tension. Any misstep could escalate the problems and cause the public to confront Beijing.

The findings in this chapter also point to the need to examine two dimensions of regime support, one that separates central government support from local government support (vertical support), and the other that distinguishes institutional support from incumbent support (horizontal support). The evidence shows a greater vertical difference than a horizontal difference, and it also shows that the former plays a more important role in explaining regime durability at the top.

Yet relying exclusively on this vertical dimension would lead one to overlook the fact that dissatisfaction with daily life and dissatisfaction with Beijing both increased public demand for democratic change. Even the authors who first developed the vertical explanation warned that if the political activists who protested against the local governments became disillusioned, they were likely to direct their blame at the center and demand fundamental political reform, such as multi-party elections (O'Brien and Li 2005a).

Departing from earlier studies that attempted to explain regime stability by showing the coexistence of high institutional support and low incumbent support, the findings in this chapter suggest that the decline of incumbent support would actually threaten institutional stability and increase popular demand for democratic change at the system level such as competitive elections, the freedom of demonstration, and ideological diversity.

Yet democratic change is taking place more slowly than many have hoped, and so far the Communist Party is firmly holding its power. Other factors that may mute the public demand for political reform must be considered. In the following chapter, I show how the demand for democratic change waxes and wanes when another political factor—nationalism—is introduced in the analysis.

CHAPTER 3

Nationalism And Regime
Sustainability

This chapter[1] builds on the discussion of the previous chapter. It further examines the relationship between public dissatisfaction and regime change (see figure 2.1) by introducing another variable—nationalism (figure 3.1). First, this chapter compares Chinese nationalism with that of 35 countries and regions. Second, it looks at the origins of Chinese nationalism as embedded in individual social and political characteristics. Third, the chapter further examines the impact of nationalism on people's political attitudes.

The Communist movement relied heavily on nationalism in mobilizing popular support and seizing political power in 1949 and has continued to do so since 1949. The overall purpose of this chapter is to discuss nationalism as an inseparable component of the contemporary Chinese political culture.

Before I show the empirical findings based on public opinion surveys, it is necessary to relate the discussion in the chapter to both the current literature and the recent development of nationalism in China.

THEORIES OF NATIONALISM

Nationalism is one of the most powerful forces of collective action, even though it is a relatively modern phenomenon that followed the birth of the nation-states in Europe.[2] As a topic, nationalism connects many disciplines in the social sciences and humanities. There are at least three influential theories of nationalism in the existing literature that can be described as functionalist, culturalist, and constructivist. While these labels may oversimplify the three theories described herein, they nonetheless summarize

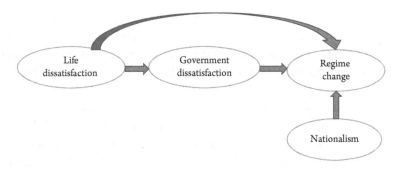

Figure 3.1:
An analytical model of authoritarian regime legitimacy with nationalism

the central focus of each, allowing us to test the importance of the central mechanisms of what drives nationalism.

In his book *Nations and Nationalism* (1983), Ernest Gellner articulates a functionalist theory of nationalism. For Gellner, economic development and modernization create the need for unified knowledge through standardized education. The cultural and linguistic diversity in traditional agrarian societies disintegrates as a result of this educational standardization within the state. The modern and standardized educational system creates social mobility between classes, a homogeneous high (literate) culture, and thus a common national identity which is imposed and protected by the nation-state in order to more smoothly make the transition to a modern, developed economy. The drive to modernize society into the ideal of the nation-state ultimately results in the creation of the nation: thus Gellner arrives at the conclusion that "it is nationalism which engenders nations, not the other way round" (1983, 55). According to this view, nationalism and its result—the nation—are functional necessities for economic development.

The Gellnerian view of functional nationalism is challenged by one of Gellner's students, Anthony D. Smith, who focuses more strongly on the cultural origins of nationalism. Smith argues that the functionalist view may be useful in industrial societies, but it fails to explain nationalism in pre-industrial, non-industrial, and post-industrial societies (Smith 1995, 1998). For him, nationalism is derived from pre-modern origins, such as kinship, religion, belief systems, and common historic territories and memories, and is thus defined as "ethnosymbolic" or even "primordial" (Smith 1983).[3] In contrast to Gellner's modernist approach, we can characterize Smith's view as premodernist: Smith sees most nations as having deep historical roots in ancestry, culture, shared history, and so forth. While modernization does work to bring about the idea of the nation, this means neither that premodern nations did not exist nor that nations are created out of thin air during industrialization. States harness *existing* ethnic and cultural identities through symbols, and the better a state can do this the better it can legitimate itself.[4]

Finally, the constructivist view argues that nationalism is a product of elite manipulation of mass publics. Many authors have noted that national identities are constructed through printed national languages that can connect people speaking different dialects (Deutsch 1953; Anderson 1991; Huntington 1993a; Said 1995). According to Benedict Anderson (1991), the rise of the printing press was a critical element in the advent of nationalism, because for the first time, people were able to imagine those who could read their language as members of their nation. In a separate but compatible vein, Paul R. Brass (1991) specifically emphasizes the role of political elites and their manipulation of cultural symbols in the building of ethnic and national identities. In contrast to culturalists like Smith, these constructivists see national identities as fluid and malleable. Unlike functionalists like Gellner, however, constructivists tend to emphasize elites' ability to *purposefully* manipulate national identity, through the use of symbols, often in order to bolster the legitimacy of the existing political order (Breuilly 1982; Brass 1991).[5] Thus, while certain elements of modernization, like media technologies, are important in the building of national identity, constructivists, unlike functionalists, do not see nationalism as a necessary functional response to modernization but as the result of the influence of elites who have incentives to create and maintain a particular national identity.

While the three theories are all plausible, the constructivist view, which focuses on the spread of printing language-based collective memory and national identity, seems to be more capable of explaining the development of nationalism in China. In addition to inventing the technique of printing, China unified the written language more than 2,000 years ago during the Qin Dynasty and continued to use the same printing language ever since, which effectively connected many highly diverse groups of people with different spoken languages and local cultures under a homogenous nationalist identity.

NATIONALISM IN CHINA

On October 1, 1949, Mao Zedong announced to the world that the Chinese people had finally stood up after repeated foreign invasions since the middle of the 19th century. It is not an exaggeration to say that the Chinese

Communist movement in the first half of the 20th century is just as much a nationalist movement, and that the Communist victory in 1949 is just as much a victory of Chinese nationalism as a victory of Communism. The Chinese Communist Party (CCP) was able to defeat the Nationalist Party (Guomindang or GMD) largely due to its ability to appeal to the sentiment of public nationalism. During the first three decades of Communist rule from the 1950s to the 1970s, Marxist ideology went side by side with nationalism.

Since the late 1970s, however, Marxism was replaced by economic pragmatism, and nationalism has served almost exclusively as the ideological instrument for political mobilization. This was especially true after the 1989 government crackdown on protests in Tiananmen Square and elsewhere. The CCP launched a nationwide campaign to promote nationalism (Zhao 2004), and anti-Western sentiment grew during the 1990s. The government tolerated and even encouraged nationalist protests in response to several events, most of which concerned China's relations with the United States and Japan. Many researchers have recognized the renewed importance of popular nationalism in China in recent years (Central Committee of the Chinese Communist Party 1994; Zheng 1999; Gries 2004a, 2004b; Guo 2004; He 2004; Zhao 2004; Gilley and Holbig 2009; Shirk 2011; Gries et al. 2011).

The study of Chinese nationalism often does not fit neatly into the study of nationalism more generally. First, China was never fully colonized, which sets it apart from most other developing countries both in East Asia and in other parts of the world. Second, China as a state has inherited the legacy of an empire. In stark contrast to the typical case of nationalism developing as a reaction to the oppression of an empire, China is itself an empire-turned-nation, or, as Lucian Pye has called it, "a civilization pretending to be a nation-state" (1996, p. 109). Despite its historical uniqueness, however, I believe that it is fruitful to consider China as one case of the broader phenomenon of nationalism. While the history of each country may have unique attributes, states always have an interest in promoting national identity, and we should be able to compare individual-level measures of national pride across national borders.

Scholars of China have identified many types of nationalism, such as ethnic nationalism, liberal nationalism, state nationalism, pragmatic nationalism, elite nationalism, mass nationalism, and so on (see Zhao 2004, chapter 1). In this chapter, I focus on public nationalism or mass nationalism defined as public sentiment toward one's country. Specifically, I measure public nationalism by four statements related to national identity in the 2003 Survey on National Identity, conducted by the International

Social Survey Programme (ISSP, www.issp.org). The statements with which respondents agreed or disagreed are as follows:

1. I would rather be a citizen of my country than of any other country.
2. The world would be a better place if people from other countries were more like people from my country.
3. My country is a better country than most other countries.
4. It makes me proud when my country does well in international sports.

The 2003 ISSP National Identity Survey contains valuable information on those four statements for more than 40,000 survey respondents from 35 countries and regions. But for some reason it missed China. Fortunately, I was able to include these statements in the 2008 China Survey, which is a project of the College of Liberal Arts at Texas A&M University, conducted in collaboration with the Research Center for Contemporary China (RCCC) at Peking University. For the purpose of this chapter, the 2008 China Survey provides rich information on national identity and attitudes toward democracy (see appendix 3.1 for further details). I draw most of the analysis from this survey for the rest of the chapter.

To begin, I examine how the Chinese respondents answered the four statements related to national identity in the 2008 China Survey. For each statement, the respondents could choose from strongly disagree (0), disagree (1), neither disagree nor agree (2), agree (3), and strongly agree (4). I converted this 0–4 scale into a 0–100 feeling thermometer by dividing the scale by 4 and multiplying it by 100. Zero means no identification, and 100 means the strongest possible identification.

In table 3.1, the findings were corrected (weighted) with the information, on age and sex from the 2000 population census. In other words, weighting based on the true population characteristics is necessary to correct any error due to sample bias. The results show that the average

Table 3.1. NATICNALISM IN CHINA (WEIGHTED)

	Feeling thermometer (max = 100)	# of respondents
Proud if my country does well in international sports	90	3,682
I would rather be a citizen of my country	85	3,687
My country is a better country	73	3,589
Other countries were more like my country	61	3,249
Nationalism (4 items combined)	80	3,076

Source: 2008 China Survey.

levels of the feeling thermometers were 61 (the world would be a better place if other countries were more like my country), 73 (my country is a better country), 85 (rather be a citizen of my country), and 90 (proud if my country does well in international sports).

Though the levels of national identity seem quite high, it is necessary to compare China with other societies to determine the relative degree of nationalism in China. To do so, the four highly correlated (correlation matrix not shown here) questions are combined into a feeling thermometer index with factor analysis. The index ranges from 0 to 100 in both the 2008 China Survey and the 2003 ISSP National Identity Survey, which contains the same four questions in 35 countries and regions. The results of the cross-society comparison of nationalism are shown in figure 3.2.

When measured by the four survey questions, China shows the highest level of nationalism among all countries and regions, with a score of 80 out of 100 (figure 3.2). The top 10 countries, in addition to China, include the United States (76), Canada (75), Australia (75), South Africa (73), New Zealand (73), Venezuela (72), Japan (72), the Philippines (71), and Austria (71). It is difficult to detect any common traits among these countries since they represent very different political systems, different cultural traditions, and different continents. At least among the top 10 countries that demonstrated the highest levels of nationalism, these high levels of nationalism seem to have their own reasons in each country and should be further analyzed within their own national contexts.

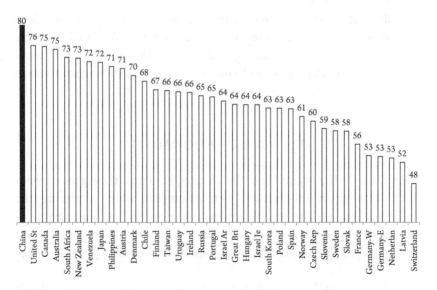

Figure 3.2:
Nationalism: an international and cross-region comparison

At the low end of figure 3.2, however, the patterns seem to be easier to discern. Nationalism tends to be low mostly in European post-industrial democracies, particularly in Switzerland, the Netherlands, West Germany, France, Sweden, and Norway. This is somewhat counterintuitive since Europe, according to most scholars, is where modern nationalism originated (Gellner 1983), and many (e.g., Inkeles 1978; Norris 2011) would expect these industrial societies to show a high level of nationalism. One possible explanation is post-materialism. In these post-industrial societies where survival values have been replaced by self-expression values or post-materialistic values (Inglehart 2007), national identity is likely to be replaced by individual identity. Another explanation may be found in the rise of a broader European identity corresponding with the adoption of the euro and the gradual institutional strengthening of the European Union.

Another group of countries that showed weak feelings of nationalism in figure 3.2 are the new democracies in Europe, including Latvia, East Germany, Slovakia, Slovenia, and the Czech Republic. Researchers have shown that civic values and nationalism evolved together in Central and Eastern Europe, which contributed to the downfall of Communism and to democratization (Wnuk-Lipinski 2007). Yet these countries were among the lowest in levels of national identity. One possible explanation lies in the distinction between elite nationalism and popular nationalism. While elite nationalism may be instrumental in democratization, popular nationalism may be more closely linked to government performance and economic conditions.

In short, it seems easier to explain at a general level why national identity is weak than why it is strong. In order to understand why China is the most nationalistic country among all the selected countries and regions, I need to further examine the individual characteristics that contribute to the sentiment of nationalism.

SOURCES OF CHINESE NATIONALISM

As discussed in the beginning of this chapter, I examine three general theories about why nationalism rises: (1) functionalism, which emphasizes the necessity of nationalism under economic development and education; (2) culturalism, which attributes nationalism to cultural myths and historic memories; and (3) constructivism, which focuses on elite political design of national identity.

In this section, I test these broad theories by examining the individual characteristics of the Chinese respondents in the 2008 China Survey.

Though these theories apply mainly to the historical roots of nationalism, they lead to corollary hypotheses at the mass level. The functionalist hypothesis, which associates nationalism with economic development, predicts higher levels of nationalism among the more educated, urban residents and higher income earners. To test the functionalist theory, I look at how individual education, urbanization, and income influence people's feelings of national identity. Education is coded as no education, primary school, junior high school, senior high school, and college and above. Urbanization is measured by urban and rural residents and rural migrants living in urban areas. Income is measured by the following question: Compared to the average household income in this county/city/district, at what level do you feel your household income is situated from 0 to 10? Zero through 2 are coded as low income (low), 3 through 5 are coded as middle income (middle), and 6 through 10 are coded as high income (high).

To test the theory of culture as the origin of national identity, I use the respondents' ethnic background. The 2008 China Survey contains such information on the respondents, including the Han majority (han), the Huis (hui), and the Uyghurs (wei)—both Muslim minorities, the Manchu minority (man) which used to rule China under the Qing empire (1644–1911), the Mongol minority (mengu) in the north which ruled China under the Mongol empire in the 13th century, southern minorities including Yi, Zhuang, Tujia, Hani, and Dai (eth_south), and other unidentified groups (eth_oth). The culturalist hypothesis, since it sees nationalism as a function of ethnic identity, expects the Han majority to show stronger nationalism than the minorities, particularly more than the religiously and linguistically distinctive groups such as the Huis, the Uyghurs, and, to a lesser extent, the Mongols and the Manchus, who each have their own written language.

Finally, to test the constructivist theory of political imagination, I use two items: Communist Party membership and age. Party members (ccp) are more indoctrinated by the official rhetoric and should demonstrate more nationalism than non-members (public). Age is divided into four groups depending on when the respondents turned 18: 1949–1965 (socialism), 1966–1977 (the Cultural Revolution), 1978–1989 (reform), or 1990–2008 (post-reform). The socialist generation includes those aged 59 and older, the Cultural Revolution generation ages from 47 to 58, the reform generation is between 36 and 48, and the post-reform generation includes those 35 and younger. The older generations have experienced more "political construction" by elites and should therefore show more nationalism than the younger generations.

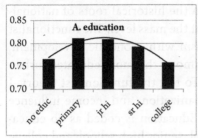

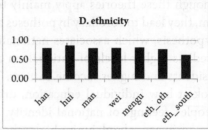

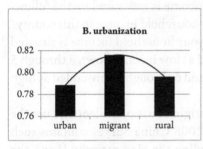

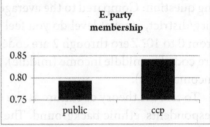

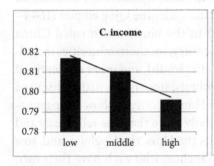

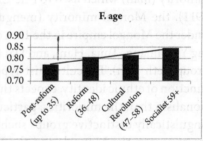

Figure 3.3A-3.3F:
Sources of Chinese nationalism

The findings show a mixed picture of the functionalist theory. In figure 3.3A, education does not have a straightforward effect on nationalism. Rather, people at both ends (no education and college education) show low levels of nationalism, and those in the middle (primary and middle school) are the most nationalistic.[6] In figure 3.3B, urban residents have the lowest level of nationalism, lower than both rural residents and rural migrants. Although rural migrants showed higher levels of nationalism than rural residents in figure 3.3B, this difference disappeared when other individual characteristics were taken into consideration, such as age, education, income, ethnicity, and gender (appendix 3.2). In other words, in the multivariate analysis, urban residents were less nationalistic than both rural residents and rural migrant workers, and there was no statistically significant difference between the latter two groups.

In figure 3.3C, income has a negative effect on nationalism, as low-income earners show more nationalism than the middle- and high-income groups. However, the high-income group becomes more nationalistic than the middle-income group in the multivariate regression analysis when other demographic variables are included in the equation. The real effect of income on nationalism seems to be U-shaped, with both low- and high-income groups demonstrating stronger feelings of nationalism than the middle-income group. Except for the high-income group, none of these findings provides strong support for the functionalist theory of nationalism. The fact that the middle-income urban residents with college education are less nationalistic seems to suggest that these groups are less likely to be affected by political mobilization and may possess more self-expression values (Inglehart 2007). Still, further tests with different measures and methods are needed before we can rule out the functionalist hypothesis. While Gellner's theory might explain how nationalism developed in its infancy, it may be less powerful as an explanation of contemporary nationalism at the mass level.

Figure 3.3D shows the impact of ethnic background on nationalism. Interestingly, the linguistic and religious minorities such as the Huis (hui), the Manchus (man), the Uyghurs (wei), and the Mongols (menggu) show just as high levels of nationalism as the Han majority. This seems to suggest that nationalism in China is not defined by the Confucian tradition, which is only popular among the Hans. Rather, it is a trans-cultural concept that can be shared by different ethnic groups. In their study of nearly 1,600 high school students in Xinjiang and Tibet, Tang and He (2010) found that the high degree of national identity among China's religious and linguistic minorities was partially created by the officially sponsored affirmative action programs. Ethnic minorities in these regions are willing to accept Chinese nationalism when and only when they enjoy a high degree of cultural and religious autonomy. Thus, at least in the current Chinese context, the culturalist theory does not explain the development of nationalism in China.

As expected in the framework of the constructivist hypothesis, Communist Party members are more nationalistic than the general public (figure 3.3E). Also as expected, age has a positive effect on nationalism (figure 3.3F). The socialist and the Cultural Revolution generations are more nationalistic than the reform and the post-reform generations. These findings seem to provide the most clear and most straightforward support for the constructivist assumption. In other words, the Chinese nation-state is an imagined multi-ethnic community constructed by the Communist Party. However, the different political socialization of these generations is not the only way to explain this finding, which may also indicate a life-cycle effect, in which a person more strongly identifies with the nation-state as he or she grows older.

These results seem to contradict the much-publicized phenomenon in China of "angry youth" (*fenqing*), but in actuality the findings help us to put this phenomenon in a larger context. The so-called angry youth are typically urban, and include not only nationalist Chinese Netizens, but also those young Chinese who take to the streets in nationalist protests, usually against a country perceived as an adversary to China. Recent protests in both China and Japan concerning the dispute over the Diaoyu/Senkaku Islands are just one example of this.[7] While these angry nationalist youth are quite visible in the news media, the findings presented here suggest that they are not representative of the broader population of youth in China. This is not to say that the *fenqing* are not important, but among everyday Chinese, the young are actually less nationalist than older generations.

The findings in this section also suggest that in the future, Chinese nationalism is likely to experience a two-stage change. In the first stage, it is likely to maintain its high level as the rate of illiteracy continues to drop and as the Communist Party continues its campaign for nationalism. In the second stage, nationalism is likely to decline as more people receive college education, as the more nationalist older generation fades away, and as more and more rural residents become urbanized. Thus, while Chinese nationalism may stay at a high level, there are reasons to expect it to ebb over the long term as China continues to modernize, since the least nationalist societies are all industrial societies in figure 3.1.

THE POLITICAL CONSEQUENCES OF CHINESE NATIONALISM

There is no consensus in the current literature in terms of what direction nationalism would lead China's political democratization in. There are roughly three views in the existing studies on the role of nationalism in regime change. The first is that nationalism simply serves as an instrument to strengthen regime stability (Zheng 1999; He 2004). According to this view, in the post-Mao ideological vacuum, Chinese leaders promoted nationalism as a substitute to Marxism-Leninism and Maoism, and claimed the CCP's representativeness of the national interest for China. Western pressure on China for democratic change hence would only backfire, because it only intensifies feelings of nationalism and may push China into political consolidation among the different elite groups within the state and between the state and the public (Zheng 1999; He 2004). Similarly, in post-Soviet Russia, researchers found that popular support for reform declined when popular nationalism rose (Miller, Reisinger, and Hesli 1996).

The second view portrays nationalism as a destabilizing factor and leads to national disintegration. In this view, nationalism leads to heightened awareness of ethnic identity in a multi-ethnic state like China, which threatens national unity and political stability (Ge 1996, quoted in Zheng 1999, 110; Wan Jun 2003, cited in Gilley and Holbig 2009, 350). Perhaps this idea of nationalism as a "double-edged sword" is best expressed by Susan Shirk (2007): "What the Chinese leaders fear most is a national movement that fuses various discontented groups—such as unemployed workers, farmers, and students—under the banner of nationalism" (62). Shirk regards nationalism as dangerous for political stability in two ways: as an instigator of protests that can turn against the state when officials tell protestors to desist, and also as possibly the only issue that can unite separate groups of people with diverse grievances against the state. Under this interpretation, strong popular nationalism is a bad sign for political stability.

Finally, others contend that nationalism promotes democracy. According to this argument, the core of nationalism is self-determination and the formation of a common identity which goes beyond parochial interests. It is in this context of nationalism, defined as self-determination and a shared community, that democracy has emerged in modern times (Guo 2004; Wang 2009). Wang Shaoguang (2009) further argued that modern Chinese nationalism since the early 20th century was rooted in the concepts that were consistent with democracy, such as the acceptance of all ethnic groups in China, the desire for self-determination and emancipation from Western colonial exploitation, individual dignity and integrity, and economic development through contact with the outside world. Recent experiences in Taiwan also seem to support this view, as self-identity played an important role in the rise of the opposition Democratic Progressive Party and in the process of Taiwan's democratization in the 1990s.

A variation of this view that connects nationalism with democracy is that popular nationalism reflects public opinion. If it doesn't heed public opinion, the Chinese government runs the risk of losing regime legitimacy which is based on its claim to nationalism. When faced with foreign aggression, the Chinese government often takes a tough stand under the pressure of popular nationalism, resulting in its compromise with public opinion (Fewsmith and Rosen 2001; Gries 2004a, 2004b; Shirk 2011). These authors all emphasize the importance of nationalism in China's political process. Their different views on the role of nationalism in China's political evolution call for a further test of the impact of popular national-ism on pro-democratic values and attitudes.

Specifically, this chapter tests the long-term and short-term effects of nationalism. The short-term effects include the public demand for de-mocracy, civil disobedience, and trust in the Beijing government. For long-term effects, the chapter examines how nationalism supports market capitalism and social and political tolerance. If nationalism leads to posi-tive political change, it should have a positive effect on the demand for lib-eral democracy and on civil disobedience but a negative impact in trusting the authoritarian single-party central government. Further, it should also have a positive influence on supporting market capitalism and on social tolerance. On the other hand, if nationalism promotes the political con-solidation of the current authoritarian political system, it should discour-age support for liberal democracy and civil disobedience, and instead promote trust in Beijing. It should further discourage support for social and political tolerance, and for market capitalism which requires the pro-tection of individual interests, sometimes at the cost of group benefit.

This chapter uses questions in the 2008 China Survey to measure pro-democracy sentiment, civil disobedience, trust in Beijing, support for capitalism, and social and political tolerance. Pro-democracy sentiment (*prodemo*) is the same combined factor index of the respondents' *disagree-ment* with the same five statements as in the last chapter: (1) public dem-onstrations can easily turn into social disturbances; (2) a system with just one main party is most suitable to China's current conditions; (3) public demonstrations should be forbidden; (4) if everybody does not share the same thinking, society can be chaotic; (5) if a country has multiple par-ties, it can lead to political chaos.

Civil disobedience (*civdisobey*) is the same combined factor index based on the respondents' *disagreement* with the same three items as in the last chapter: (1) never evading taxes; (2) always obeying laws and regulations; (3) willing to serve in the military.

Trust in Beijing (*trustbj*) is based on a single question: How much do you trust the leaders in the central government?

Support for capitalism (*procap*) is another combined factor index of the respondents' *disagreement* with the following two statements:

1. market competition is harmful to social stability;
2. social stability will be harmed if the economy grows too fast.

Social and political tolerance (*tolerance*) is an imputed factor index of the respondents' acceptance of political dissidents, prostitutes, homosex-uals, and drug addicts.

Table 3.2. NATIONALISM AND REGIME CHANGE (OLS COEFFICIENTS)

	prodemo	civdisobey	trustbj	procap	tolerance
nationalism	−0.357***	−0.258***	0.437***	−0.119***	−0.203***

***p<=.01.

Source: 2008 China Survey.

Notes: The dependent variables are pro-democracy (prodemo), civil disobedience (civdisobey), trust Beijing (trustbj), pro-market (procap) and social tolerance (tolerance). The independent variable is nationalism. Other independent variables included in the equations but not shown: age, party membership, education, family income, family income squared, urbanization, ethnicity, and gender (see appendix 3.2).

Some of the preceding questions have missing values (those who answered "don't know"). I estimated these missing values with the respondents' valid answers to other questions (imputation) before I constructed the indices for pro-democracy, civil disobedience, and support for market capitalism. This technique of imputation allows me to keep as many respondents as possible by utilizing the information from their valid responses in the survey. All variables have the same scale ranging from 0 (minimum) to 1 (maximum) (see appendix 3.1).

In table 3.2, nationalism shows a strong anti-democratic, pro-authoritarian, and anti-capitalist tendency. When nationalism increased from minimum (0) to maximum (1), support for democracy decreased by about 36%, civil disobedience decreased by about 26%, trust in the authoritarian government increased by 44%, support for the individual interest-based market capitalism decreased by 12%, and social and political tolerance also decreased by 20%. The effects of nationalism are independent of other individual characteristics, including age, party membership, education, family income, urbanization, ethnic background, and gender.

The preceding results can be compared to the findings in chapter 2. In that chapter, both life dissatisfaction and the dissatisfaction with the central government promoted pro-democratic attitudes and civil disobedience (figures 2.1 and 2.6, chapter 2). If we introduce nationalism into the equation (figure 3.1), the results show that when nationalism was added to the OLS regression equations, it played an overwhelming role in reducing the demand for democratization and civil disobedience by 28.6% and 18.6%! Although life dissatisfaction and dissatisfaction with Beijing continued to encourage regime change attitudes, their roles on pro-democracy declined from 10.7% (figure 2.6) to 7% (figure 3.4) for life dissatisfaction, and from 9.1% (figure 2.6) to 6.1% (figure 3.4) for dissatisfaction with Beijing. With nationalism in the equation, the impact of dissatisfaction with Beijing on civil disobedience also declined from 17.8%

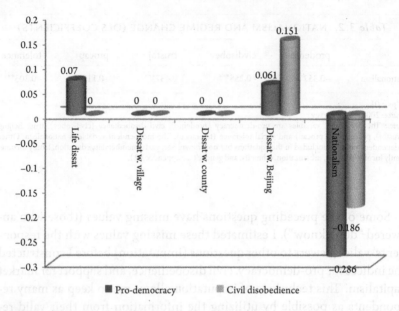

Figure 3.4:
Prodemocracy and civil disobedience by nationalism (OLS)
Source: 2008 China Survey.
Notes: The dependent variables are pro-democracy and civil disobedience. The independent variables in each OLS equation are central government dissatisfaction, county/city government dissatisfaction, village/neighborhood government dissatisfaction, the overall life dissatisfaction factor index of 21 items, and nationalism. Controlled variables include age, age-squared, education in year, welfare benefits, Han ethnicity, female, rural, urban, migrant, group membership, imputed 2007 family income (log), and occupation. The effect of political fear is controlled by including whether there was any nonfamily-related adult present during the interview. PSU dummies are controlled. All shown non-zero coefficients are statistically significant at $p < 0.001$. See appendices 1 and 5 for further details.

(figure 2.6) to 15.1% (figure 3.4). Clearly, nationalism played a more important role in preserving political stability than the role played by public dissatisfaction in speeding up regime change.

If nationalism is measured differently, for example, elite nationalism, it may play a positive role in democratization. However, as long as nationalism is measured by the four survey items in table 3.1, it clearly hinders the development of democracy and promotes the sustainability of the current authoritarian political system in China.

CONCLUSIONS

Four findings in this chapter can be highlighted. First, China had one of the highest levels of popular nationalism in the world by the end of the first decade of this century. Second, Chinese nationalism was not so much rooted in its cultural tradition as it was in the imagined multi-ethnic community designed by the Communist Party. Third, nationalism in China is likely to decline over time as levels of urbanization and education continue to increase. Fourth, nationalism had a strong positive effect on regime stability and legitimacy. It also prevented the public from demanding liberal political change. The negative effect of nationalism on the demand for liberal democracy confirms earlier studies which showed that nationalism was designed by the CCP to maintain its legitimacy (Zheng 1999).

Meanwhile the West remains fixated on political change in China. Many people in Western democracies believe that if they keep pushing, China will become a democracy. The international community, including news media, Western governments, political activists, and nongovernment organizations, does so by offering support for anyone who wants to challenge the Communist Party's rule, such as financing the separatist movements in Tibet and the Muslim region of Xinjiang, hosting the religious dissident group the Falungong, which is banned in China as a cult, awarding the Nobel Peace Prize to the political dissident Liu Xiaobo, and financing the art exhibits by dissident artists like Ai Weiwei. One obvious example is the U.S. Congress–funded National Endowment for Democracy, which specializes in financing the separatist and dissident groups from China and pro-separatist international organizations such as International Campaign for Tibet, Students for a Free Tibet, the Uyghur American Association, and the World Uyghur Congress (http://www.ned.org/publications/annual-reports/2009-annual-report/asia/description-of-2009-grants/china-tibet).

However, criticism of China's human rights violations by industrial democracies is often perceived in China through the lens of nationalism (Gries 2004a, 2004b). Such a nationalistic response in China potentially creates a dilemma for those on the outside. On one hand, few Western democracies and human rights organizations would want to stop criticizing the authoritarian regime and pushing it to change. On the other hand, continued political pressure from outside seems to further fuel nationalism, which ironically serves the CCP by diverting the public demand for democratization.[8]

While Chinese civilization is an ancient concept, Chinese nationalism is a relatively new idea in contemporary China. It is constructed by the CCP to incorporate a multi-ethnic state that was inherited from the Qing dynasty. It has been used by the CCP to justify its resistance to liberal democracy which is often associated with Western imperialist invasion of China in the 19th and early 20th centuries. More importantly, nationalism is an inseparable component of contemporary Chinese political culture that provides the soil for the CCP to nurture its legitimacy.

CHAPTER 4
Interpersonal Trust
and Regime Sustainability

This chapter discusses another element of the Chinese populist authoritarian political culture—interpersonal trust and group solidarity. It examines the seeming puzzle of how high interpersonal trust coincides with the lack of democracy in China. Using the data from the 2008 China Survey and the 2004 Legal Reform Survey, this chapter divides interpersonal trust into three categories: parochial, communal, and civic. Each type of trust is related to regime support and liberal values and attitudes in different ways. The findings indicate that interpersonal trust promotes liberal values and attitudes as well as regime solidarity in a populist authoritarian society like China.

THE PUZZLE

In *The Civic Culture*, Almond and Verba (1963) pioneered the study of interpersonal trust and democracy by using public opinion survey data from the United States, the United Kingdom, Germany, Italy, and Mexico. They found that interpersonal trust led to a sense of cooperation, which in turn created stable democracy. In their 1959 five-country survey, people in the United States and the United Kingdom consistently showed higher levels of trust than in Germany, Italy, and Mexico. This was why, according to the authors, historically democracy worked well in the United States and the United Kingdom but failed in Germany, Italy, and Mexico (Almond and Verba 1963). Interpersonal trust, according to Almond and Verba, is derived from group membership in civic organizations. Putnam, Leonardi and Nanetti (1993) revived the study of civic culture by their research on civic traditions in modern Italy. They found that in Italy, regions with more citizen associational group activities developed more social capital based on trust and tended to have more stable democracy. The social capital theory has been applied to explain democratization in other societies in Europe (Perez-Diaz 1994), Eastern Europe (Di Palma 1991; Bernhard 1993), the United States (Putnam 1995), Africa (Gyimah Boadi 1996), the Middle East (Kubba 2000), and in Central and Latin American countries (Pearce 1997; Stolle and Rochon 1998; Booth and Richard 1998). Inglehart made the most serious empirical attempt to establish the link between trust and democracy by analyzing the data from the multi-national World Values Surveys (www.worldvaluessurvey.org, accessed Jan. 18, 2011). He found that there was a statistically significant positive relationship between trust and the level of freedom ranked by the Freedom House in 60 societies (Inglehart 1999). Thus, trust provides the necessary social capital for the formation and successful functioning of democracy (Cohen and Arato 1992).

Yet this theory of interpersonal trust and democracy becomes problematic when China is included. Seligson (2002) found that among the 53 countries in the 1990–1996 World Values Surveys, interpersonal trust had a positive effect on the Freedom House Rating. One of the most striking outliers was China, where an exceptionally high level of interpersonal trust was associated with an exceptionally low level of freedom (Seligson 2002). In fact, China had one of the highest levels of interpersonal trust and one of the lowest freedom scores (figure. 4.1).

According to the civic culture literature, there are a number of reasons to believe that the level of trust in China should be low. First, modernization leads to trust (Putnam 1993; Inglehart 1999). China is a developing country and thus should have less trust than industrial societies. Second, trust is closely associated with democratic institutions (Almond and Verba 1963). Given the lack of democratic institutions, China again should have less trust. Third, post-socialist societies all had low levels of trust due to previous bureaucratic control (Inglehart 1999). Again, China was subjected to socialism and thus should have developed less trust (Fukuyama 1996). Inglehart attributed the high level of trust in China to Confucianism (1999), yet it is unclear why and how Confucianism would increase trust. Even if we accept that it does increase trust, more than five decades of Communist rule should have reduced the Confucian influence. Further, other Confucian societies, such as Japan and South Korea, all had lower levels of trust than China (figure 4.1). Thus, the extent to which Confucianism creates trust in China needs further scrutiny.

One potential problem for China's high level of interpersonal trust presented in figure 4.1 is survey reliability. The Chinese sample of 1,000 respondents in the 1990 World Values Survey could be biased and therefore

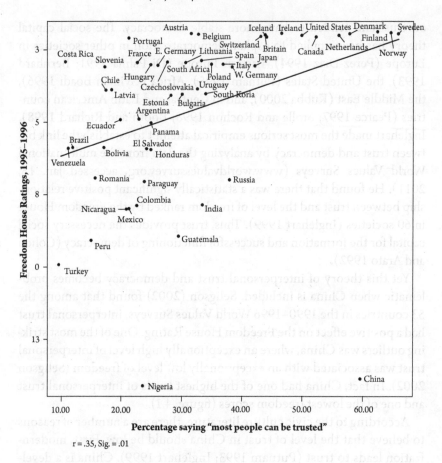

Figure 4.1:
Freedom by interpersonal trust

not representative of the national average. Table 4.1 shows the average levels of interpersonal trust in twelve Chinese surveys in 1990, 1992, 1999, 2000, 2004, 2005, 2008, 2012, 2013, 2014 (twice), and 2015. These surveys were conducted in different years by both Chinese and foreign researchers and organizations, covered either urban or national populations, and used both the traditional household registration sampling method and the GPS-based spatial sampling method. Interpersonal trust has been consistently high among these surveys, ranging from 49% to 69%. This consistency suggests that survey error is not the problem for China's exceptionally high interpersonal trust, and therefore, its sources have to be further explored.

This chapter attempts to address the puzzle of why China is so high in interpersonal trust but has little democracy. To that end, it explores the meaning of trust and its social and political origins. The second goal of

Table 4.1. "MOST PEOPLE CAN BE TRUSTED," CHINA
1990–2014 (WEIGHTED %)

1990 World Values Survey China ($n = 985$)	60
1992 Chinese Urban Survey ($n = 2,395$)	60
1999 Chinese Six-City Survey ($n = 1,831$)	69
2000 World Values Survey China ($n = 963$)	55
2004 China Values and Ethics Survey($n = 7,105$)	51
2005 World Values Survey China ($n = 1,873$)	52
2008 China Survey ($n = 3,858$)	54
2012 World Values Survey China ($n = 2,300$)	60
2013 Urban Survey ($n = 2,000$)	57
2014 Urban Surveys ($n = 4,000$)	49
2015 Urban Survey ($n = 2,000$)	58

Sources: The World Values Surveys 1990, 2000, and 2005 (www.worldvaluessurvey.org), the 1992 ESRIC Urban Survey (Tang and Parish 2000), the 1999 Six-City Survey, the 2004 Chinese Values and Ethics Survey, the 2008 China Survey, the 2012 World Values Survey China, and the 2013 and 2014 Urban Surveys (see appendix 1.1).

this chapter is to examine the impact of trust on a wider range of political values and attitudes than promoting cooperation, such as social tolerance, political efficacy, and regime support. The effect of trust on these values and attitudes will broaden the civic culture literature by establishing the relationship between the different elements of political culture.

INTERPERSONAL TRUST AND DEMOCRACY

On the surface, the civic culture literature claims that trust can only stabilize but not create democracy. For example, although Inglehart (1999) finds a strong relationship between trust and democracy, he is cautious and tries not to claim that trust is able to create democratic institutions. Yet a closer reading suggests that Inglehart strongly implies in several different ways that trust does more than simply stabilize democracy. First, in his statistical analysis, trust is used as an independent variable against both democratic stability and the level of democracy. The latter is measured by the Freedom House Rating, which is an index of institutional political rights and civil liberties in different societies.[1] Methodologically, Inglehart shows us an effect of trust (independent variable) in increasing the level and stability of democracy (dependent variables). Second, Inglehart argues that "economic development is conducive to democracy ... because it encourages supportive cultural orientations [trust]" (Inglehart 1999, 97). In this statement, trust seems to be the catalyst of democratization under modernization. Third, Inglehart carefully separates elite-initiated democratization from the successful functioning of democratic institutions. He seems to say that the latter requires trust and the former does not necessarily require trust. Yet he agrees that democratic elections will possibly not be initiated if the elite do not believe in trust-based cooperation and loyal opposition (loyal to democracy while opposing each other). Again, this connection between the elite and trust suggests that trust is conducive to the rise of democratic elections.

Inglehart is also cautious about asserting that democracy creates trust. Instead, he makes a distinction between Protestant and Confucian societies on one hand and Catholic, Christian Orthodox, and Islamic societies on the other. The former group is associated with high trust and the latter with low trust. But in other places, he implies that the political system matters. One example is the lack of trust in post-socialist countries due to their previous bureaucratic authoritarian political systems. The other example of Inglehart's belief in democracy promoting trust is the explicit statement that "democracy makes people happy and trusting" (Inglehart 1999, 118).

Empirically, the lack of democracy in some high-trust societies such as China and the lack of trust in some democratic societies (figure 4.1) cast serious doubts on the supposedly close tie between trust and democracy and on the ability of trust to create democracy (also see Seligson 2002).

Although Inglehart claims that his findings about the close relationship between trust and democracy is based on more than 70% of the world's population, including China, this empirical foundation is shaken if China's 20% of the world's population is excluded. Based on the remaining 50% of the world's population, the likelihood of a positive relationship between trust and democracy is about half and half.

Conceptually, it is limiting to think that trust is only an asset for democratic regimes. Why can't it be good for any regime? For the populist authoritarian regime in China, more trust reduces the need for coercion and thus increases regime legitimacy. If anything, too much trust may not be good for democracy, since trust may discourage citizens from directly challenging the state (Newton 1999; Norris 1999; Newton and Norris 2000).

As mentioned previously, one of the civic culture school's findings is that trust is based on subjective well-being, which in turn is created by democracy. Yet there is no reason to believe that subjective well-being and trust exist only in a democracy. Trust may reduce political conflict in both democratic and authoritarian regimes, as it may encourage certain values and behaviors that serve as lubricants in state–society relations.

In the following pages, I show that neither is interpersonal trust created only by democracy nor would interpersonal trust necessarily lead to democracy. Trust can also promote regime stability and social solidarity in an authoritarian country.

ORIGINS OF INTERPERSONAL TRUST

Early studies defined interpersonal trust in China as "traditional" (Inglehart 1999; Tang 2005). This definition of traditional trust requires further clarification. Relative to pre-Communist China, tradition can mean Confucianism. Compared to post-Mao China, tradition can mean socialism. Even if trust remains rooted in the socialist tradition (see chapter 1), recent economic booms and marketization may reduce the level of interpersonal trust and change its meaning of trust from traditional to modern. In other words, the trust we see in China today may be based on new meanings compared to the trust in earlier studies.

Confucian Tradition

At least three factors are related to trust. The first is Confucian tradition. Some studies suggest that Confucian societies can promote interpersonal trust (Inglehart 1999). In such societies, there is a clear distinction between insiders and outsiders based on family and kinship ties. For example, Lieberthal (2004) vividly illustrates this distinction in China. According to him, a Chinese family would ignore a starving beggar but take in any distant relative who shows up at the door. Liberthal notes that Chinese visitors to the United States in the 1980s had to be specifically instructed not to stand around and laugh but help someone injured in an accident (p. 16). One objective of this chapter is to examine the current level of kinship trust in China and how it is related to the overall level of interpersonal trust.

Socialist Legacy

The second important component of Chinese social life is the legacy of socialism. Studies of the Soviet Union suggest that the Soviet era left a more noticeable impact on today's mass political attitudes in Russia than did traditional Russian culture. In addition, the Soviet period contributed to democratization more than did Russian tradition (Reisinger 1993, 274). Similarly in China, the Communist Party attempted to replace traditional economic and social institutions with a socialist system in which public ownership, central production plans, employment security, and centrally controlled wealth distribution were put in place to eliminate individual and family interests and promote political loyalty to the collective. As a result, in the early years of the People's Republic, society was organized into residential communities such as the people's communes and work-unit housing compounds with low residential mobility and a high degree of equality in income and consumption (Whyte and Parish 1984). Studies indicate that this communal culture continued to exist under market reform. For example, although income stratification rose rapidly in the 1990s, most of the inequality can be explained by between-group difference rather than by within-group difference (Wang and Wang 2007), suggesting a persistent group coherence. In other words, while market reform may have created greater differences among occupational sectors, the gap among members of the same work unit remained small. The question is whether this state-defined communal environment encourages or discourages interpersonal trust. On one hand, the monolithic control by the party in distribution of wealth and services and planned production based on societal need would create alienation. The low career and residential mobilities and the close interaction among residents would provide greater knowledge of one another which could be used against people during political campaigns. As a result, the socialist social institutions would create more interpersonal distrust. On the other hand, socialist policies such as job security, income equality, low residential mobility, and the priority of group interest would discourage individual competition and promote the feeling of solidarity, resulting in greater interpersonal trust (Whyte and Parish 1984; Bryant 2005).

Existing empirical studies show that it is possible for civic values and behavior to grow in the Soviet-type societies. For example, even though interpersonal trust in the Soviet Union in 1980 was low, it was nevertheless higher than in France, Italy, Belgium, Germany, and the more Western-oriented Lithuania (Reisinger, Miller, Hesli, and Maher 1994). Although there was a lack of associational activities, the levels of conventional political participation and community self-government in the Soviet Union and China were at least as high as in established democracies (Reisinger, Miller, and Hesli 1995; Shi 1997; Tang and Parish 2000; Tang 2005; and Chen and Lu 2007).

Economic Growth and Marketization

The third important component of Chinese life is economic growth and marketization. Marketization brings back individual interest and intensified interpersonal competition. Consequently, trust should decline. On the other hand, market economy leads to social diversification and cooperation, which may result in greater interpersonal trust. The impact of economic growth and rapid improvement of living standard on trust is also unclear. On one hand, modernization would seem to discourage group-based social interaction and increase the sense of privacy as more and more people are moving from the traditional single-story interconnected communal living quarters into separated apartments in guarded residential areas. After all, many developed societies showed lower levels of trust than China (figure 4.1). Yet economic modernization increases education and income. These factors will increase individual citizens' involvement in civic activities such as membership in associational groups and other types of civic participation (Inkeles 1974; Verba, Nie, and Kim 1978; Read 2003). In the Soviet Union and post-Soviet societies in the early 1990s, education had a clear impact in promoting public support for democratic changes, and its effect was independent of regime type (Miller, Hesli, and Reisinger 1994; Miller, Reisinger, and Hesli 1996). Accordingly, modernization, as reflected in increased education, income, and urbanization, should promote interpersonal trust, even in an authoritarian society.

With newly available survey data, I examine the roles of the preceding factors in explaining interpersonal trust. I address the question of why trust is so high in China and what is its exact meaning. Finally, I also examine the impact of different types of trust on other political attitudes.

Most of the data in this chapter are drawn from the 2008 China Survey. The 2008 survey includes both rural and urban residents, while earlier studies on trust only included urban residents.[2]

FINDINGS I: CLASSIFICATION OF INTERPERSONAL TRUST

This section explores the meaning of trust with survey data. The 2008 survey contains the same interpersonal trust question "Can most people be trusted?" as in the previous surveys. As shown in table 4.1, 54% (weighted) of the 2008 respondents answered "yes," indicating a continuous high level of interpersonal trust in China. In order to further examine the meaning of trust, we designed a set of questions in the 2008 survey about how much each respondent trusts each of 12 groups of people. Each group has a trust thermometer from 0 (no trust) to 100 (most trust) based on the 3,989 respondents' ratings. The 0–100 trust thermometer for each group is the average value of the respondents' ratings for that group. The most trusted groups are family members (96) and relatives (84), followed by neighbors (71), villagers (70), schoolmates (69), coworkers (67), and home-towners (*tongxiang*, 66). At even lower levels are urbanites (49), businessmen (36),

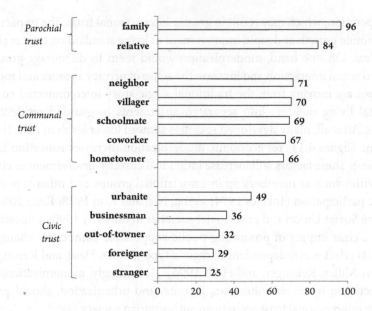

Figure 4.2:
Trust thermometers

out-of-towners (32), foreigners (29), and strangers (25). Overall, trust seems to decrease as the distance between one's immediate family and a given group increases.

A visual display of the trust ratings (figure 4.2) indicates that the 12 groups fall into three clusters. Family and relatives are in the first group, with the highest trust ratings. Neighbors, villagers, schoolmates, coworkers, and people with the same geographic origin (home-towners) are in the second group, with the second highest ratings. Urbanites, businessmen, out-of-towners, foreigners, and strangers are in the third group and have the lowest ratings. This classification is confirmed by a factor analysis which nicely categorizes the 12 groups under three factors (appendix 4.1).

Three Types of Interpersonal Trust

The factor analysis results indicate that family and relatives are most closely related to each other and fall in the same category. This category is based on traditional kinship ties which are the closest to one's immediate self and can be described as *parochial trust.*

Neighbors, villagers, schoolmates, coworkers, and people with the same geographic origin (home-towners) are more related to each other than to other groups and thus belong to another category. This category is about one's immediate social and work environment. As mentioned earlier, China's socialist tradition is conducive to fostering state-defined group ties. Trust developed in this environment can be described as *communal trust*. It is no surprise that the factor analysis puts rural residents (villagers) in this category, since rural life still creates greater community solidarity than urban life, partially as a result of the remaining rural communal dwelling arrangement.

The third category of related groups contains urbanites, businessmen, out-of-towners, foreigners, and strangers. This category is in the third zone away from one's immediate self. It is the most abstract type of trust based on one's civic awareness and can be defined as *civic trust*. For the same reason that trust for rural residents was categorized as communal trust, it is no surprise that urbanites are defined as part of civic trust, since urbanites may represent the modern lifestyle such as cars, single-family dwelling, and the Internet that creates less traditional community solidarity but more modern civic awareness.

Three Types of Trust and General Interpersonal Trust

The three types of specific trust (parochial, civic, and communal) in figure 4.2 provide further understanding of interpersonal trust. It may be obvious that the three types of specific trust are related to interpersonal trust. What is not immediately clear, however, is which of the three types of trust has the strongest effect on interpersonal trust. If the Confucian explanation is correct, parochial trust should be most closely related to interpersonal trust. On the other hand, if the modernization explanation is true, civic trust in China should instead be most closely associated with interpersonal trust. Again, if the civic culture school of thought is right, communal trust based on bureaucratic control should not promote interpersonal trust. Further, it is also necessary to examine the impact of the three specific trusts on interpersonal trust when individual characteristics are controlled. The three types of trust are indices derived from the factor analysis results (appendix 4.1). Each type of the specific trusts is converted into a 0–1 scale. They are then examined against interpersonal trust (dependent variable).

Interpersonal trust is measured by the question "Generally speaking, would you say that most people can be trusted or that you need to be very careful in dealing with people?" Two choices were given: "Most people can be trusted" (coded 1) and "Need to be very careful" (coded 0). The first choice indicates more interpersonal trust. This is the same question used in the World Values Surveys and in Almond and Verba's (1963) 1959 five-country surveys.

Table 4.2. INTERPERSONAL TRUST BY TRUST TYPES
(OLS COEFFICIENTS)

	Interpersonal trust
Communal trust	0.549***
Civic trust	0.310***
Parochial trust	0.126***
Constant	−0.195***
Observations	7,594
R^2	0.111

***$p<=.01$. *Source:* The 2004 Legal Reform Survey.
Notes: Age, gender, education, income, ethnicity, party membership, urbanization,
and township are controlled but not shown (see appendix 4.2b).

Table 4.2 contains the multivariate regression results of interpersonal trust.[3] It shows how communal, civic, and parochial trusts affected the overall interpersonal trust while controlling for age, ability to speak Mandarin, education, group membership, welfare, ethnicity, gender, urbanization, family income, and geographic region (see appendix 4.2 for the full model). Interestingly, among the three specific types, communal trust had the strongest impact on interpersonal trust, followed by civic trust and parochial trust.[4]

In short, the findings in this section are worth repeating. First, the classification of trust makes an important distinction between different types of trust. It shows that trust has at least three dimensions—parochial, civic, and communal. Parochial trust is associated with kinship-based traditional social and economic lifestyle. Communal trust carries the characteristics of China's traditional socialist legacy. Civic trust is probably the closest to the kind of trust described in the civic culture literature. Judging by the broad range of groups that it encompasses, this type of trust has the broadest scope.

The second interesting and somewhat unexpected finding in this section is that, while the three types of trust all have positive influence in the overall interpersonal trust, the strongest source of interpersonal trust clearly comes from communal trust, rather than from parochial trust or civic trust. The civic culture literature and the Confucian explanation of China's high level of interpersonal trust are only correct to a certain extent in predicting the positive affect of civic trust and parochial trust, yet they did not foresee the unique influence of communal trust which is a direct product of Chinese political culture under the CCP's rule (see chapter 1). In the next section, I examine the social and political implications of these three types of specific trust.

FINDINGS II: TRUST AND POLITICAL ATTITUDES AND BEHAVIOR

The preceding section examined what creates trust. This section looks at what trust creates. The data analysis is based on the 2004 Legal Reform Survey which includes a random sample of 7,714 respondents. The 2004 survey has the same questions related to interpersonal trust and trust in the specific groups as the 2008 China Survey, but the 2004 survey contains more questions related to political attitudes and behavior than the 2008 China Survey and can be used to examine the effects of the three types of trust on a greater range of political attitudes and behavior. Specifically, this section examines the impact of the three types of interpersonal trust on regime support, nationalism, political interest, social activism, efficacy, volunteerism, and tolerance.

First, interpersonal trust is expected to promote *regime support* in democratic societies (Brehm and Rahn 1997; Rice 2001; Keele 2007; Denters, Gabrie, and Torcal 2007). The question is whether it also promotes regime support in an authoritarian state. If so, what type of trust would do so? Following the civic culture argument (Almond and Verba 1963), in an authoritarian society, both parochial trust and communal trust should increase regime support while civic trust should not.[5] Regime support is measured by an index of the respondent's confidence in the following organizations: consumers' association, court, people's congress, legal defense, ombudsman's office, work unit, the Communist Party, public prosecutor's office, government, labor union, media, women's federation, and public security. A factor analysis indicates that these items are highly correlated with each other and only one factor is generated (results not shown). Therefore, the factor index based on these items is an indication of regime support. The system support factor scores are converted into a 0–1 scale.

Second, another possible measure of regime support is *nationalism*. It may be true that not every nationalist supports the current regime. One reason to believe that regime support and nationalism are closely related is the fact that the post-Mao Chinese government has added a significant element of nationalism in its guiding ideology. This tactic is designed to incorporate those nationalists who did not identify with the Communist Party. Nationalism is measured by the following four statements in the 2004 survey (also see chapter 3):

1. I would rather be a citizen of China than of any other country in the world.
2. Our country's shame would result in each citizen's inferiority in the eyes of foreigners.

3. The world would be a better place if people from other countries were more like the Chinese.
4. The individual should sacrifice for the benefit of our country.

Agreement with the preceding statements indicates more nationalism. A factor index using the four items is created, and the factor scores are converted into a 0–1 scale. Zero is no nationalist feeling, and 1 is maximum nationalism.

Third, one precondition for active citizen participation in politics is *political interest*. It is necessary to examine whether trust would increase political interest. The civic society literature would expect a positive influence of civic trust on political interest. Similarly, it would expect a negative effect of parochial trust on political interest. It is not clear whether communal trust would promote political interest, depending on whether community solidarity is a top-down control or a more contractual relationship between the public and the state. Top-down control would lead to political disinterest, whereas a mutually obligatory relationship would lead to more interest. Political interest is measured by the question "Some people are very interested in government affairs and others are not very interested. Please tell us whether you are very interested [coded 1], relatively interested [coded 0.666], not very interested [0.333], or not interested at all [coded 0]."

Fourth, another way trust can promote citizen participation is through *social activism*. We expect that civic trust and communal trust would increase social activism while parochial trust would not. One common method to measure social activism is through citizen participation in social and political groups. Such a measure is less effective in China due to the lack of autonomous social groups such as political parties and labor unions. The 2004 survey asked the respondents whether they had participated in the following social activities in the past two years: going to a movie, going to an opera, or attending a live concert. The combined factor index of the three activities measures social activism (0 = none and 1 = maximum).

Fifth, the feeling of *political efficacy* is an important prerequisite of a successful democracy. Political efficacy can assure citizens' active participation in government decision making. Again, we expect that political efficacy should be encouraged by civic trust but discouraged by the inwardly oriented parochial trust. If the consequence of bureaucratic control is alienation, communal trust should not promote political efficacy. Efficacy is measured by nine questions in the 2004 survey:

1. Hiring a lawyer can win a lawsuit more easily.
2. People like myself can affect government decision making.

3. Local people's congresses listen to the opinions of people like myself.
4. People are capable of expressing their opinions on the complex issues in a modern society.
5. In most times the government can solve the problems for people like myself.
6. Government should not decide whether ideas can be circulated in a society.
7. In most times the police can solve problems for people like myself.
8. Ordinary people should question the government.
9. One should not simply obey the government.

For each question, "strongly agree" indicates more efficacy, "agree" shows some efficacy, "disagree" means less efficacy, and "strongly disagree" is equal to no efficacy. These nine questions are combined into a single factor index with a 0–1 scale where 0 means no efficacy and 1 is maximum efficacy.

Sixth, *volunteerism* is a valuable component of American democracy (Tocqueville 2000). It is a channel for citizen participation. Civic trust is expected to encourage volunteerism, and parochial trust should discourage it. If communal trust is confined to one's immediate communities, it should not encourage volunteerism beyond one's immediate social circles. The 2004 survey asked the respondents whether they had donated blood, volunteered in social campaigns, made a donation to the Hope Project, or made a donation to disaster-stricken areas. Responses are coded 0 if none of the activities is chosen, 0.25 if only one item is chosen, 0.5 if two items are chosen, 0.75 if three are chosen, and 1 if the respondent participated in all four activities.

Seventh, *tolerance* is an important prerequisite for the successful functioning of democracy. Tolerance may lead to willingness to compromise, respect for diversity, and cooperation with others. We should expect that civic trust would encourage tolerance and that parochial trust would discourage tolerance. It is unclear whether communal trust would create tolerance. If the communal control is rigid, communal trust should not encourage tolerance for diversity. Yet a communal culture is significantly different from the traditional kinship network. It represents a higher level of socialization that should be more tolerant of diversity. Tolerance is measured by the following question in the 2004 survey: "Can you tolerate the following people as your neighbors?" The respondent was asked to choose from (1) absolutely not, (2) difficult to tolerate, (3) possibly can tolerate, and (4) can completely tolerate for each of the following groups: criminal record holders, foreigners, conservative ideologues, drunks, radicals, mentally ill patients, other ethnicities, migrant workers, drug addicts, AIDS patients, homosexuals, and religious fanatics. These items are combined into a factor index with a 0–1 scale. Zero indicates no tolerance, and 1 is the most tolerance.

OLS regression is used to examine the role of each type of trust on the aforementioned values and behavior: interpersonal trust, regime support, nationalism, political interest, social activism, political efficacy, volunteerism, and tolerance (table 4.3).

In table 4.3, as expected, civic trust plays a significant role in promoting tolerance. It also discourages regime-promoted nationalism. According to the civic culture school, these are desirable attitudes and behavior for creating democracy. Somewhat unexpected is the lack of clear impact of civic trust on political interest, efficacy, and volunteerism. One possibility is that civic trust is associated with the desire to create a new set of civic institutions and the respondents with civic trust are ambivalent about the existing single-party-controlled decision-making process. It is also somewhat unexpected that civic trust has a negative effect on social activism, at least not on the social activism measured by going to a movie, opera, or concert.

Also as shown in table 4.3, parochial trust does not seem to promote democracy and participation. It strengthens passive regime support and nationalism while discouraging social tolerance. Its effect on increasing interpersonal trust is the smallest compared with civic trust and communal trust (table 4.2). This last finding does not support the Confucian explanation of China's high level of interpersonal trust.

Perhaps the most interesting and ambivalent results in table 4.3 are about communal trust. On the one hand, it strengthens regime sustainability of the authoritarian state by encouraging regime support and nationalism. On the other hand, communal trust plays a strong role in promoting democratic values and behavior including political interest,

Table 4.3. POLITICAL VALUES AND BEHAVIOR BY TRUST TYPE, OLS REGRESSION COEFFICIENTS

	System support	Nationalism	Political interest	Social activism	Efficacy	Donation	Tolerance
Parochial trust	0.144**	0.103**	0.027	0.143**	0.023	–0.013	–0.030**
Communal trust	0.437**	0.247**	0.273**	0.121**	0.269**	0.044**	–0.007
Civic trust	0.017	–0.039**	0.034	–0.148**	0.020	0.015	0.053**

Source: 2004 Legal Reform Survey.
Notes: In the seven OLS regression equations, each of the seven attitude and behavior variables serves as the dependent variable, and the three types of interpersonal trust are independent variables. Age, gender, education, income, ethnicity, party membership, urbanization, and township are controlled but not shown (see appendix 4.2).

policy efficacy, and volunteerism. Its impact on promoting China's high level of interpersonal trust is the strongest compared with civic trust and parochial trust (table 4.2). In other words, communal trust serves a dual function, promoting limited democracy while preserving political order and regime solidarity.

CONCLUSIONS

Now I return to the questions proposed earlier in this chapter: why trust is so high in China and whether trust creates favorable conditions for a civil society. Although parochial trust is the highest in China, it is neither the only nor the strongest reason for the high level of interpersonal trust. Instead, interpersonal trust in China is derived from the same "civicness" as in democratic societies. Another unexpected source of interpersonal trust is China's bureaucratic-communal political environment. In fact, communal trust makes the strongest contribution to China's high level of interpersonal trust. Its effect is even stronger than civic trust. The findings in this study support the prediction by the civic culture school of thought about the positive relationship between civic trust and interpersonal trust. They provide no proof, however, of the predictions derived from the civic culture literature that civic culture can only grow in a democratic society, that authoritarian societies discourage trust, and that Confucianism supports civic culture.

Similarly, the findings about the impact of the three types of specific trust also address the second question of whether trust creates civic values and attitudes. The findings about how civic trust promotes support for democracy back up the assertion that trust is closely associated with liberal democratic values such as social tolerance. But the question is why an authoritarian society like China can develop civic trust in the first place. Clearly, democratic institutions are neither a necessary nor a sufficient condition for trust. The strong effect of communal trust on regime support further weakens the association between civic culture and democracy. A trust-based political culture can grow in both democratic societies and non-democratic societies and can serve to improve regime stability in any political system, not only in democracy. For the time being, trust by itself is unlikely to create a democratic revolution in China because it is based on communal trust that facilitates regime support, national identity, social activism, political efficacy, and volunteerism. In the long run, whether trust will bring democratization or authoritarian regime stability depends partially on how fast the state-dependent social groups transform themselves into autonomous social groups during China's economic modernization.

Political Trust in China and Taiwan (with Joseph (Yingnan) Zhou and Ray Ou Yang)

Measured by liberal democratic standards, China in many ways is a repressive state that does not respect human rights. It restricts the freedom of expression by media censorship and by jailing political dissidents. It limits religious freedom by arresting Catholic priests and by shutting down underground churches. It denies people's free choice of having more than one child. It harshly cracks down on any separatist movement in the ethnic minority regions. The list goes on.

Yet public opinion surveys consistently show high levels of popular trust of the Chinese government (chapter 2). In the meantime, studies show that public support for the political system is also high in many Western democracies, although support for politicians and specific institutions has declined (Dalton 1999). It is difficult to isolate the cause of any difference in political trust between China and Western democracies, since they differ culturally as well as politically.

This chapter compares political trust in authoritarian China and democratic Taiwan. The two societies share similar Confucian cultural values and authoritarian political tradition, but they followed very different political paths in the 1980s. By controlling for cultural tradition, the difference in political trust between these two societies can be interpreted as the results of the different political systems.

WHAT IS POLITICAL TRUST?

The study of political trust is almost as old as political science itself. Political trust is a desirable commodity that all political systems want to acquire.

It is probably more easily understood and expected under democracy than under autocracy. Democracies create political trust because they guarantee their citizens' rights to freely compete for ideas and for offices. Even autocratic regimes are often associated with using force; these regimes also feel more secure and legitimate if their citizens show more trust in them (Rousseau 1762).

Several concepts can be used to describe public opinion regarding the political environment people live in. In addition to political trust, political support and political legitimacy are also frequently used to measure people's sentiment about their political system and their government. People have to trust their political system first. Political trust leads to public belief in the legitimacy of the political system. Both political trust and political legitimacy make the public support the political system. Although these concepts carry slightly different meanings, they are highly related to each other and are used interchangeably in this chapter. Some people tend to focus on the differences between these concepts. As we show herein, as long as the *measures* of these concepts stay clearly defined and unchanged, it may not be so critical what label is used.

One way to measure political trust is to ask people about their support for democracy (Chu, Nathan, and Shin 2010). Researchers have shown that support for democracy is high throughout the world in established democracies, in new democracies, and even in autocracies (Dalton and Shin 2007; Inglehart and Wetzel 2009). The underlying assumption is that in democratic societies, political legitimacy is high because people support their political system, whereas in autocratic societies, support for democracy means low political legitimacy because people want a different system. The problem with such an assumption is that some autocratic governments also claim to be democratic (Diamond 2010; Shi and Lu 2010; Lu and Shi 2015). Even North Korea claims to be a "people's democratic republic." This is not to say that North Korea is really democratic by Western standards, but its people may believe in its own version of democracy. The high level of support for democracy in these societies actually means support for and legitimacy of the autocratic regimes. As a result, the same concept of democracy measures different things, and this creates the problem of "concept stretching" (Sartori 1970; Collier and Mahon 1993; Peters 1998).

This chapter goes beyond the concept of democracy and examines political trust in four dimensions, including (1) public perception of the political system as a whole, (2) national identity, (3) trust in key political institutions, and (4) trust in the leaders who run the government.

These four components cover the two categories of political support defined by Easton (1975), namely diffuse political support (system support and national identity) and specific support (trust in institutions and in leaders). The advantage of these measures is that they can be applied to both democracies and autocracies while avoiding concept stretching.

Previous studies show that while diffuse support (support for democratic principles) is high, specific support has declined in post-industrial Western democracies (Dalton 1999; Norris 1999, 2011) and also in new democracies such as Taiwan (Shyu 2010). Similarly, in autocratic China, O'Brien and Li in their studies explain how rural residents use the central government as a shield to fight against power abuse by their local governments (O'Brien and Li 2005a, 2005b, 2006). Other studies of Chinese regime legitimacy more directly apply the Eastonian concepts and show a similar distinction of high diffuse support and low specific support in China as in Western democracies (Chen 2004; Shi 2009). From the existing studies, one knows more about the difference between central government support and local government support (chapter 2), and between diffuse and specific political supports, but less about the difference between democracy and autocracy.

COMPETING THEORIES OF POLITICAL TRUST

By examining the existing literature, one can identify several reasons for the rise and fall of political trust. These include (1) political mobilization, (2) economic satisfaction, (3) internal efficacy, (4) external efficacy, and (5) Confucian tradition. These factors require further elaboration.

Political Mobilization

The first explanation of political trust lies in the regime's own effort at promoting public support. One way to do so is through the officially controlled or sanctioned media (Brady 2007; Shirk 2011; Norris 2011; Hong 2012). One problem with political mobilization is its unintended consequences. Huntington (1968) shows that mobilized political participation can become autonomous participation. In China, Tang (2005) shows that political mobilization through the media can also create unintended consequences by making people more critical of the government and acceptable of Western liberal ideas. In addition, media commercialization and the development of communication technologies make information control more difficult and encourage freedom of speech and autonomous political action (Shirk 2011; Stockmann 2012; Lei 2012).

Other means of political mobilization are through officially granted channels of citizen *political participation*. Citizens are expected to show more support for the political system when they feel free to voice their concerns, to replace their leaders in elections, and to influence government decision-making through contacting government officials (Almond and Verba 1963; Verba, Nie, and Kim 1978; Gilley 2006).

Economic Satisfaction

In democratic societies, one important factor for voters when choosing their candidate is the assessment of their economic well-being (Gilley 2006; Bovens and Wille 2008; Lewis-Beck, Jacoby, Norpoth, and Weisberg 2008; Lewis-Beck, Tang, and Martini 2014). In an autocratic society like China, regime legitimacy can be boosted by the government's success in promoting economic development and in improving people's living standards (Wang 2006; Wright 2010; Norris 2011; Pei 2012). This success explains why China has so far survived the collapse of Communism and the Arab Spring (Pei 2012). Likewise, its future stability and sustainability will also depend on its ability to create a positive public outlook for further economic benefits. While the economic view seems to be a powerful predictor of political trust in China, it does not explain the difference between China and other fast-growing economies. For example, in the 5th Wave of the World Values Survey, China still ranks at the top of political trust among other fast-growing economies such as India, Brazil, and Russia (see Yang and Tang 2010). Others predict that economic modernization will eventually lead to the collapse of the Communist regime in China when per capita income reaches a certain level (Rowen 1996; Diamond 2012).

Internal Efficacy

Campbell, Gurin, and Miller (1954, 187–94) define political efficacy as "the feeling that individual political action does have, or can have, an impact upon the political process." This concept represents the extent to which people are willing to embrace and participate in a political system. As Lane (1959) suggests, the concept of political efficacy incorporates two separate but interrelated components. One is the image of oneself as effective, and the other is the image of a responsive government (Lane 1959, 149). Lane's argument initiates the differentiation between internal efficacy and external efficacy.

To be more specific, internal efficacy refers to beliefs about one's own competence to understand and to participate effectively in politics

(Balch 1974; Craig, Niemi, and Silver 1990). Even if people do not actually participate in politics, political support will increase when they *feel* that they can make a difference if they want to (Almond and Verba 1963). Conversely, the feeling of powerlessness creates hostile feelings toward the authority (Stokes 1962). In addition, internal efficacy can influence political trust through mechanisms that are more complex. Scholars have identified a three-way interaction between internal efficacy, political trust, and participation. Research finds that an efficacious and trustful individual tends to be more active in conventional participation (Pollock 1983), which reinforces the individual's political trust (Finkel 1987).

While internal efficacy can be created in a democratic society where there are institutional channels for political participation, political apathy may be the norm in an authoritarian society where such channels of participation are under-developed. However, it should be noted that even in a democratic society, socioeconomic inequality in political participation is still likely to exist. It has been shown that this inequality can lower disadvantaged people's internal efficacy (e.g., Abramson 1983).

The second dimension of internal efficacy is interpersonal trust. With some interesting exceptions in South Korea (Kim 2005), existing studies show that interpersonal trust leads to more political support for democratic principles in democratic societies (Almond and Verba 1963; Putnam, Leonardi, and Nanetti 1993; Inglehart 1999; Fukuyama 2000). As discussed in chapter 4, interpersonal trust also makes people support the authoritarian government in China. The question is whether interpersonal trust continues to promote regime support in China when other competing explanations are taken into consideration.

External Efficacy

External efficacy refers to people's belief that their government will respond to their demands (Balch 1974; Craig, Niemi, and Silver 1990; Hutchison and Johnson 2011). Regime trust is high when such belief is strong. The conventional wisdom is that a democratic government must respond to public opinion if it wants to win in competitive elections, while an autocratic government does not have to respond to public demands due to the lack of competitive elections. Consequently, regime support must be higher in democratic states than in autocratic states. But some studies show that representative democracy actually makes elected politicians less likely to respond to public opinion between elections. Once elected, their jobs are guaranteed until the next election. As a result, the public may become apathetic toward such a system (Dalton 1999).

In an earlier attempt to compare China and Taiwan, Shi (2001) shows a higher level of government responsiveness in China than in Taiwan. Shi's study uses data collected in 1993 when Taiwan did not have competitive elections. What remains unanswered is whether Taiwan's implementation of competitive elections in recent years leads to improved government responsiveness. The other unanswered question in Shi's earlier study (2001) is whether government responsiveness leads to political trust.

Another line of research focuses on scapegoating in China. It shows that the people voice their demands at the local level, while using the central government policy to legitimize their rebellious behavior against local governments (Li 2004; O'Brien and Li 2006). The focus of these studies is local politics; they do not provide a clear answer to the question about central government support. The underlying assumption is that the central government in Beijing does not need to respond with policy change as long as it can blame the local officials for any wrongdoings and unsatisfactory implementation of the central policy. As we show in this and the next chapters, however, scapegoating itself is a response, and such a tactic is often effective in promoting political trust in the central government.

Confucian Tradition

According to the culturalist view, regime legitimacy tends to rise in cultures that emphasize social hierarchy and group orientation (Ma 2007), such as Confucian tradition. For example, Shi (2001, 2015) measures social hierarchy and group orientation by survey questions related to the respondents' respect for social hierarchy and their tendency to avoid open conflict, and finds significant effects of both hierarchical orientation and conflict avoidance in promoting regime legitimacy particularly in China but also in Taiwan. Other studies dispute the influence of culture (Mishler and Rose 2001, 2005). For example, Wong, Wan, and Hsiao (2011) measure cultural values by public attitudes toward cultural tradition and find insignificant effect of "traditionalism" in political trust in China, Hong Kong, Singapore, South Korea, Japan, and only a weak effect in Taiwan. The anti-culturalists argue that economic and political performance by the government is a much more important determinant of political trust (Mishler and Rose 2001, 2005; Wong, Wan, and Hsiao 2011).

COMPARING CHINA AND TAIWAN: METHODS AND DATA

This chapter examines political trust in China and Taiwan. These two societies share a common cultural heritage of Confucianism but very different recent political experiences (Chu 2012). China has been ruled by the Communist Party since 1949. Until around the time of Mao's death in 1976, China was under rigid economic planning and tight political control. Since the late 1970s and early 1980s, China has experienced significant economic liberalization but no fundamental political change. Although there is greater freedom at the individual level, the country is still under the single-party rule with state-controlled media. There have been relatively free village elections, but there is no legitimate political opposition to effectively challenge the Communist Party's monopoly of political power at the national level.

On the contrary, Taiwan has experienced fundamental changes in both economic and political spheres. After being defeated by the Communists in the mainland in 1949, the Nationalist Party retreated to Taiwan and ruled the Island under the Martial Law until 1987, while promoting an economic takeoff during the same period of time. After the Martial Law was lifted in 1987, Taiwan experienced a remarkable political transformation to democracy. In the first truly competitive presidential election in 2000, the opposition Democratic Progressive Party (DPP) candidate Chen Shuibian defeated the Nationalist Party candidate and became Taiwan's first democratically elected president. After eight years of DPP rule which was tainted by political scandals of corruption, the Nationalist Party candidate Ma Ying-jeou defeated Chen in 2008 and regained the Nationalist Party's control of presidency and was reelected in 2012. In this process of party competition and political turnovers, Taiwan's democratic politics matured, and its media have become independent of state control (Fell 2005, 2008).

Studying political trust in these two societies allows one to focus on the impact of the different political systems while controlling for cultural similarities. Such a method of "most similar systems design" is commonly used in comparative political research (Przworski and Teune 1970). Some people may be quick to point out the differences between the two societies, such as Taiwan's smaller size and higher level of economic development than China. Yet Taiwan is by no means a homogenous society even if it is much smaller than China. Taiwan has its own geographic, ethnic, religious, and economic diversities perhaps just as much as mainland China. More importantly, the two societies have been ruled by two separate governments since 1949. Regardless of what the two governments say about their relationship to each other, these are two de facto separate political entities for the purpose of political science research. The research question is whether and how the two very different political systems generate political support in these two societies that share the same cultural tradition, similar social and economic diversity, and the same Leninist political tradition of single party rule.

Data for this chapter are drawn from the Wave II Asia Barometer Survey (ABSII) which was co-directed by Profs. Fu Hu and Yun-han Chu and received major funding support from Taiwan's Ministry of Education, Academia Sinica, and the National Taiwan University (www.asianbarometer. org). The survey includes both Mainland China and Taiwan. The random sample for the Taiwan survey contains 1,587 respondents who were 20 or older, and the survey was conducted in 2006. The probability sample for the China survey includes 5,098 respondents who were 18 or older, and the survey was conducted in 2008. The two surveys used the same questionnaire which includes questions on political support, cultural values, economic attitudes, political mobilization, internal and external efficacies, as well as the respondents' demographic information.

In addition to the ABSII data, this chapter also relies on the information from the 4th and 5th World Values Surveys (http://www. worldvaluessurvey.org/). These surveys were conducted in China in 2001 ($n = 1,000$) and 2007 ($n = 2,015$) and in Taiwan in 2000 ($n = 780$) and 2006 ($n = 1,227$). The data from the two waves of the World Values Survey are used to examine the change over time in political trust in the two societies.

Perhaps the most frequently asked question about political trust in China is whether the respondents are telling the truth. While political sensitivity is indeed a factor in public opinion surveys in China, people are becoming quite outspoken and candid in responding to survey questions as long as the questions are not about whether they should overthrow the government. For example, the reader may suspect that Chinese respondents lied when they showed an extremely low level of distrust (5%) of national government in the ABSII survey (55% in Taiwan). In the meantime, however, distrust of local government in China jumps to 39% (40% in Taiwan) even if it is perhaps riskier to show open dissatisfaction with the local authorities that have more direct impact in one's everyday life. Such a gap between trusting central and local governments should give the reader more confidence that the respondents' high support of the central government is probably not a lie.

The second example that Chinese respondents are not afraid of answering politically sensitive questions concerns their attitude toward the government when they think it is wrong. If the Chinese are as coerced as commonly expected, one would expect more Chinese to say that they would support the government even if it is wrong. As shown in figure 1.1, in the 2008 China Survey, 46% of Chinese respondents would support their government even if they think it is wrong. Among the 25 countries where the same question is asked in the 2003 National Identity II Survey (http://www.issp.org/), Venezuela ranks the highest (69%) in supporting the wrong government and Sweden ranks at the bottom (34%). When China is added to the list, it ranks the 17th (46%), after Portugal (59%), Switzerland (58%), Poland (52%), Spain (51%), the United States (50%), and Denmark (48%). Again, the large number of Chinese (54%) who feel free to openly show their opposition to the government that they think is wrong further gives the reader more confidence in survey responses in China.

The third way to deal with political sensitivity is to approach "don't know" responses more conservatively. Researchers often treat "don't know" as random missing values and exclude them from analysis. Yet some studies show that Chinese respondents sometimes answer "don't know" to the politically sensitive questions that they don't feel comfortable answering (Ren 2009). The reader should feel more confident about the reported level of political trust in China if the "don't know" answers are treated as negative responses. Such a treatment should effectively weigh down the overall level of regime trust in the sample (see notes in tables 5.1A and 5.1B).

Finally, the high level of regime trust in China is more likely a result of other reasons, such as cultural values, economic benefit, political mobilization, and political efficacy. These factors are further examined in the rest of this chapter.

MEASURING AND COMPARING POLITICAL TRUST IN CHINA AND TAIWAN

This section examines the level of political trust in China and Taiwan. It takes a multidimensional approach to measuring political trust. It uses four indicators:

1. Trust in political institutions including the national government, parliament, political parties, police, military, civil service, and courts.
2. Trust in political leaders.
3. Trust in the nation.
4. Trust in the political system.

Perhaps the most commonly used measure of regime trust is public confidence in the key political institutions (Shi 2001; Wang 2006; Yang and Tang 2010; Wong, Wan, and Hsiao 2011). Trust in political leaders is part of "specific" political support defined by Easton (1975). Trusts in the nation and in the political system echo "diffuse" political support again defined by Easton (1975), as well as the components of civic culture described by Almond and Verba (1963).

As shown in table 5.1A, When China in 2008 and Taiwan in 2006 are compared using the data from the Asian Barometer Survey II, they demonstrate a huge gap in political trust. China scored 61 out of 100 on the institutional trust index, while Taiwan only reached 21 out of 100. In China, 51% respondents trusted their leaders "quite a lot" or "a great deal," but only 22% did so in Taiwan. While 42% of the mainland Chinese respondents were very proud to be a citizen of China, only 28% respondents in Taiwan felt that way. The big jump for Taiwan is diffuse support for the democratic system. Sixty-two percent of Taiwanese respondents agreed or strongly agreed that their political system was the best. But the diffuse support for the autocratic system in China was even higher (73%). Overall, China outperformed Taiwan in every dimension of political trust (table 5.1A).

The findings in table 5.1A confirm the existing studies about the high level of political trust in China (Norris 2011) and the low level of trust in democratic societies (Dalton 1999). Before looking into the sources of political trust, it is necessary to look at the change in political trust over time in the two societies. Since 2000, China's autocratic political system remained mostly unchanged. In Taiwan, however, political democratization took off during the same period of time. The highly competitive presidential election in 2000 resulted in a narrow win by Chen Shui-bian

Table 5.1A. POLITICAL TRUST IN CHINA IN 2008 AND TAIWAN IN 2006 (WEIGHTED %)

	China	Taiwan
Trust in institutions (max = 100)	61	21
Trust in leaders (% agreed/strongly agreed)	51	22
Trust in nation (% very proud to be a citizen)	42	28
Trust in system (% agreed/strongly agreed)	73	62

Asian Barometer Survey II.
Notes: (1) Trust in institutions is an additive index of one's feelings in seven key political institutions (national government, parliament, political parties, police, military, civil service, and courts. "A great deal of trust" and "quite a lot of trust" are coded as 2 and 1, respectively; "not much trust" and "none at all" are coded as 0. The resulting trust index is converted into a 0–100 scale ($x/14*100$). (2) Trust in leaders is based on the statement "You can generally trust the people who run our government to do what is right". (3) Trust in nation is derived from the question "How proud are you to be a citizen?" (4) Trust in system is drawn from the statement "Whatever its faults may be, our form of government is still the best for us". (5) For all four items, missing values are included in the total numbers of respondents (see notes in table 5.1b).

with only 39.3% of the votes (Soong Chu-yu won 36.8% and Lien Chan 23.1%). In 2004, the challenging Nationalist Party candidate, Lien Chan, had a comfortable lead prior to the election but eventually lost to the incumbent Chen Shui-bian due to an alleged assassination attempt against Chen the day before the election. Chen survived the shooting with only minor skin scratches and was reelected the next day with an even narrower margin of 0.028% more votes (50.11%) than Lien Chan (49.89%; Hsieh 2010; Rigger 2010). It will be interesting to compare the changing public opinion over time in the politically stagnant mainland China and in the rapidly democratizing but sometimes chaotic Taiwan.

The 4th and 5th Waves of the World Values Survey provide an opportunity for comparing institutional trust in China and Taiwan over time. In China, the 4th Wave and the 5th Wave were conducted in 2001 and 2007. In Taiwan, they were conducted in 2000 and 2006. The 2006 Taiwan survey was important because it was implemented after the controversial 2004 presidential election.

As shown in table 5.1B, although trust in specific institutions fluctuated slightly from item to item between 2001 and 2007 in China, the overall institutional trust index remained almost at the same level (66) with a negligible 1% increase. The picture is quite different in Taiwan, where trust in each of the seven key institutions experienced a double-digit drop. The overall institutional trust index dropped 18 points from 55 in 2000

Table 5.1B. INSTITUTIONAL TRUST OVER TIME IN CHINA AND TAIWAN (WEIGHTED, MAX = 100)

Trust in	China 2001	China 2007	China 2001–2007	Taiwan 2000	Taiwan 2006	Taiwan 2000–2006
Government	77	72	−5	58	38	−20
Congress	72	67	−5	51	25	−26
Party	69	73	4	45	22	−23
Police	59	63	4	55	42	−13
Military	79	66	−13	63	44	−19
Civil service	41	60	19	55	44	−11
Court		63		56	41	−15
Average	66	66	1	55	37	−18
N	1,000	2,015		780	1,227	

Source: 4th and 5th World Values Surveys.
Notes: (1) The original scale of 0 = no trust, 1 = not much trust, 2 = quite a lot of trust, and 3 = a great deal of trust is converted into a 0–100 scale ($x/3*100$). (2) Missing values are coded as 0 (no trust). Another option is to assume that missing values are random and code them as the mean. This method will result in higher levels of trust. The advantage of coding "don't know" (missing) as "no trust" is to avoid the problem caused by political fear in China when the respondents answered "don't know" (missing values) to politically sensitive questions, while trying to hide their lack of trust in the institutions.

to only 37 in 2006 (table 5.1B). One possible explanation for the decline in political trust in Taiwan is the confusion and frustration with the controversial 2004 presidential election. Another possible explanation is the emergence of the free and often polarized press in Taiwan that made people more suspicious of the government. More generally, the decline of political trust may be a reflection of the negative public reaction to the political chaos created by the democratic transition in Taiwan.

In sum, the findings in this section confirm the earlier studies about the strong regime support in autocratic China and the weak support in democratic Taiwan. One new finding in this section is that such a gap has widened since 2000. The weak political trust in Taiwan in the 2006 ABSII survey is unlikely to be a temporary reaction to the 2004 shooting incident during Taiwan's presidential campaigns. In fact, political trust in Taiwan continued to be low in the 2010 ASBIII survey (see notes in table 5.1A). Another new piece of information is that such a gap exists even if political trust is measured in different ways, in addition to the commonly used measure of institutional trust. The third new finding is that the gap exists in a shared Confucian cultural environment while the two societies differ in their political systems. Without controlling for cultural environment, it is difficult to determine whether the difference in political trust is caused by political system or by culture.

MEASURING AND COMPARING THE SOURCES OF POLITICAL TRUST IN CHINA AND TAIWAN

Before examining the impact of the various factors in promoting regime trust, this section first looks at how these factors themselves differ in autocratic China and in democratic Taiwan. Specifically, it compares five items in these two societies: (1) political mobilization, (2) economic satisfaction, (3) internal efficacy, (4) external efficacy, and (5) Confucian values. As described earlier, these concepts represent the competing theories of political trust. The next section examines how these factors strengthen and weaken political trust in China and Taiwan.

One way to measure *political mobilization* is political participation, which can potentially increase one's sense of regime support if one is able to use different channels to voice one's opinions. In the ABSII survey, the respondents were asked (1) if they voted in the last elections, (2) whether they ever contacted their elected officials, (3) whether they ever contacted government officials, and (4) whether they joined any petitions and demonstrations. Not surprisingly, democratic Taiwan provided more opportunities for citizen participation, as more Taiwanese respondents voted

(80%), contacted their elected officials (10%), and joined petitions and demonstrations (4%) than in China where only 56% voted, 2% contacted elected officials, and 1% petitioned and demonstrated. What is interesting, however, is that people in China did not seem to want to stay quiet even if their political system did not permit them to vote or protest freely. They found their way to participate through contacting government officials. A significantly higher percentage of Chinese respondents (17%) contacted their government officials than in Taiwan (9%, table 5.2–1a). Combining the two contacting questions together, China (2 + 17) scored the same as Taiwan (10 + 9) in political contact.

Political mobilization can also be measured by membership in formal political organizations. In China, formal organizations are sanctioned by the government. These organizations include the Chinese Communist Party, the Labor Union, Women's Federation, and several youth organizations. In Taiwan, where political organizations are not sanctioned, people have the option of joining different political parties and other political organizations. Only 3% of the Chinese respondents belonged to any formal organizations in the ABSII data.[1] A much higher number of Taiwanese respondents (28%) were members of formal organizations, correctly reflecting the existence of much greater degree of political freedom in Taiwan (table 5.2–1b).

Another measure of political mobilization is by watching TV for political news. Unlike the internet and print media, television is the most tightly controlled media channel in China. In Taiwan, while the media are not officially controlled, they are nevertheless highly polarized along party lines. In both societies, acquiring political information through TV news exposes one to political mobilization either by the government in China or by political parties in Taiwan. As shown in table 5.2–1b, while 54% of Taiwanese respondents relied on TV for political news, a significantly larger number of respondents did so in China (82%), suggesting a greater level of political mobilization through the media in China than in Taiwan (table 5.2–1b).

Economic satisfaction is measured by the respondents' assessment of their current and future economic situations. On both measures, Chinese respondents were more satisfied than their Taiwanese counterparts. Fifty-one percent of Chinese respondents thought their current family economic situation was good or very good, while only 40% respondents thought so in Taiwan. The gap was even wider for future economic expectation. More than twice as many respondents in China (76%) than in Taiwan (34%) expected their family economic situation to be better or much better in the next few years (table 5.2–2). These findings confirm the common impression about the continuous high rate of economic growth

Table 5.2. SOURCES OF POLITICAL LEGITIMACY IN CHINA
AND TAIWAN (WEIGHTED)

1a. Political participation:	China	Taiwan
Voted in the last election (%)	56	81
Contacted elected officials (%)	2	10
Contacted government officials (%)	17	9
Petition/demonstration (%)	1	4
1b. Political mobilization:		
Are you a member of any organization or formal groups? (%)	3	28
TV as main source of political information (%)	82	54
2. Economic satisfaction:		
As for your own family, how do you rate your economic situation today?	51	40
(% "good" or "very good")		
What do you think the economic situation of your family will be a few years	76	34
from now? (% "better" or "much better")		
3. Internal efficacy:		
Factor index (0–100) of (1) political interest, (2) "I have ability to participate	57	38
in politics", (3) "Politics is not too complicated" ("d/k" coded as missing and		
imputed, weighted)		
"Most people can be trusted." (% yes)	55	33
4. Confucian values:		
Even if parents' demands are unreasonable, children still should do what parents	49	27
ask.		
(% "agree" or "strongly agree")		
Being a student, one should not question the authority of their teacher.	57	38
(% "agree" or "strongly agree")		
When one has conflict with a neighbor, the best way to deal with it is to	58	28
accommodate the other person (% "agree" or "strongly agree")		
5. External efficacy:		
Government responds to what people want. (% very/largely responsive)	77	36
Last election was unfair. (% "not fair" or "fair but with major problems")	23	41
People are free to speak what they think without fear. (% agree/strongly agree)	76	74
People can join any organization they like without fear. (% agree/strong agree)	54	77

Source: ABSII 2006 (Taiwan) and 2008 (China).
Note: "Don't know" answers are included in the total sample (not coded as missing).

and its social benefit in China. In contrast, Taiwan experienced slow growth during the first four years of Chen Shui-bian's presidency. From 2001 to 2004, the average annual GDP growth was only 2.6% in Taiwan, while China scored a remarkable 9.5% from 2001 to 2008 (http://www.indexmundi.com/g/g.aspx?c=tw&v=66, accessed March 7, 2013).

Internal efficacy. The next likely source of political trust is internal efficacy. As discussed earlier, internal efficacy refers to the *feelings* of one's competence to understand and to participate effectively in politics (Almond and Verba 1963; Craig, Niemi, and Silver 1990). The ABSII survey includes two questions related to internal efficacy: (1) "I have the ability to participate in politics," and (2) "Politics is not too complicated to understand." In addition, the ABSII also contains a third commonly used question about internal efficacy: "How interested are you in political issues?" In order to save space, the three questions are combined into a single factor index ranging from 0 (minimum) to 100 (maximum). The small number of missing values in each question is estimated using the information from the other two questions (imputation). On this internal efficacy index, China scored an impressive 57, and Taiwan only scored 38 (table 5.2–3).

Internal efficacy can also be measured by interpersonal trust. Previous studies suggest that interpersonal trust is a social capital that can make a democratic political system function more smoothly (Almond and Verba 1963; Putnam 1993). The standard question to measure interpersonal trust is "Do you think most people can be trusted?" which has been repeated in many different surveys throughout the world since the 1950s (Almond and Verba 1963). In the ABSII data, China showed a higher level of social capital than Taiwan. Similar to the level of general interpersonal trust shown in Chapter 4, 55% of Chinese respondents thought most people could be trusted, as compared to only 33% in Taiwan (table 5.2–3).

In short, China outscored Taiwan on both dimensions of internal efficacy. One possible explanation for such a gap is that the Chinese respondents were made to believe that their opinions mattered and that their society was harmonious. In Taiwan, people were more cynical due to the fierce political competition and polarization between political parties.

External efficacy. The fourth likely source of political trust is external efficacy, which refers to people's feelings about whether their government would respond to their demands (Craig, Niemi, and Silver 1990; Hutchison and Johnson 2011). In addition, external efficacy can also be measured by whether people *believe* that their electoral system is free and fair, and that they possess the freedoms of speech and organization, regardless of whether they can actually vote and freely speak and join organizations. External efficacy and political trust are not endogenous. People may feel that their needs are met by the government, that the electoral system is free and fair, and that they generally enjoy the freedom of speech and organization, but they may not necessarily support or trust the specific government and the politicians running it.

As shown in table 5.2–5, more than twice as many Chinese respondents (77%) thought their government was responsive to what they wanted, as compared to only 36% in Taiwan. This is somewhat shocking if one expects that democratic governments are more likely to respond to public demand than autocratic governments. One possibility is that democratic governments enjoy relative security once they are elected. This sense of relative security makes them less responsive than autocratic regimes that do not have such luxury. As a result, autocracies are more on their toes in watching public opinion than democracies.

Next, when measured by public perception of fairness of elections, Taiwan again showed a lower degree of external efficacy than China even though the elections were much freer in Taiwan but were limited to the local levels in China. Forty-one percent of Taiwanese thought their last election was not fair or had major problems, while only 23% thought so in China (table 5.2–5). The more positive assessment in China is probably due to the fact that two-thirds of the respondents in the 2008 ABSII survey were in rural areas (appendix 5.2) where village elections were more competitive and better institutionalized than urban residential council elections. The negative assessment in Taiwan is probably a reaction to the shooting that took place the day before the highly controversial presidential election in 2004 as well as the much more open and often critical coverage of the elections in Taiwan by the media.

As expected, more Taiwanese respondents (77%) felt free to join political organizations than mainland Chinese respondents (54%), given the difference in the actual political reality between the two societies. Somewhat unexpected is that the numbers of those who felt free to speak were roughly equal in China (76%) and Taiwan (74%). Even though the autocratic regime in China prohibits organized political opposition, it seems to allow free speech at the individual level (table 5.2–5).

Confucian values. The last likely source of political trust is Confucian values. Three items in the Asian Barometer Survey II are related to Confucian values: (1) obeying parents, (2) obeying teacher, and (3) avoiding open conflict. China ranks higher on all of them. In examining the percentages of respondents agreeing or strongly agreeing with these Confucian values, 49% in China and 27% in Taiwan were willing to obey parents, 57% in China and 38% in Taiwan respected teacher's authority, and 58% in China and only 28% in Taiwan wanted to avoid open conflict (table 5.2–4). The fact that China is more "Confucian" than Taiwan is somewhat unexpected. The six-decade Communist rule in China was often hostile to Confucian social hierarchy even though the Chinese government has attempted to revive traditional values in recent years. In Taiwan, cultural continuity seems to be less interrupted. One possibility is that Taiwan's higher level of economic modernization than China may have led to the growth of post-modern values that emphasize individualism (Inglehart 2007).

In sum, the analysis in this section demonstrates that mainland Chinese respondents in the ABSII survey held stronger Confucian values, expressed more economic satisfaction, were under more political mobilization through the media and through the opportunity to contact government officials, and possessed more internal and external efficacies than the respondents in Taiwan. In the meantime, the democratic political system in Taiwan resulted in more political participation in competitive elections, contacting elected officials, and freely joining political organizations. The remaining question is how the factors examined in this section affect political trust in the two distinctive political systems.

MULTIVARIATE ANALYSIS OF POLITICAL TRUST IN CHINA AND TAIWAN

This section relies on multivariate regression analysis to detect the relative importance of the different factors in table 5.2 on political trust in table 5.1A. Specifically, the multivariate regression models use political trust as the dependent variable and treat Confucian tradition, economic satisfaction, political mobilization, and internal and external efficacies as independent variables. China and Taiwan are studied in separate regression models. Combining the two societies in a single data set may simplify the analysis (results available upon request), but it may not allow for straightforwardly exploring the different effects of the same independent variables in different societies.

Political trust is defined by the four items in table 5.1A, namely, trust in the key political institutions, trust in political leaders, trust in the nation, and trust in the political system. In order to reduce the number of regression equations, the four items are combined into a single-factor index of political trust. Even though these concepts may represent different dimensions of political support,[2] such as diffuse and specific political supports defined by Easton (1975), they are highly correlated with each other, and the factor analysis only detected a single dimension among the four variables (appendix 5.1). The missing values in each item are estimated (imputed) using the respondents' answers in the other three items. The resulting factor index of political trust for the entire sample containing both societies is converted into a 0–1 scale where 0 = no trust and 1 = maximum trust (appendix 5.2).[3]

Political participation is based on three actions: (1) voting, (2) contacting, and (3) protesting (table 5.2–1a). Voting is whether the respondent voted in the last election (0 = no and 1 = yes). In addition to "contacting elected officials" and "contacting government officials" shown in table 5.2–4, the new contacting variable includes two more questions: "contacting party officials" and "contacting other influential people." "No contact" is coded 0, "contacted once" is coded 0.5, and "contacted more than once" is coded 1. The sum of the four contacting items is divided by 4, resulting in a 0–1 index of political contacting. Zero means never contacted anyone, and 1 means having contacted all four types of people more than once. "Petition" is coded 0 if the respondent never participated in any petition or demonstration, 0.5 if participated once, and 1 if more than once.

Political mobilization is measured by two separate items in table 5.2–1b, (1) membership in formal organization (0 = no and 1 = yes), and (2) watching TV as the main source of political information (0 = no and 1 = yes).

Economic satisfaction is measured by the two questions in table 5.2–2, namely, the respondent's satisfaction with current family economic situation and future family economic conditions. The missing values in each question are imputed with information in the other question. The two variables are not combined and are examined separately in case they have different effects on regime trust.

Internal efficacy is measured by the same factor index of the three questions (imputed) in table 5.2: (1) interest in politics, (2) understanding politics, and (3) ability to participate in politics (table 5.2–3). The index ranges from 0 (no internal efficacy) to 1 (maximum internal efficacy). Interpersonal trust is an alternative measure of internal efficacy. It is the respondent's answer to whether most people can be trusted (0 = no and 1 = yes).

External efficacy includes items in table 5.2–5: (1) government responsiveness, (2) fairness of elections, and (3) freedom to speak and to join organizations. Government responsiveness is coded 0 for "not responsive at all," 0.33 for "not very responsive," 0.66 for "largely responsive," and 1 for "very responsive." Fairness of elections is coded 0 for "not fair," 0.33 for "fair with major problems," 0.66 for "fair with minor problems," and 1 for "completely fair." The third measure of external efficacy is a factor index of the two freedom items in table 5.2–6: freedom of speech and freedom of organizations, ranging from 0 to 1.[4]

Confucian tradition is measured by the three questions in table 5.2–4: (1) obeying parents, (2) obeying teacher, and (3) avoiding open conflict. The missing values in each item are imputed with information in the other two, and the three variables are combined into a single-factor index of Confucian tradition ranging from 0 (minimum) to 1 (maximum).

Finally, the respondents' demographic and socioeconomic characteristics are included in the regression analysis, including age, gender, education, urbanization, and Buddhism, which is the most popular religion in both China and Taiwan.

Appendix 5.2 shows the summary statistics for all the variables just discussed.

The OLS regression begins with the base model of only demographic and socioeconomic variables (model 1, tables 5.3A and 5.3B). Age has a positive effect on regime support, as the older groups are all more supportive than the youngest group (32 and younger, comparison group) in both China and Taiwan. Gender has no significant impact in China, but interestingly, women are less enthusiastic about the regime than are men in Taiwan. Education has a negative effect on regime legitimacy in both societies. In China, the college-educated (some college, college graduates, and post-graduate education) are less supportive of the regime than those with high school (incomplete and complete) and primary school (complete and incomplete and none) educations. Similarly, primary (and less) education shows a higher level of regime support than the other two higher education groups in Taiwan. Urbanization does not have a significant effect in promoting political trust in either society. Interestingly, Buddhism shows the opposite effects in China and Taiwan. In China, Buddhism seems to be more "otherworldly," as it has a weak but statistically significant negative effect on regime trust. In Taiwan, Buddhism is more "this-worldly," with a weak but statistically positive effect on political trust.

In model 2 of tables 5.3A and 5.3B, somewhat unexpectedly, political participation through voting and contacting does not increase political trust in China and Taiwan, as none of the regression coefficients for the two participation variables is statistically significant, and the adjusted R^2 does not increase at all after adding the three political participation variables to the equation (model 2, table 5.3A). Similarly, the three political participation variables contribute a negligible 5% to the total increase in the value of adjusted R^2 in Taiwan (model 2, table 5.3B). Interestingly, protesting (petition) causes political support to decrease in both China and Taiwan. One possibility is the lack of responsiveness by the government, which is further discussed later.

In democratic Taiwan, political mobilization through membership in formal organizations and through television programs plays no role in increasing regime legitimacy (model 3, table 5.3B). This is expected, since these channels are not directly controlled by the government but tend to be partisan. Similarly, in Israel, where the media operate in a democratic environment, researchers find that there is no clear relationship between watching the news and political trust (Tsfati, Tukachinsky, and Peri 2009). In autocratic China, although formal group membership and

Table 5.3A. POLITICAL SUPPORT IN CHINA (OLS COEFFICIENTS)

A. China	1	2	3	4	5	6	7
BIOLOGICAL & SOCIOECONOMIC TRAITS:							
Age 33–45	0.019***	0.018***	0.015***	0.019***	0.020***	0.018***	0.013***
Age 46–58	0.038***	0.037***	0.035***	0.038***	0.039***	0.033***	0.028***
Age 59–75	0.053***	0.052***	0.050***	0.055***	0.054***	0.049***	0.041***
Age 76 & up	0.039***	0.040***	0.043***	0.045***	0.045***	0.040***	0.032***
Female	−0.002	−0.001	−0.001	0.000	0.004	0.004	0.004
Primary school	0.030***	0.028***	0.024***	0.029***	0.043***	0.041***	0.033***
High school	0.034***	0.033***	0.026***	0.030***	0.037***	0.034***	0.030***
College (comparison)							
Urban (compared to rural/migrant)	−0.008**	−0.009**	−0.009**	−0.006	−0.005	−0.002	0.003
Buddhist	−0.016***	−0.017***	−0.014***	−0.015***	−0.013***	−0.012**	−0.007
POLITICAL PARTICIPATION:							
Voted		0.010***	0.007**	0.005*	0.003	0.001	−0.002
Contact		0.000	−0.001	−0.003	−0.016	−0.018*	−0.004
Petition		−0.047**	−0.047**	−0.040*	−0.045**	−0.039*	−0.032*
POLITICAL MOBILIZATION:							
Group membership		0.026***	0.023**	0.017*	0.013	0.007	
TV		0.037***	0.032***	0.027***	0.025***	0.020***	
ECONOMIC SATISFACTION:							
Income current (imputed)				0.030***	0.023***	0.028***	0.019***
Income future (imputed)				0.087***	0.077***	0.079***	0.055***
INTERNAL EFFICACY:							
Internal efficacy					0.083***	0.087***	0.058***
Interpersonal trust					0.027***	0.027***	0.014***
CONFUCIAN VALUES:							
Confucian tradition						0.140***	0.126***
EXTERNAL EFFICACY:							
Fair elections							0.049***
Free speech/org							0.117***
Gov. responsiveness							0.142***
Constant	0.592***	0.589***	0.565***	0.479***	0.436***	0.362***	0.224***
Observations	4,748	4,748	4,748	4,720	4,670	4,534	4,534
R^2	0.037	0.039	0.056	0.085	0.109	0.142	0.265
R^2 change		0.002	0.017***	0.029***	0.024***	0.033***	0.123***
% of total change		0.88	7.46	12.72	10.53	14.47	53.95

Source: ABSII 2008.
Notes: (1) The dependent variable, political support, is an imputed factor index of institutional trust, trust in leaders, national identity, and support for political system. (2) The independent variables were entered in different orders from the above and no significant differences were observed in the results. (3) The statistical significance of the R^2 change is obtained by TEST, which is a post-estimation command in STATA 12 after the OLS regression. (4) The % of total change is calculated by $x/(0.265-0.037)*100$, where x is the value of each R^2 change.
*p<=.1, **p<=.05, ***p<=.01

Table 5.3B. POLITICAL SUPPORT IN TAIWAN (OLS COEFFICIENTS)

B. Taiwan	1	2	3	4	5	6	7
BIOLOGICAL & SOCIOECONOMIC TRAITS:							
Age 32 & younger (comparison)							
Age 33–45	0.016**	0.017**	0.017**	0.023***	0.022***	0.020**	0.024***
Age 46–58	0.033***	0.037***	0.036***	0.042***	0.041***	0.037***	0.030***
Age 59–75	0.053***	0.055***	0.054***	0.063***	0.062***	0.051***	0.043***
Age 76 & up	0.041***	0.043***	0.042***	0.052***	0.050***	0.040**	0.035**
Female	−0.017***	−0.018***	−0.018***	−0.017***	−0.017***	−0.015***	−0.012**
Primary school	0.047***	0.043***	0.044***	0.049***	0.050***	0.036***	0.020**
High school	0.025***	0.023***	0.023***	0.024***	0.025***	0.017**	0.011
College (comparison)							
Urban (compared to rural/migrant)	−0.011	−0.01	−0.01	−0.012	−0.01	−0.004	0.003
Buddhist	0.01	0.01	0.01	0.009	0.008	0.007	0.010*
POLITICAL PARTICIPATION:							
Voted		0.001	0	−0.002	−0.001	−0.007	−0.006
Contact		−0.017	−0.019	−0.021	−0.017	−0.007	0.005
Petition		−0.069***	−0.069***	−0.069***	−0.068***	−0.068***	−0.041***
POLITICAL MOBILIZATION:							
Group membership			0.007	0.004	0.003	0.002	0
TV			0.006	0.005	0.005	0.005	0.006
ECONOMIC SATISFACTION:							
Income current (imputed)				0.040***	0.037***	0.035**	0.005
Income future (imputed)				0.061***	0.061***	0.061***	0.023*
INTERNAL EFFICACY:							
Internal efficacy					−0.024	−0.015	−0.026
Interpersonal trust					0.018***	0.019***	0.014***
CONFUCIAN VALUES:							
Confucian tradition						0.145***	0.104***
EXTERNAL EFFICACY:							
Fair elections							0.061***
Free speech/org							0.087***
Gov. responsiveness							0.143***
Constant	0.450***	0.453***	0.450***	0.391***	0.395***	0.341***	0.253***
Observations	1,584	1,584	1,584	1,579	1,571	1,560	1,560
R^2	0.08	0.092	0.093	0.113	0.118	0.15	0.31
R^2 change		0.012**	0.001	0.020	0.005**	0.032***	0.160***
% of total change		5.22	0.43	8.70	2.17	13.91	69.57

Source: ABSII 2006.

Notes: (1) The dependent variable, political support, is an imputed factor index of institutional trust, trust in leaders, national identity, and support for political system. (2) The independent variables were entered different orders from those shown in the table, and no significant differences were observed in the results. (3) The statistical significance of the R^2 change is obtained by TEST, which is a post-estimation command in STATA 12 after the OLS regression. (4) The % of total change is calculated by $x/(0.32–0.08)*100$, where x is the value of each R^2 change.
*p<=.1, **p<=.05, ***p<=.01

watching the news on TV have statistically significant effects on promoting regime support, these effects are weak, and adding them to the equation only contributes about 7% of the total improvement in the overall explanatory power of the model (model 3, table 5.3A). This is somewhat unexpected, since earlier studies show that political mobilization through media control partially explains the high level of regime support in China, together with culture and economic benefit (Norris 2011).

Economic satisfaction (model 4, tables 5.3A and 5.3B) also significantly increased regime support in both places. Its effect is stronger in China than in Taiwan. The two economic variables together contribute to a 12.7% increase in the goodness of fit in China, but only 8.7% in Taiwan (model 4, tables 5.3A and 5.3B). In both places, the expected future economic benefit plays a stronger role than current economic satisfaction.

Both the internal efficacy index and interpersonal trust slightly increase political trust in China, but they add relatively little to the overall explanation of political trust (adjusted R^2 only improves by 10.5%; model 5, table 5.3A). In Taiwan, internal efficacy is not even statistically significant, and the adjusted R^2 almost does not change (2.2%), although interpersonal trust plays a weak but positive role (model 5, table 5.3B).

Next, the Confucian values index is added to the equation (model 6 in tables 5.3A and 5.3B). Consistent with earlier studies (Shi 2001, 2015), it shows a significant effect of increasing political trust. But somewhat different from the earlier study by Shi (2001, 2015), even though Confucianism is more visible in China than in Taiwan, its role in promoting regime support is about the same. The addition of Confucianism in model 6 improved the overall adjusted R^2 by about 14.5% in China and 13.9% in Taiwan. The relatively small change in the value of the adjusted R^2 suggests that tradition plays a relatively small role (Lewis-Beck and Skalaban 1990).

External efficacy turns out to be the most important factor in predicting political trust. Adding the three external efficacy variables (fair elections, freedom of speech and organization, and government responsiveness) greatly improves the adjusted R^2 by 54% in China and 69% in Taiwan (model 7, tables 5.3A and 5.3B). Among the three variables, government responsiveness is the single most important predictor. For example, when the three variables are added separately to model 6 in tables 5.3A and 5.3B, government responsiveness increases the adjusted R^2 by 0.09, fairness of elections by 0.02, and freedom of speech and organization by 0.03 in China. In Taiwan, government responsiveness improves the adjusted R^2 by an even more impressive 0.11, fairness of elections by 0.07, and freedom of speech and organization by 0.04 (regression results are available upon request).[5]

Since the effect of belief in government responsiveness is so strong in explaining political trust, it is necessary to further explore what contributes to such belief. Three factors are possible sources: (1) political mobilization through media and membership in formal organizations, (2) political mobilization through political participation (voting, contacting, and protesting), and (3) internal efficacy (interest in politics, understanding politics, and belief in one's ability to participate). Some of these factors performed poorly in predicting political trust at least in one of the two societies, but they may be related to government responsiveness.

In table 5.4, political mobilization through TV news and voting in China have significant effects on the belief in government responsiveness. Contacting elected and government officials leads to less belief in government responsiveness in China, while petition/protesting has a negative impact on the belief in government responsiveness in both China and Taiwan. In other words, the more one contacts officials or petitions in China or protests in Taiwan, the more one learns about the lack of government responsiveness. Internal efficacy significantly improves the belief of government responsiveness in both China and Taiwan.

Table 5.4 can also serve as an endogeneity test between political trust and government responsiveness. The reader may be suspicious of the strong effect of the perceived responsiveness on political trust in tables 5.3A and 5.3B and conclude that these two concepts are not causally related but are two sides of the same coin. Indeed, scholars recognize this problem and try to distinguish political trust from external efficacy both conceptually and empirically. Gamson (1968) argues that political trust is the belief that the political system will bring desired outcomes

Table 5.4. EXTERNAL EFFICACY IN CHINA
AND TAIWAN (OLS REGRESSION COEFFICIENTS)

	China	Taiwan
Group	0.034	0.014
TV	0.074***	0.000
Voted	0.019**	0.006
Contact	−0.053*	0.012
Petition/protest	−0.099*	−0.089***
Internal efficacy	0.249***	0.077***
Observations	4695	1575
R^2	0.0557	0.0320

Source: ABSII 2006–2008.
Notes: Age, gender, education, urbanization, and Buddhism are controlled but not shown.

even if left untended. This implies that citizens may perceive little responsiveness yet still trust a government. Empirically, Craig, Niemi, and Silver (1990) find that external efficacy, measured by fairness of political procedures and outcomes, is distinct from political trust.

In this chapter, we make an additional effort to disentangle external efficacy from political trust in China by the method of two-stage least squares (2SLS). 2SLS is a powerful tool for causal inference with cross-sectional data (Wooldridge 2010). In our 2SLS analysis, the first step is to find an instrumental variable that is correlated with external efficacy but is uncorrelated with political trust. One such variable is "contact," which is significantly correlated with external efficacy in table 5.4 for mainland China but not with political trust in China in table 5.3A.

We use the same additive index as in table 5.3A as the instrumental variable, which combines the respondents' reported action of contacting government officials, elected officials, party leaders, and other influential people. In the first stage of 2SLS, the instrumental variable (contacting) and the control variables are regressed on external efficacy, and the predicted values of external efficacy are estimated with the results of the first-stage regression. In the second stage, the predicted values of external efficacy and control variables are regressed on political trust. Table 5.5 shows the results of the second stage. The predicted external efficacy has a significant influence on political trust. Such a result provides further evidence that external efficacy has a causal effect on political trust, at least in mainland China.

In sum, this section compared the competing theories for political trust. The findings support the culturalist and economic theories, but only to a limited extent. Both only improved political trust in China and Taiwan to a limited extent. The findings do not support the political mobilization hypothesis, as the variables related to political mobilization played a weak or no role in increasing political support. This is probably not a big surprise in Taiwan, where government-initiated political mobilization is no longer very important. In China, where political mobilization is supposedly a fact in everyday life, it is somewhat surprising that political mobilization is not the most important reason for political support. Next, the findings in this section show that external efficacy, particularly when measured by the belief in government responsiveness, is by far the most important reason for regime support. Such belief in government responsiveness is related to media mobilization and participation in voting and individual internal efficacy. These effects are particularly visible in China. Finally, through a two-stage least-squares test, we provide evidence that external efficacy has a causal effect on political trust.

Table 5.5. POLITICAL SUPPORT BY EXTERNAL EFFICACY
IN CHINA (TWO-STAGE LEAST-SQUARES)

Political support (imputed factor index of institutional trust, leader trust, nationalism, and system trust)

External efficacy (instrumented by contact)	0.012*
Age 32 & younger (comparison)	
Age 33–45	0.005
Age 46–58	0.022
Age 59–75	0.022
Age 76 & up	−0.012
Female	0.008
Primary school	0.083*
High school	0.075**
College (comparison)	
Buddhist	−0.01
TV	0.007
Income current (imputed)	0.008
Income future (imputed)	0.001
Internal efficacy	−0.054
Interpersonal trust	−0.025
Confucian tradition	0.277***
Fair elections	−0.003
Freedom of speech/freedom of association	0.094
Voted	0
Petition	−0.066
Urban (compared rural/migrant)	0.023
Constant	−0.521**
N	4,150

Source: ABSII China 2008.
Notes: Contact is the instrumental variable. External efficacy is the instrumented variable.
*$p < 0.1$, **$p < 0.05$, ***$p < 0.01$

CONCLUSION AND DISCUSSION

The goal of this chapter has been to explain why political trust is so much higher in autocratic China than in democratic Taiwan. Rather than treating it as a unidimensional concept, the chapter defines political trust as trust in political institutions, trust in political leaders, trust in the nation, and trust in the political system. It shows that on each of these dimensions, political trust in China is significantly higher than in Taiwan. The high level of regime trust in China is unlikely a result of political fear, since the Chinese respondents are outspoken and critical on other politically sensitive survey questions.

In a review of the existing literature, this chapter identified several sources of political trust, including political mobilization, economic satisfaction, Confucian values, and internal and external political efficacies. The empirical findings suggest that external efficacy, particularly when measured as the respondents' belief in government responsiveness to public demand, is more important in predicting political trust than the other competing theories.

The reason for perceived government responsiveness in China is rooted in the institutional deficiency of lacking free and competitive elections. As is further elaborated in chapter 8, the populist authoritarian government claims to represent "most" people's interest, but it cannot prove it by elections. It is the instinct of survival that compels the government to respond.

This chapter has shown the importance of perceived government responsiveness in promoting regime support. Yet government responsiveness is only reflected in people's perception in surveys. Some readers may still question whether it actually exists. This is the topic of the next chapter.

CHAPTER 6

Regime-Inspired
Contentious Politics

This chapter describes another important element of populist authoritarianism—direct public involvement. It shows that the Chinese government selectively uses public protest to consolidate its rule. Through both case studies and statistical analysis of survey data, it demonstrates that the central and provincial governments often bypass lower level governments and legal procedures and directly intervene in local protests. Such a tactic is effective in reducing public anger and increasing central government support, but it is detrimental to the rule of law and the development of civil society.

THE RISE OF CONTENTIOUS POLITICS IN CHINA

Public protests have become widespread in China in recent years. Some target land grabs by developers and power abuses by local officials, and others are against firms with unpaid wages and bad work conditions (Orlik 2011). Although it is difficult to obtain the exact numbers, sporadic studies indicate the rapid increase of collective protests. For example, Hu, Hu, and Wang (2006) quote an authoritative study by the Central Party School[1] about how the number of "mass incidents" such as collective petitions, protests, demonstrations, strikes, rallies, sit-ins, boycotts, and violent clashes (*qunti shijian*) increased more than seven times from 10,000 in 1994 to 74,000 in 2004, and how the number of people involved increased more than five times from 730,000 to 3.76 million during the same period of time. The *New York Times* reports as many as 180,000 mass incidents in 2010, as counted by "a prominent Chinese sociologist at the government-run Research Center for Social Contradictions" (Jacobs 2011a, 2011b).

Many people see the rise of contentious politics as a reflection of the political tension between the regime and Chinese society, caused by the gap between the rich and the poor, the widespread official corruption, the lack of accountability, and the non-responsiveness of the legal system (Jacobs 2011b; Lemos 2012). The conventional wisdom holds that such growing tension between the regime and society is a sign of the vulnerability and weakness of the Chinese Communist Party (CCP). Several authors have predicted the coming collapse of the Communist regime in the near future (Chang 2001; Wines 2011; Sun 2011; Pei 2012; Shambaugh 2015).

Proponents of this crisis view base their explanation of the intensified protests on the combination of political repression and economic modernization: As living standards improve, people demand political rights that have been denied by the CCP. While such a hypothesis can be useful in explaining some protest activities, particularly those associated with political dissidents, it fails to account for the high levels of regime support which has been found repeatedly in various public opinion surveys conducted by independent scholars, such as the 5th and the 6th Waves World Values Survey China, the 2008 China Survey, the 2008 Asian Barometer Survey II, the 2010 Chinese General Social Survey (CGSS), and a 2012 PEW survey.[2]

THE CONTENTIOUS POLITICS LITERATURE

The literature on contentious politics provides some insights into the rise of protests in China.[3] For example, Tilly's effort at theory building provides useful ways to define the forms of protests by their organization, format, types of claims, and types of participants (Tilly 2004; Tilly and Tarrow 2007). While Tilly correctly shows that protests in non-democracies do not necessarily lead to advocating democracy or democratization, he argues that only in democracies can social movements pick up their momentum by guaranteeing the rights to free speech, assembly, and association (also see Rucht 2007). This last point makes Tilly's and other related studies less useful in explaining why non-democracies sometimes have more protests and why these protests can also gain momentum.

Other scholars have also advanced useful insights in explaining collective action. For example, Olson (1971) argues that collective action is a rational behavior and people participate when they see the benefit of doing so. He further points out that the free-riding problem in which nonparticipants benefit from the outcome of other people's collective action can be solved by the provision of selective incentives. But the rational behavior explanation still needs to account for the "irrational" behavior of those

who participate in protests based on considerations beyond their immediate interest. In other words, the rational behavior theory still needs to
address why some protest participants join collective actions regardless of
whether their immediate interests are affected.

Gurr (1970) offers a refreshing argument of relative deprivation. He
argues that demonstrations occur not in places with absolute poverty,
when people have nothing to lose. Instead, people rebel when they feel
that they are unfairly treated and that they are not rewarded according
to their expectations. While relative deprivation is a powerful theory in
explaining why people rebel, there is still the need to look at how the state
frames the opportunities of protest that is the basis of the perceived unfairness and, more importantly, examine why some people are more likely
to rebel than others when they feel equally unfairly treated.

In one of the most illuminating studies on contentious politics in
China, O'Brien and Li (2006) develop the concept of "rightful resistance"
to explain contentious political behavior against local governments in
rural China. They show that such behavior is tolerated by Beijing because
the protestors often cleverly take advantage of the inconsistency between
central government policies and the lack of local implementation. Rural
protestors often press local officials to meet their demands in the name of
the center. While the concept of "rightful resistance" provides a nuanced
explanation about the existence of protests in China's authoritarian political system, it leaves people to wonder about the extent to which Chinese
citizens support the central government. Merely using its name does not
mean people really support the central government. In fact, many people
would believe that protesting against the local governments is a way for
people to express their dissatisfaction at the center. What about the strong
support of Beijing shown in many Chinese surveys? The simple answer is
that people lied in these surveys (Li 2013).

REGIME-MOBILIZED CONTENTIOUS POLITICS
IN CHINA

This chapter presents an alternative explanation of the rise of contentious
political behavior in China and shows that such behavior is partly a result of
regime mobilization in order to strengthen its position and consolidate its
power. Regime mobilization is defined broadly, ranging from direct persuasion and organization to indirect encouragement, tolerance, and cultivation.

Regime-mobilized patriotic protests against foreign pressure and criticism are well-documented as a way for the government to gain public
support, such as the government-encouraged protests against the U.S.

bombing of the Chinese Embassy in Belgrade in 1999, the anti-Japanese protests in various years, and the protests against Western media for demonizing China during the 2008 riots in Tibet (Perry 2001; Gries 2004a and 2004b; Tang and Darr 2012).

Meanwhile, other scholars have recognized that the CCP also uses protests against domestic targets in order to strengthen its power (Saich 2007; Stockmann and Gallagher 2011; Kennedy 2012; Tong and Lei 2014). One study shows that protests against domestic targets are the most tolerated as long as they are localized (Perry 2001). This chapter goes even further by showing that contentious political behavior is cultivated by the regime to serve the purpose of shifting the public attention and anger from one sector of the government to another, such as from the center to local authorities, from the government to business enterprises, from the general government policy to specific officials, and from one official to another.

In a formal model, Lorentzen (2013) shows that authoritarian regimes are compelled to allow and even encourage limited expression of discontent in order to target its response to public demand and to avoid potential political instability. Such tactics have by and large helped the regime to maintain public support.

Tilly (2004) shows that the state is not merely a target of protests; it also creates the opportunities and frames the scope for protests. In China, the role of the state becomes even more important and more effective where the state and society are linked directly without the intermediate buffer zones of a civil society. It is relatively easy for political elites to mobilize public protests in order to clean out the undesirable elements in the system. In this *populist authoritarian society*, there is a general tendency to encourage, tolerate, and respond to popular protests, and only repress them when they go out of control. Even in some protests that ended with repression, such as the 1989 Tiananmen protest, the 1999 Falungong protest, and the 2008 Lhasa riots, the initial government responses were more conciliatory than repressive.

In their study of social protests in contemporary China, Tong and Lei (2014) compiled a data set of 548 large-scale mass protests with 500 or more participants from 2003 to 2010. They found that repression was extremely rare, consisting of only 2.8% of protests, and more than 90% of these cases were either tolerated or compensated by the government. Their explanation of such tolerance is the principle of moral responsibility that is deeply rooted in Chinese political culture. Such a principle encourages the masses to demand justice from the rulers and urges the rulers to respond in order to maintain political legitimacy (Tong and Lei 2014).

INSTITUTIONAL DEFICIENCIES AND POPULIST AUTHORITARIANISM

In a populist authoritarian state, the underdevelopment of political institutions results in the direct link between political elites and the masses. As discussed in the previous chapter, one example is the lack of meaningful elections. Elections are effective ways to provide political legitimacy for the state, regardless of how small the winning margin is. Without elections, the state feels paranoid about its legitimacy and tends to be overly responsive, because it also wants to rule by claiming to represent the interests of the majority, and the only way to show its legitimacy and to gain political support is by responding to public demand, and not through elections. In a democracy, politicians only need to respond to enough public demand so that they win elections. Consequently, the response rate is likely to be higher in a populist authoritarian state than in a democratic society. As shown in the last chapter, in the Asian Barometer Survey II, 77% of respondents in China in 2008 agreed or strongly agreed that their government responded to what they wanted, as compared to only 36% of respondents giving the same answers in democratic Taiwan in 2006. Thus, weak electoral institutions seem to make the authoritarian Chinese government more responsive.

Weak institutional development is also reflected in the problems of the legal process. Gallagher and Wang (2011) found that users of the legal system actually demonstrate less "legal consciousness" due to the lack of effectiveness and responsiveness of the legal institutions. While these users gain little sense of external efficacy (how the law works) after going through the legal process, Gallagher and Wang (2011) show that their sense of internal efficacy (how to work the law) tends to increase. The implication of such a finding is that these people are likely to develop the habit of using extra-legal and even extra-system means for problem solving.

In his study of the Chinese legal system based on interviews with dozens of judges, Liebman (2011) depicts the numerous practices when public justice takes over legal justice. For example, judges are frequently ordered by the government to make themselves more accessible to the public by publishing their cell phone numbers and by holding trials in the open air (even in the rain) in villages. Court petitioners are allowed to select their own judges by reading the judges' resumes. Court petitioners who do not accept the courts' rulings are regularly compensated by the courts or by the local governments, regardless of the legal ground of their petitions (Liebman 2011).

The predominant channel of conflict resolution in China is still through government-sponsored mediation or simply taking the matter into one's own hands, not the court system. For example, Michelson (2008) found that most issues are resolved locally in rural China without going to court. In a 2004 public opinion survey of a random sample of 7,774 respondents, among the 2,290 respondents who had legal disputes and who took actions, only 11% relied on the courts to solve their problems; the remaining 89% of disputants used other channels, including mediation (32%), mutual negotiation (31%), the government (14%), the media (7%), fights (4%), and the legislature (1%; Tang 2009). In short, the absence of a well-functioning legal system, the disrespect for procedural justice, and a culture of substantive justice all encourage a direct relationship between the state and society in conflict resolution.

The Internet is becoming an effective outlet to vent public dissatisfaction with the government (King, Pan, and Roberts 2013). It is expected to bring down authoritarian rule by breaking through its information control and mobilizing and organizing anti-regime activities, as it did during the Arab Spring, but it sometimes plays a counter-productive role. It also facilitates Internet users taking justice into their own hands and forming mob attacks. Downey (2010) describes how the Chinese netizens use the Internet as a "human flesh search engine" (*renrou sousuo*). They use the Internet to expose the private information about "guilty" suspects such as alleged animal killers, people allegedly committing extramarital affairs, and those who advocate a softer approach to Tibet. Consequently, these "accused offenders" are fired from their jobs, forced to move away from their hometowns, and even physically harassed. Without a strong and effective legal system, the Internet forces the government to react directly to whatever the netizens see as unjust. Downey calls such a direct relationship between the state and the masses "Red Guard 2.0" (Downey 2010).

Further, weak institutions in China are also reflected in the ineffectiveness of the types of social organizations which in a civil society can serve as a buffer zone between the state and the public. For example, in a democracy, politically autonomous labor unions play important roles in elections and in negotiations between labor and capital. In China, by contrast, the official All-China Federation of Trade Unions and its local branches are often unable to represent the interests of workers, forcing the workers to directly confront their employers. The government often has to intervene as a mediator in labor disputes, and as a result the trade union sometimes becomes irrelevant.

Finally, the fragmentation of bureaucracy also provides room for the public to challenge different segments of the government. Tarrow (2011) argues that divided elites provide political opportunities for collective action. There are several studies on the bureaucratic fragmentation in China. Lieberthal (2004) discusses the protracted Chinese decision-making process is due to the competing interests of various bureaucratic agencies. Manion (2004) shows how the center deliberately exposes the corruption at the local level so that public anger can be directed from the central government. Landry (2008) describes the gap in the quality of bureaucratic recruitment between the central and local levels. O'Brien and Li (2005) use the term "rightful resistance" to show how protesters justify their causes against local officials by citing central government policies and regulations. Shi and Cai (2006) show that the fragmentation of the local government provides opportunities for Shanghai's homeowners to protest.

EXAMPLES OF REGIME-MOBILIZED CONTENTIOUS POLITICS

Regime mobilization has a long tradition in modern Chinese history. The Communist revolution before 1949 was a successful social movement in which Mao Zedong appealed directly to rural residents while bypassing the Nationalist government. The eventual defeat of the Nationalist government in 1949 created tremendous confidence for Mao and his followers to continue their populist approach in the post-1949 era. They repeatedly relied on mass campaigns to purge political opponents. In 1966, within less than three months from August to November, Mao appeared on the Gate of Heavenly Peace eight times and inspected more than 11 million Red Guards. The result was the Cultural Revolution—the largest scale social movement in the history of the People's Republic of China, in which the revolutionary masses eliminated Mao's political opponents and their bureaucratic institutions.

Not all of the attempts of elite direct mobilization are successful. One failed example of elite mobilization was the then CCP General Secretary Zhao Ziyang's highly risky appearance in Tiananmen Square during the 1989 urban protests. He made a speech and told the protesting students to go home because he couldn't help them even if he wanted to. The hidden message in Zhao's speech was that the elites at the top were split between his reform faction and the hardliners, and that the students should continue to protest in order to support his reform faction. Zhao's failed attempt was partly because of his lack of charisma and partly due to the limited scope of his appeal only among the students, rather than the general population. However, such direct contact and interaction between the General Secretary of the Communist Party and the masses is consistent with the tradition of China's populist authoritarian regime and with Zhao Ziyang's own style as a longtime student of the Mass Line (Zhao 1944).

In addition to the cases of top-down elite mobilization, in recent years there have been many examples of bottom-up appeal from the masses to the central government for direct intervention in local disputes. One such example is the use of the national flag during the 2009 Xinjiang protests by the Uyghur and Han ethnic groups. Both sides were demanding their equal rights under the same political framework, rather than pushing for separate states. The use of the national flag is symbolically important in showing the consequence of political mobilization. In this case, the symbolic importance is the willingness to demand national-level intervention when a group feels that its rights are threatened. This assertion of ethnic groups was a remarkable event in the early stages of the Xinjiang protests, although it was overshadowed by the violence that dominated news headlines and thus came to characterize the protests.[4]

In the 2011 high-profile protest against village officials' decision to sell land to real estate developers in Wukan, Guangdong Province, villagers demanded compensation and held banners which asked the central government to save the people in Wukan village. The protest resulted in the intervention from the provincial government, the partial return of the village land, the election of a new village council, and disciplinary action against local officials.[5] The significance of the Wukan protest is not that it serves to weaken CCP rule as a "harbinger" of democratization. It was utilized by the central government to gain more local support.[6]

Similarly, in another high-profile protest in Shifang in 2012, Sichuan Province, local protesters demanded the central government's intervention in the Shifang city government's decision to construct a copper plant. The protesters charged that the local officials had been paid off by the copper company without creating adequate measures for environmental protection. Again, the protesters' banners demonstrated the public demand for direct central government intervention: "Long Live the Communist Party! Drive out the Copper Plant!" Consequently, the construction plan was canceled, and most arrested protesters were released.[7]

The preceding cases suggest that China's populist authoritarian tradition is still playing a role in the country's political life. Due to the weakness of political institutions and the underdevelopment of civil society, political elites often directly appeal to the public, bypassing the intermediate organizations. For their part, the masses are often too impatient to go through the bureaucratic and legal steps to voice their dissatisfaction and are much more willing to reach the top directly. In this process, the central government is busy responding to bottom up public demands; in return, the masses offer their political support and loyalty to the center.

CASE STUDIES AND LARGE-*N* ANALYSIS

Almost all of the existing contentious politics research projects are based on case studies (Scott 1979; Tilly 1986, 1995; Perry 2001; Shi and Cai 2006; O'Brien and Stern 2008). Even when these studies are based on a few cases, their unit of analysis is still at the level of protests, and is not about their participants. Such a qualitative approach, while being capable of developing "thick" descriptions of each case (Geertz 1973), nonetheless runs the risk of generalizing about individual behavior at the group level. The case study approach suffers from the problem of external validity or generalizability. We know through case studies what the participants want in each case, but we cannot generalize about what participants share in common across cases. While protests are few, participants are abundant. But few studies based on individual attitudes and behavior are available or even possible until large-scale social survey data have become available.

In the remaining part of this chapter, I use survey data to further analyze protest behavior in China. The data are drawn from the 2010 (CGSS) conducted by Renmin University in China.[8] It contains a national random sample of 10,192 respondents covering all of the 31 provinces, autonomous regions, and provincial-level cities (Wang 2012). The survey includes a number of questions regarding the respondents' awareness and participation in mass incidents (*qunti shijian*).

The sample seems to contain a slightly more under-educated population than the 2010 Population Census. Weighting is used to correct this under-representation of education.

THE SCOPE OF COLLECTIVE ACTION

The first goal of analyzing the data from a national survey is to get a sense of the scope of mass incidents, since official statistics are often very sketchy. Although a few existing studies report the numbers of mass incidents (Hu, Hu, and Wang 2006; Jacobs 2011a, 2011b), it is never clear in these studies how the researchers obtain their numbers. The lack of transparency and verifiability in these studies casts doubt on the credibility and reliability of their findings. The 2010 CGSS dataset contains two questions about the respondents' awareness of and participation in mass incidents:

1. In everyday life, people often witness collective activities and actions, such as jointly
   boycotting unreasonable fees, coordinated opposition to land acquisition and building

removal, collective resistance to the implementation of certain projects, collective petitions, collective strikes, rallies, demonstrations, protests, and so on. In the past three
years, did any of these events happen around you?

2. During these events, what role did you play? (1) organizer, (2) participant, (3) indirect participant through material and moral support, (4) did not participate.

Overall, 10.8% of the respondents were aware of any local mass incidents around them ($n = 1,313$, weighted). The 95% confidence interval is
between 10.73% and 10.87%. If this range can be used to represent the national population, that means a total of 118 million (1.1 billion[9] × 0.1073 =
118 million) to 120 million (1.1 billion × 0.1087 = 120 million) people
lived in the mass-incident-affected regions in the past three years. These
are large numbers even if they only consist of relatively small percentages
of the total population.

In terms of the rate of participation in collective action by the affected population, among all the respondents knowing about collective
events in the sample ($n = 1,313$), the majority of them did not participate
(69%); 9% participated indirectly by providing material and moral support; and 22% reported that they directly participated in these group
actions. In other words, almost 1 out of 3 people participated either directly or indirectly (9% + 22% = 31%). Nationwide, if we use the 119
million people living in the protest zones as a base, 10.7 million of them
participated indirectly (119 million × 0.09), and 26.2 million (119 million × 0.22) participated directly. The combined number of direct and
indirect participants is 36.9 million. Although this is only about 0.3% of
the national population over the age of 15, it is a large group in absolute
number.

GROUP LEADERS

Among the 357 participants in the mass incidents in the sample, there are
understandably only 14 leaders/organizers. Though the group is too small
for multiple regression analysis, simple bivariate analysis shows some distinctive characteristics of this group: They are noticeably younger, more educated, more likely to be male, and in the higher income group. And, most
interestingly, they are more likely to be party members. For example, 26%
of the group leaders are party members, while only 8% are party members
in the entire sample (table 6.1).

Clearly, these organizers of mass incidents are social *and* political elites.
This finding is consistent with O'Brien and Li's (2005a) study.

Table 6.1. GROUP LEADERS' CHARACTERISTICS

	Group Leader	Sample
Age (year)	42.7	48.8
Education (year)	7.5	6.9
CCP (%)	25.7	7.7
Income09 (10,000 yuan)	1.8	1.2
Male (%)	72	49

Source: CGSS 2010.
Note: All results are weighted by education in the 2010 Population Census.

REGIONAL DISTRIBUTION

Since the sample is representative of the provinces, and its respondents are also representative of each province's population, it is easy to compare the percentage of mass incidents-affected population in different provinces. As shown in figure 6.1, the least affected three provinces are Liaoning (1.6%), Yunan (2.8%), and Helongjiang (4.1%). The top five most affected provinces are Guizhou (28.9%), Jiangsu (24.6%), Qinghai (23.3%), Hubei (20.3%), and Shandong (16.9%). It is difficult to pinpoint the exact causes of mass incidents in these high-occurrence regions without digging into the specific cases. At first glance, these regions don't seem to share much in common. Perhaps some anecdotal examples will help the reader to understand the sources of the mass incidents in these provinces.

Guizhou is a relatively poor province. Its high frequency of group actions is consistent with the anecdotal accounts in the media, and is perhaps related to the problems of institutional deficiency discussed earlier. In a 2008 high-profile incident in Weng-an, for example, a 17-year-old girl drowned, but her family refused to accept the medical examiner's report and claimed that it was a homicide. Several hundred protesters occupied and burned the county government building. In the end, several government officials were dismissed, including the county party secretary and the county head, and the family was compensated by the government.[10]

Jiangsu is one of the most affluent areas in the country. Its high rate of mass incidents is probably related to the diverse economic activities in the region. One highly publicized incident in 2012 took place in the city of Qidong. Tens of thousands of protesters surrounded the city government, stripped topless the mayor and the party secretary, and eventually forced the city to cancel a wastewater processing facility.[11]

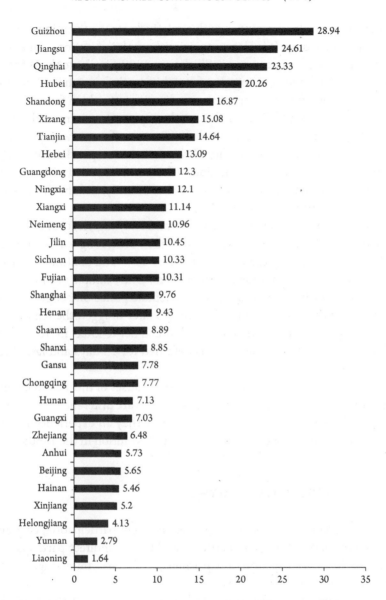

Figure 6.1:
Percent of population knowing about collective action in past 3 years by province (weighted %, CGSS 2010)

Qinghai is one of the most ethnically diverse areas in China. One source of mass incidents is dissatisfaction with the provincial government's ethnic policies. For example, in 2010, Tibetan high school students in Hainan and Huangnan prefectures reportedly protested against the government's decision to teach Chinese, and they demanded to keep Tibetan as the language of instruction in teaching math, geography, and history.[12]

Hubei is an inland province with a relatively strong tradition of state-controlled economy. It is also a region with weak institutions. One well-known mass incident occurred in Shishou in 2009. Similar to the Weng-an incident in Guizhou, a young chef fell to his death from a hotel building, but his family refused to accept the medical report, which found suicide as the cause of death. Tens of thousands of protesters burned the hotel and set up road blocks. *People's Daily*, the Party's official newspaper, intervened by urging the Shishou City Government to respond more quickly to the public demand for information.[13] This incident ended with the hotel and city government compensating the chef's family, and the dismissal of Shishou City's party secretary.[14]

Shandong is a coastal province with a relatively high level of economic development. Similar to Guizhou and Hubei, Shandong was a Communist stronghold during the Civil War before 1949 and continued to have a strong populist orientation in recent years. One example of a mass incident took place in Jinan in 2011 when a female police officer got into an argument with a street vendor. Bystanders later dragged the female cop out of the police car, assaulted her, and forced her to kneel in front of the elderly woman. The female cop was detained for 15 days and later fired from her job.[15]

These examples provide some clues to the causes of the mass incidents in the top five provinces. Although these causes are different, one thing all of them share in common is that historically they all experienced large-scale factional fighting during the Cultural Revolution in the 1960s.

MULTIVARIATE ANALYSIS

In a multivariate regression analysis, mass incident participation, or group action, is coded as 0 for non-participation, 0.5 for indirect participation, and 1 for direct participation (*group action*), and then examined against the following independent variables.

Government trust at the central and local levels. In the 2010 CGSS, the respondents were asked the extent to which they trusted the central and local governments. These two variables are coded from complete distrust (0), relative distrust (0.25), between trust and distrust (0.5), relative trust (0.75), and complete trust (1) (*trust_central gov* and *trust_local gov*). If the central government in Beijing is successful in consolidating its power by channeling the public anger to local governments, protest behavior should be provoked by low trust in local government but high trust in the central government. On the other hand, the conventional view of China's hierarchical authoritarian political system should lead one to believe that there is no clear distinction between central and local governments, and protest behavior should be expected when distrust is high in both local and central governments.

The target of group action. The 2010 CGSS includes questions about the specific targets of mass incidents for those respondents who answered that they were aware of mass incidents around them in the past three years. The respondents were given five choices as the targets of protest incidents, ranging from (1) economic organization such as companies, firms, and businesses (*against_firm*); (2) non-government and non-profit organizations (*against_org*); (3) state cadres including village officials (*against_cadre*); (4) government bureaus (*against_bureau*); to (5) state policy (*against_policy*). Each of the five targets is coded as a dummy variable (0 = no, 1 = yes). These variables should test what types of tension are more likely to provoke group action. If the government is effective in shifting public anger away from itself, group action should be triggered by non-government actors such as economic and social organizations. For a similar reason, public anger at specific officials, rather than government institutions and policies, is expected to play a more significant role in creating group action.

Unfair treatment. In the 2010 CGSS survey, the respondents were asked whether they experienced unfair treatment by local governments in the past year (coded 0 if no and 1 if yes, *unfair treatment*). It is expected that such unfair treatment plays a major role in causing group action. In addition, it would be more interesting to know who is more likely to experience unfair treatment, using the respondents' social and demographic variables.

Social and demographic variables, including age (five age groups and the youngest as comparison), education (four education groups and college as comparison), gender (*female*), individual income in 2009 measured in 10,000 yuan (*indinc10k*), urban residents (*urban*), party membership (*ccp*), and ethnic minority status (*non-han*), are included in the regression equations, with group action and unfair treatment as dependent variables. These variables are expected to play a consistent role in causing unfair treatment and group action. For example, if a particular age group reports unfair treatment, it's also more likely to engage in group action, and vice versa.

The statistical characteristics of the preceding variables are displayed in appendix 6.1.

Ordered-logistic regression is used for the two equations since both dependent variables (*group action* and *unfair*) are coded as ordered categorical scales. Both regression equations only include the subsample of the respondents who lived in the protest-affected areas, since people are likely to participate in group action only if they are aware of such mass incidents around them. The results are shown in table 6.2.

Table 6.2. COLLECTIVE ACTION PARTICIPATION AND UNFAIR TREATMENT BY GOVERNMENT (ORDERED LOGIT REGRESSION COEFFICIENTS, PROTEST-AFFECTED SUBSAMPLE ONLY)

	Group Action	Unfair treatment
Trust_Beijing	0.157***	
Trust_local gov	−0.524***	
Against_firm	0.295***	
Against_cadre	0.224***	
Against_org	0.169***	
Against_bureau	−0.259***	
Against_policy	−0.579***	
Unfair treatment by gov.	1.126***	
Age 17–34 (comparison)		
Age 35–48	0.031***	−0.325***
Age 49–60	−0.253***	−0.003
Age 61–77	−0.241***	−0.819***
Age 78–96	0.710***	0.244***
Primary	−0.156***	−0.715***
Jr. hi	−0.449***	−0.978***
Sr. hi	−0.622***	−0.982***
College (comparison)		
Female	−0.431***	−0.250***
Ind inc 10 k	−0.038***	−0.010***
CCP	−0.082	−0.444***
Urban	0.269***	−0.032*
Non-Han	0.380***	−1.023***
Pseudo R²	0.056	0.027
N	1,267	1,279

Source: CGSS 2010.
Note: Both equations are weighted by a weight variable constructed with the information on education in the 2010 Population Census.

Central and Local Governments

The first set of interesting results in the regression analysis in table 6.2 concerns the opposite effects of government trust. As expected, participation in group action is significantly reduced when the trust in local government goes up. In contrast, however, trust in the Beijing government increases group action participation. These results seem to confirm the anecdotal examples that show the alliances between the protesters and the national government against the local officials in Urumqi, Wukan, and Shifang.

Targets of Group Action

Certain targets are likely to draw more group action than others. Economic organizations are the easiest targets and attract the heaviest participation (*against_firm*). The second easiest target is government officials (*against_cadre*), followed by non-government and non-profit organizations (*against_org*). Conflicts with government agencies and official policies significantly weaken group participation (*against_bureau* and *against_policy*). As expected, the possible explanation of the differences is that the center is successful in redirecting public anger from the government itself and its policies to other scapegoats, especially economic and social organizations and individual officials' wrongdoings.

Unfair Treatment

Experience with any unfair treatment understandably plays the strongest role in promoting group action participation (*unfair treatment by gov.*). If there is anything unusual, it is the lack of fear for people to act when they perceive any unfairness in a populist authoritarian state.

Age

Regarding the age effect, one group that stands out is the oldest cohort (age 78–96). This group reported the highest level of mistreatment and the highest possibility to engage in group action. While it is not clear why this group experienced the most mistreatment, their political activism may be a result of their political socialization. The respondents in this age group completed their political socialization, defined as when they became 16, during the Revolutionary Era before 1949. They have experienced the longest time of political mobilization and thus are the most prone to join social movements. The second age group that stands out is the age 35–48 cohort. This group reported a low level of mistreatment but a high probability of group action. One possibility is that this age cohort was politically active because they completed their political socialization between 1976 and 1989 (when they became 16). This period was China's initial market reform era, and it witnessed the relative political openness that eventually led to the 1989 urban protests. Finally, the two middle groups (*age 49–60* and *age 61–77*) were quite comfortable, feeling neither unfair treatment nor the need for group action.

Education

The three less educated groups (*primary, jr. hi, sr. hi*) felt less unfairly treated than the college educated and, accordingly, demonstrated less interest in group action than the college educated. College graduates complained the most about being unfairly treated and were the most likely to participate (*college*). It seems that this group was "relatively deprived" (Gurr 1970). They felt that they deserved more than what they got.

Gender

Females, higher income earners, and Communist Party members saw themselves as more fairly treated than males, low income earners, and non-Party members. As expected, these groups are also less participative, although the coefficient for party members is not statistically significant (but with the correct sign).

Urbanization and Ethnicity

The last two groups are urban residents (*urban*) and minorities (*non-Han*). Interestingly, neither of these two groups felt more unfairly treated than their counterparts (rural residents and Han majority), yet they both were more likely to participate in collective action. Urbanites (including migrants) were more participative, perhaps because they possessed more information and resources (money, transportation, etc.). Ethnic minorities were more likely to take part in collective action even if they didn't feel unfairly treated, perhaps because of their stronger awareness of group identity in China's "state-sponsored" affirmative action policy (Tang and He 2010). In other words, minority collective action was a response to the state's call for ethnic equality.

CONCLUSIONS AND DISCUSSION

This chapter has shown that contentious politics in China is partly a result of the country's populist authoritarian tradition, in which political institutions and autonomous social organizations are weak, the bureaucracy is fragmented, and the elites and the masses can reach each other in a relatively direct way without the interference of the intermediate institutional procedures.

The rationale for the CCP to maintain and encourage such populist relationships is to test its policies, to eliminate unqualified officials, to play the role as a mediator between conflicting social and economic interests, and, more importantly, to promote political support for the CCP regime.

For the time being, China's populist authoritarianism seems to generate a fairly high level of regime support while allowing selective expression of public anger. This model of populist authoritarianism explains the seeming contradiction between mass protest and regime support. In the long run, however, such a relationship is fragile and can quickly turn into nationwide social movements that can serve to topple the regime.

Some people may still be suspicious of the strong support for the central government found in Chinese public opinion surveys. They continue to believe that people habitually lie in these surveys and that most of them are actually very unhappy about their government and are ready to explode. While this suspicion is well justified, and proving the reliability of the survey responses poses a true challenge for those who rely on survey data, one assurance is that Chinese people never hesitated to rise and overthrow their unpopular governments, as has happened many times in Chinese history. As long as the current Communist government is not overthrown, it is possible that people are not so fed up with it and that their support is not a lie.

This chapter relied on both case studies and large-N survey data to show how regime-mobilized contentious politics plays out in contemporary Chinese society. The combined qualitative and quantitative methods compliment each other nicely without sacrificing the "thick" description of the specific cases and the generalizability of the findings.

Future research needs to rely more on the increasingly available survey data with tremendously improved quality. In addition, lab experiments can also be used to test the various hypotheses in the study of collective action. Another direction for future research is to further separate protest behavior by its incentive structure (direct compensation of land acquisition vs. uncertain environmental impact) and risk levels, and how these factors influence protest behavior.

CHAPTER 7
Individual Dispute Resolution

This chapter continues the discussion of conflict resolution from the last chapter. The last chapter estimated the number of people who lived in protest-affected regions as 11% of the total population above age 15, and about one-third of the 11% were directly or indirectly involved in some form of protest. But there are at least three unanswered questions from the findings in the last chapter. The first is the actual number of disputes before they escalate into protests. Second, the last chapter only focused on protest as a channel for problem solving. But the unanswered question is whether people use other channels and the effectiveness of these other channels comparing to protest. Third, the last chapter was only interested in collective action; it did not include conflict resolution at the individual level. With additional survey data, this chapter addresses these questions, namely, the scope of dispute and the channels of dispute resolution at the individual level.

Specifically, this chapter examines the following issues: (1) scope and types of disputes; (2) the channels of dispute resolution and their effectiveness; (3) the role of ownership type in dispute resolution.

Data used in this chapter are from the 2012 China Labor-Force Dynamics Survey (CLDS) by the Center for Social Science Survey at Sun Yat-Sen University in Guangzhou, China (http://css.sysu.edu.cn). The multi-stage stratified random sample includes 17,885 respondents in 370 villages and neighborhoods (*juweihui*) in 151 cities and counties in 29 provinces.[1] Among all of the respondents, 4,394 are non-agricultural employees and the others are either employers, self-employed, farmers, or not working. This chapter uses the subsample of the 4,394 employees and analyzes their workplace dispute resolution. The CLDS contains a module of questions on labor dispute, channels of problem solving and the result (appendix 7.1). The information on labor dispute can be compared in different types of ownership.

Another source of empirical evidence is drawn from the 2004 Institutionalization of Legal Reform Survey supported by the Ford Foundation and Peking University (*Zhongguo Gongmin Sixiang Daode Guannian Zhuangkuang Diaocha*).[2] This survey contains a national random sample of 7,714 respondents in 200 townships and urban neighborhoods located in 100 counties and urban districts. It includes a wide range of questions related to the respondents' attitudes and behavior in dispute resolution.

SCOPE AND TYPE OF DISPUTES

A number of studies have reported the rapid increase in various types of dispute in China, reflected in the court-accepted cases (Ho 2004; Shen 2007; Tang 2009; Gallagher and Wang 2011). Chinese national statistics show that the courts accepted nearly 16 times more civil cases in 2003 than they did in 1978, nearly 60 times more economic cases in 2001 than in 1981, and almost 170 times more administrative cases in 2003 than in 1983 (Tang 2009, figure 1).

Yet the rapid increase in court-accepted cases does not necessarily indicate the institutionalization of the rule of law in China when compared with other societies. One study (World Bank 2002) lists the numbers of court-filed disputes per 100,000 population in 12 countries in 1995, including Austria (29,294), Ecuador (10,467), England and Wales (4,718), Portugal (3,719), Brazil (2,739), Germany (2,655), Peru (2,261), France (2,242), the Netherlands (2,031), Spain (1,898), Panama (1,656), and Italy (1,227). In the same year, the courts in China filed 4.55 million disputes, resulting in only 371 disputes per 100,000 population.[3] Thus, even though the number of court-accepted disputes increased rapidly, it was still at the bottom in China compared with other societies where statistics are available.

However, not all disputes end in courts. For example, among the total number of 2,671 disputes in the past 20 years reported by the 7,714 respondents in the 2004 Legal Survey, only 17% were taken to court; the majority of them were resolved through other channels. The average number of disputes per respondent was 0.35 (2,671/7,714), or there was one dispute for every three respondents.

In the 2012 Labor Survey, 52% of the 4,394 employees in the sample never had any disputes, but 48% of them had some sort of dispute related to overwork, unfair pay, bad work conditions, delayed pay, or injury; these included 24% with one dispute, 14% with two, 7% with three, 2% with four, and 0.4% with all five types of disputes (weighted). Since each respondent's number of disputes is known, it is possible to calculate the total number of disputes in the sample by summing up each respondent's reported number of disputes. As a result, there are 3,743 total disputes among the 4,394 employees, or 0.85 disputes per employee on average; that is, about 4.5 out of every 5 employees had a dispute.

This level of dispute more than doubled the 0.35 disputes per respondent in the 2004 Legal Survey, particularly considering that the 2004 survey asked about the past 20 years while the 2012 survey was about the past two years. Three reasons may contribute to such a high level of disputes. One possibility is that the 2012 Labor Survey was conducted among non-agricultural employees rather than the general population. The workplace is where people spend most of their awake time besides eating and sleeping. It is where most social, economic, and political interaction and conflict take place. It is understandable that there are more disputes at the workplace than among the general population. The second possibility is that some of the disputes in 2012 were likely to be perceived rather than realized, such as unfair pay and bad work conditions. The third possibility is the real increase of disputes initiated by employees. Regardless of the reasons, such a surprisingly high level of disputes suggests mass political activism in China, which is far beyond the numbers reflected in the court-accepted cases.

The 2012 Labor Survey also contains the types of labor disputes and whether they were resolved. Among the 3,743 reported disputes, 19% were about work-related injury, 26% were related to pay delay, 22% were about overtime work, 25% were about bad work conditions, and 8% were about unfair compensation.

Figure 7.1 shows the rates of problem solving among the five types of dispute. For work injury, over 75% of the disputes were resolved or partially resolved. Similarly, over 60% of disputes related to pay delay were either resolved or partially resolved. In contrast, the problem solving rates were only about 35% for both overwork and bad work condition, and only about 30% for unfair compensation. The determining factor seems to be whether the problem requires immediate attention, such as injury and pay delay, or whether it can be postponed as related to overtime work, bad work conditions, and unfair pay. The problem solving rate is quite high in the former cases. Such a high response rate is also reflected in the 2004 Legal Survey; among the 2,671 reported disputes, only 24% cases were not resolved. Among the 76% resolved cases, the most popular result was compromise (25%), followed by win (16%), lose (18%), and other outcome (17%).

In summary, the findings from the two large-scale national surveys in this section suggest that disputes are widespread in China. This spread is both a reflection of the growing social tension in a transitional society

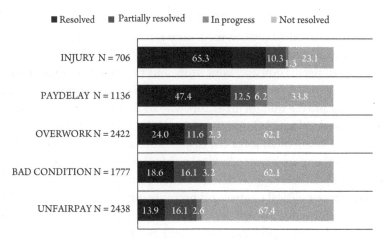

Figure 7.1:
Problem solving outcome by type of problem (weighted %, 2012 CLDS)

with fundamental restructuring of various social interests and the widespread political activism in Chinese society, particularly at the workplace.

CHANNELS OF DISPUTE SETTLEMENT

Studying the channels of problem solving is important, because they are reflections of how a political system functions. Broadly speaking, they can be divided into formal and informal channels. The former can be further divided into two categories, the ones that were established and used regularly prior to market reform, such as mediation and ombudsman, and the new institutional channels that are gaining importance in dispute settlement since the 1980s, including the courts, the media, and the People's Congresses (Tang 2005). Informal channels include individual negotiation and protest. Therefore, once in dispute, one has four options: established institutional channels, newly emerging institutional channels, extra-system informal means, or taking no action.

Established Official Channels

Perhaps the most popular option is through established official channels, including mediation and administrative channels. Mediation is an established channel for dispute resolution (Womack and Townsend 1996). Traditionally, mediation was preferred over litigation. The 1982 Constitution further institutionalized this system by requiring residential and village committees to create People's Mediation Committees. Unlike court rulings that tend to follow the law, mediation is more ad hoc in nature and requires different solutions for different cases. It often involves criticism and self-criticism, persuasion and education, and imposed solutions (Perkovich 1996). In 2003, for example, China had 870,000 People's Mediation Committees and 6.8 million mediators who dealt with 5.7 million disputes (Law Yearbook Editorial Committee 2004). Critics of mediation argue that Chinese mediators often force the disputant to accept a solution and that this process therefore blurs individual rights (Ludman 1999, 2000; Fu and Cullen 2011). Others suggest that mediation is simply a mechanism for the state to enforce political control and promote official norms (Clark 1991). As market reform increasingly legitimizes individual interests, it is unclear whether mediation would adequately address individual needs and continue to be a preferred mechanism for dispute resolution.

Another popular mechanism for conflict resolution is through the Letters and Visits system (*xinfang*).[4] According to the 1996 State Council Regulations on Letters and Visits, all citizens have the right to voice their criticism, suggestions, and requests to administrative, legislative, and judicial organizations at all levels, to reveal the wrongdoings of officials, and to protest any violation of their legal rights.[5]

It is important to note that although the Letters and Visits (or petitioning) system is an officially designed system, it is intended for the individuals to solve their problems by bypassing one's immediate supervising organization or the normal bureaucratic procedure. One study on *xinfang* found that even though this system was widely used by the public, it is fundamentally an instrument to rule by the party, rather than a legal institution that protects individual rights (Minzner 2006).

Administrative review is another official channel for problem solving. The 1999 Administrative Review Act passed by the Standing Committee of the National People's Congress[6] states that all citizens can request administrative reviews concerning administrative rulings against them. In 2003, nearly four million letters and visits were accepted by the courts alone, and there were 76,000 administrative review cases (Law Yearbook Editorial Committee 2004, pp. 1056, 1072). Clearly, these channels are widely used for dispute resolution.

Emerging Institutional Channels

The second group of institutional channels for dispute settlement includes the newly emerging channels such as courts, the media, and the legislature (national and local People's Congresses). Although these are still under the monolithic control of the Communist Party, they may attract public attention due to their increasingly active role in government supervision and legal reform since the 1980s. Court is the ideal channel for dispute resolution if the rule of law is in effect. Although nearly 5.13 million cases were accepted in courts nationwide in 2003,[7] the courts may not be the preferred channel for dispute resolution if the pessimist view of Chinese courts as corrupt, under-trained, and ineffective is true (Woo 1997, 1999; Lubman 1999, 2000; Zheng 2014a, 2014b). The Chinese media are filled with discussions of controversial legal cases, corruption, abuses of power, and legal education programs. People's Congresses at different levels are asserting their constitutional responsibilities of supervising the administrative and judicial branches of government.[8] Compared to the traditional official channels, these are relatively new institutional channels of dispute resolution.

Non-Institutional Channels

The third category consists of non-institutional channels, including mutual negotiation, protest, and violence. Disputants may use these channels when the institutional channels are ineffective or inaccessible. The final category is no action, reflecting the most pessimistic assessment of the effectiveness of all existing channels, or a feeling of apathy.

Admittedly, the items in each category are different from each other and should not be discussed in the same group. For example, one could argue that mutual negotiation is different from protest and does not belong in the same category. The distinction here is based on institutions, however. Mutual negotiation and protest may be different, but they are both extra-system means.

Hypothetical and Actual Channels

Figure 7.2 shows the channels the respondents used to solve their disputes in the 2004 Legal Survey. If the respondents never had any disputes, they were asked to pick a channel they would use in case of a dispute. In a hypothetical dispute, the top three channels to solve it were mutual negotiation (36%), court (26%), and do nothing (16%). This mixture of the top three channels seems to point to the simultaneous consequences of the lack of a legal-institutional culture (mutual negotiation), the impact of market reform on emphasizing the role of the courts (court), and apathy under authoritarian control (no action).

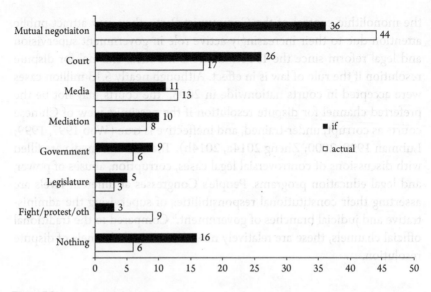

Figure 7.2:
Hypothetical and actual channels of dispute settlement (weighted %, 2004 Legal Reform Survey)

The differences between hypothetical and actual channels are also worth noting (figure 7.2). First, fewer respondents said that they would use mutual negotiation or force/protest in a hypothetical dispute, but they were more likely to use these channels if they were in a real dispute. There seems to be a contrast between the encouragement to use institutional channels and the public suspicion of the effectiveness of those channels. Consistent with this suspicion, the respondents seemed to prefer the court in a hypothetic dispute but were less likely to take an actual dispute to court. These findings are not in favor of the rule of law. They suggest that once in trouble, people could easily resort to non-institutional channels, although fewer would openly admit it. Thus, it is still too early to say that conflict resolution is "institutionalized" in China. The final difference is that the respondents were more apathetic in theory than in reality. Sixteen percent said they would do nothing if they had a dispute, but a much smaller number (6%) of those who were actually involved in disputes took no action. This gap seems to suggest a high level of political activism.

Similar trends continued in the 2012 Labor Survey. The respondents in the 2012 survey were asked the channels through which they resolved each of the five types of dispute (injury, overwork, pay delay, unfair pay, and bad work conditions). The channels include individual negotiation with the firm; collective negotiation; official channels such as courts, labor unions, and the media; contentious behavior such as protest, petition, strike; and resorting to violence. In figure 7.3, overwhelming majorities

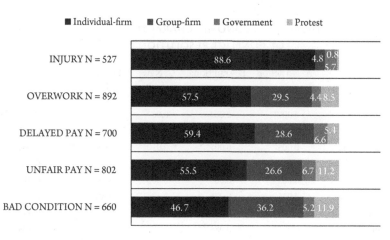

Figure 7.3:
Problem solving channels by problem type (weighted %, 2012 CLDS)

of the respondents used non-institutional channels for problem solving at the workplace. For each type of dispute, over 80% of the disputants tried to solve their problems through individual or group negotiations, and a sizable percentage of disputants engaged in protest behavior, particularly in solving problems related to work conditions, unfair pay, and overwork. The disputants largely ignored the institutional channels, including courts, labor unions, and the media, as only about 5% of them tried to go through these channels.

Socio-Economic Characteristics of Dispute Resolution

The next step is to examine who are more likely to use what channels for problem solving. The 2004 Legal Survey is a better source for this purpose since it contains more detailed information about the channels. In an ordinary least squares (OLS) multivariate regression analysis, each type of channel is treated as a dependent variable, including no action, traditional official channels, new official channels, mutual negotiation, and protest. The determinants (independent variables) of each type of action include the respondents' age, gender, education, party membership, income, legal knowledge, and urbanization (coded as migrant, urbanite, and ruralite).

As shown in table 7.1, when examining the socio-economic background of the disputants who did not take any action, there was a strong modernizing effect; namely, the more educated, Party members,[9] migrant workers, and urban residents were more likely to take action than the less educated, non-Party members, and rural residents (column A, table 7.1).[10]

Table 7.1. SOCIAL AND ECONOMIC CHARACTERISTICS AND CHANNELS
OF CONFLICT RESOLUTION (OLS)

	A. No action	B. Traditional official	C. New official	D. Mutual negotiation	E. Fight/protest
Age/10	−0.007**	−0.004	0.007	−0.036***	0.004
Female	−0.005	−0.008	−0.010	0.028	−0.001
Education (yrs)	−0.005***	−0.007***	0.010***	−0.003	0.000
Party member	−0.060***	−0.043	0.043	−0.012	0.026
Indinc03/10 k	0.002	−0.008	−0.006	−0.001	0.010***
Legal knowledge	−0.025	−0.076	0.326***	0.016	−0.079**
Migrant	−0.073**	0.081	−0.097	−0.152*	0.099***
Urbanite	−0.026*	0.085***	−0.087**	−0.063	0.005
Rural (comparison)					
_cons	0.147	−0.036	−0.297	1.232***	0.033
Adjusted R²	0.224	0.093	0.263	0.224	0.155
N	2445	2445	2445	2445	2445

Source: 2004 Institutionalization of Legal Reform Survey.
Notes: Each dependent variable is coded 0 or 1. Zero presents taking action and not using any of the other four channels, and 1 means not taking action or using any of the other four channels. Logistic regression results are consistent with the OLS results, which make comparisons easier between findings in this table and elsewhere in the chapter. Official channels (mediation and government Letters and Visits and Administrative Review) are combined into a factor index ranging from 0 to 1; new channels (court, media, and People's Congress delegates) are also combined into a factor index ranging from 0 to 1; and protest/fight is another factor index ranging from 0 to 1. OLS regression is used to provide better comparison among the five regression equations, although the dichotomous variables such as "no action" and "mutual negotiation" are best estimated by logistic regressions. Logistic regression is used to double check the OLS results, and the two techniques produced very similar results. "Age/10" is age divided by 10; "education" is measured in years; "indinc03/10k" is the respondent's 2003 income in yuan divided by 10,000; legal knowledge is an index of the respondent's correct answers to the legality of 12 items including coresidence before marriage, extra-marital affairs, land ownership, child labor, signed contract, parental care by married daughter, suspect's right to be silent, inheritance by married daughter, court's lawmaking function, law suit by prosecutor's office, forced confinement of SARS patients, and local government's right to interfere with court's decisions. Township is controlled for all equations.
*p < = 0.1, **p < = 0.05, ***p < = 0.01. See appendix 6.1 for further statistical details of these variables.

The same modernizing effect also applies to using institutional channels. Education decreased the use of traditional official channels but encouraged the use of new institutional channels (columns B and C, table 7.1). Similarly, legal knowledge reduced fight and protest while promoting the use of new institutional channels such as the courts, the media, and the legislature (columns C and E, table 7.1). The militant tendency among migrant workers is noticeable. Not only did they have a high number of disputes (Tang and Yang 2008) but they were less likely to engage in mutual negotiation and more likely to fight and protest (columns D and E, table 7.1).

In sum, at least five findings in this section need to be highlighted. One interesting finding is the strong tendency for people to take action in dispute resolution in China's contentious political cultural environment. The second is the lasting legacy of Maoist populism in conflict resolution, as people still tended to take issues into their own hands rather than rely on institutional channels. The third, a somewhat disappointing finding, is how under-utilized the courts were in dispute resolution and how much people still sought solutions through extra-institutional channels. The fourth, an unexpected finding, is the militancy shown by the migrant workers who were conventionally described as a politically weak group. Fifth, traditional channels of conflict resolution (mediation) remained dominant. These findings may disappoint the reader who is expecting the institutionalization of the rule of law in the growing marketization in China's economic modernization.

ECONOMIC ORGANIZATIONS AND THE POLITICS OF DISPUTE RESOLUTION

This section compares different types of economic organizations and their effects in labor dispute resolution. Different economic organizations provide specific institutional environments in which power relations are structured and are likely to generate distinctive patterns of dispute resolution.

China's economic transformation in the past several decades has created a diverse economic environment in which the state sector has given away its traditionally dominant role to the private sectors. For example, in the weighted sample of 12,207 respondents of the 2012 Labor Survey, only about 10% of the employees worked in state-owned and collectively owned enterprises, and about 9% worked in party-state or nonprofit organizations. Nearly half (49%) of the employees in the survey worked in the private sector, including firms owned by private individual entrepreneurs, by private groups, and by foreign investors, while 29% still worked as farmers and 3% in other types of organizations. While the private-sector employees were on average several years younger than the other groups, the party-state and nonprofit organizations still attracted the most educated in China's labor force.

Studies of workplace political participation and political activism under different types of ownership have shown very different and sometimes opposing results. One view sees private ownership as the product of market economy and economic freedom, and economic freedom will have a spillover effect in political freedom (Friedman 1962; Dahl 1985), which will lead to a greater level of workplace participation and political activism. Others, however, argue that private ownership widens the class distinction between labor and capital (Braverman 1974; Edwards 1979) and strengthens the latter's "despotic control" (Burawoy 1979). In his quantitative study of Chinese local industries in the 1990s, Tang (1993) found that workers in private firms demanded less participation in managerial decision-making than those in more centralized forms of ownership. In recent years, political activism seems to be on the rise in private firms and particularly in foreign-owned private firms (Cheng 2014). Therefore, it is necessary to reexamine this issue in private firms after 20 years of phenomenal economic growth.

Others have suggested that state-sector employees were more likely to demonstrate political activism. Under central planning, supply shortage was a chronic problem for state-owned enterprises. Factory managers had to exercise a greater degree of flexibility in order to fulfill their quotas at the end of the month, giving employees more bargaining power in this process (Burawoy and Lucas 1985). In addition, the ideological propaganda of egalitarianism under Mao Zedong was designed to eliminate class distinction and promote working class political participation (Tang 1996). Such political indoctrination has provided the political will and skill as well as the organizational resources for labor political resistance against private owners (F. Chen 2008) and for fighting for ideologically based justice in the post-Mao market reform (Gallagher and Wang 2011). In addition to studying these former state-sector employees, it is also necessary to look into the current state-sector employees and compare them with those in other types of organizations.

One way to compare organizations is to look at the difference between the specific disputes in these organizations. Table 7.2 compares two kinds of disputes (pay delays and overtime work) in four types of organizations including the party-state sector, foreign or jointly owned firms, state-owned enterprises, and firms owned by private entrepreneurs. In the weighted sample, employees in firms owned by private entrepreneurs were more likely to face pay delays (30%) than those in other types of firms (17% in SOEs, 8% in foreign/joint firms, and 3% in party-state organizations), but these private-firm employees complained the least (31%) about overtime work than the employees in the other organizations (42% in SOEs, 45% in foreign/joint firms, and 51% in party-state sector). Employees in party-state organizations were the least likely to experience pay delay (only 3%), but they complained the most about overtime work (51%). Pay delay is an immediate problem, whereas overtime work can be seen as a hidden form of exploitation. Interestingly, the party-state sector can be best protected from the overt mistreatment (pay delay) but not necessarily from the hidden mistreatment (overtime work). The private sector is the least protected from pay delay, which is an explicit violation of employees' rights, but these workers can be relatively free from being

Table 7.2. DISPUTE TYPE BY ORGANIZATION TYPE (% YES, WEIGHTED)

	A. Pay delay		B. Overtime work
Party-state	3%	Privately owned	31%
Foreign/jointly owned	8%	State-owned (SOE)	42%
State-owned (SOE)	17%	Foreign/jointly owned	45%
Privately owned	30%	Party-state	51%

Source: 2012 CLDS.
Notes: Party-state n = 269; Foreign firm n = 310; SOE (State-owned enterprise) n = 914; private entrepreneur n = 910.

coerced into doing overtime work. It may be disappointing news for the impatient reader who is looking for a simple answer, but unfortunately each type of organization has its own flaw.

The second way to compare organizations is by examining the channels for problem solving. In the 2012 Labor Survey and also in figure 7.3, these channels include (1) individual negotiation with the firm; (2) official institutions including trade unions, courts, and the media; (3) group negotiation; and (4) protest, also including fights, sit-ins, and petitions. Petitions are treated as a form of protest here, rather than an institutional solution, because it encourages the adoption of "extra-system" means by bypassing one's immediate supervisors or supervising organization.

Figure 7.4 compares the employees' conflict resolution behaviors in four types of organizations, namely individually owned firms, state-owned enterprises, foreign or jointly owned companies, and the party-state sector. Interestingly, each type of organization demonstrated a distinctive behavioral pattern.

Although everyone used individual negotiation, employees in individually owned firms stood out among others. Forty-five percent of the employees in individual-owned firms used individual negotiation for dispute resolution, as compared to 35% in SOEs, 25% in foreign firms, and only 13% in party-state organizations. This is perhaps due to the fact that workers in individually owned firms are the least organized and most of the firms are probably small in size.

For institutional channels, the party-state sector (8%) outperformed SOEs (3%), foreign firms (2%), and individually owned firms (2%). This is understandable since this sector is the most closely integrated into the system.

For group negotiation, SOEs showed the most willingness (26%) over individually owned firms (13%), foreign firms (11%), and the party-state sector (10%). This seems to confirm Feng Chen's 2011 study about the socialist legacy in state-owned enterprises. During market transformation,

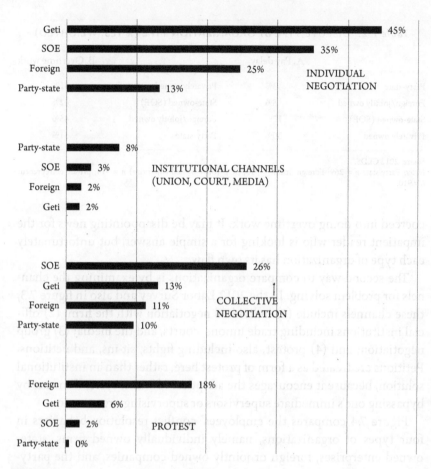

Figure 7.4:
Dispute solving channels by firm type (weighted %, 2012 CLDS)

employees in these firms continued to demonstrate their group solidarity, organizational resources, and the political skills for collective bargaining.

And finally, for protest, employees in foreign and jointly owned firms showed the strongest desire to engage in openly confrontational behavior (18%) over individually owned firms (6%), SOEs (2%), and the party-state sector (0.5%). This is consistent with the frequent media coverage of protests in foreign companies such as Nike and Adidas in China (Cheng 2014). One possible explanation is that such protest behavior is more tolerated since it is not pointing fingers at the Chinese government but at foreign investors.

The third and final way to study the organizational effect is by comparing their success rates of dispute resolution in the 2012 Labor Survey. Table 7.3 is a multiple regression analysis of the dispute resolution success rates among the different types of organizations, while controlling for dispute type, respondents' age, gender, education, party membership, local residency, and income.

The winners were the employees in foreign or jointly owned firms, domestic privately owned firms, and in state-owned companies, as they showed significantly higher success rate in problem solving than the other types of organizations. There was no statistically significant difference between the other types of firms including the party-state sector, nonprofit organizations, individually owned firms, agricultural organizations, and collectively owned firms.

As mentioned previously, the higher success rates in SOEs and in foreign firms are likely the results of the SOE employees' group solidarity and superior collective bargaining power and the greater government

Table 7.3. SUCCESS RATES OF DISPUTE RESOLUTION
BY FIRM TYPE (OLS)

	solvedpct
Foreign/joint	0.039**
Private firm	0.035**
SOE	0.034**
Party-state	−0.013
Nonprofit	0.02
Individual (geti)	0.007
Agriculture	0.009
Firm_other	0.026
collective (comparison)	
Injury	0.134***
Pay delay	0.136***
Unfair pay	0.002
Bad env	0.034***
Overwork	0.047***
Age	−0.001***
Female	−0.015**
Degree	−0.002
CCP	0.007
Local household registration (hukou)	−0.005
Loginc11 (2011 logged income)	0.005
Constant	0.078***
Observations	3,624
R^2	0.252

Source: 2012 CLDS.
Note: The dependent variable (solvedpct) is a percentage of dispute resolution (see appendix 7.2 for further details).
*p<0.1, **p<0.05, ***p<0.01

tolerance for open confrontation with foreign investors. Similarly, the success in domestic private firms is also the likely result of greater official tolerance of open confrontation against the private investors as long as it is not directed against the government.

In summary, the findings in this section demonstrate the organizational consequences in workplace conflict formation and dispute resolution. One interesting finding is the "hidden" conflict as reflected in overtime work in the party-state organizations. Such conflict is often less noticed, as the public attention is more easily focused on the explicit conflicts such as pay delays. The second interesting finding is the distinctive patterns of conflict resolution behavior due to the nature of different ownership types, such as individual negotiation in the loosely organized individually owned firms, institutional behavior in the highly organized party-state sector, collective bargaining in the state enterprises with traditional working-class ideological legacy, and protest in foreign firms where the Chinese state is motivated to direct public dissatisfaction away from itself. The third finding is that success in dispute resolution is not found in the organizations that are highly centralized, as in the party-state and nonprofit organizations, nor in firms with little or no organization, such as individual-owned companies. It seems that success has to satisfy one of two conditions: group solidarity, as in SOEs, and/or not directly confronting the state, as in foreign firms.

CONCLUSION AND DISCUSSION

The preceding chapter focused on protest as a form of collective action in conflict resolution. This chapter continues the discussion of conflict resolution by addressing two unanswered questions in that chapter, namely, how many disputes actually take place before they express themselves in protests, and what are the other channels and their effectiveness in conflict resolution besides protest? These questions are discussed by drawing evidence from two large-scale national representative surveys, the 2012 China Labor Survey and the 2004 China Legal Survey. These two surveys together contain more than 25,000 respondents throughout the country.

Concerning the first question, the number of disputes, a comparison between the two surveys suggests a rapid increase in recent years. There was one dispute for every three respondents in the 2004 Legal Survey. In the 2012 Labor Survey, there were 8.5 disputes for every 10 employees, that is, 85% of the employees had labor disputes. This number seems extremely high. One possibility is that some of these disputes were not real but only perceived as a problem, such as unfair pay, overtime work, and bad work conditions. Regardless of whether these disputes were real or only "imagined," such a high ratio of disputes at least suggests one thing, namely, the respondents' willingness to see and approach their problems in a contentious way. Such willingness to engage in confrontation is further supported in this chapter by the high level of political activism. In both surveys, the majority of the respondents would take action and only a very small percentage of them would do nothing.

Next, the two surveys are quite consistent in showing the high rates of problem solving. In the 2012 Labor Survey, 75% of the disputes were related to injury, and 60% of pay delay problems were resolved. In the 2004 Legal Survey, only 24% of the disputes were left unresolved. Such high rates of problem solving echo the findings in chapter 5, in which mainland Chinese respondents in the 2008 Asian Barometer Survey thought their governments at different levels were more responsive than did the Taiwanese respondents.

Regarding the second unanswered question from the last chapter, namely, the channels of problem solving, the main finding in this chapter is how under-developed and under-utilized the newly emerging institutional channels are, such as the courts, trade unions, the media, and the legislature. Sometimes people may think that these channels are fashionable but still avoid them when it comes to real problem solving. This finding continues the discussion of the weak institutional development from the last chapter.

On the other hand, however, traditional official channels such as mediation are exerting their lasting effectiveness after several decades of market reform. Even though mediation is being constantly criticized by both Western and Chinese legal scholars as blurring human rights, Chinese disputants nevertheless still preferred mediation over litigation.

The third finding concerning the channels of dispute resolution is the importance of informal channels, including individual negotiation, group negotiation, petitioning, and protest. These informal channels and the traditional official channels together consist of over 90% of dispute resolution in China.

The final section of this chapter explores the relationship between economic organization and conflict resolution behavior. State-owned enterprises and foreign-owned companies seemed to produce more political activism and success in dispute resolution than the highly controlled party-state organizations and the individual-owned small firms with little worker solidarity. Employees in the SOEs perhaps benefited from the ideological and organizational legacy of workers' rights from the socialist era. Those in foreign firms were likely taking advantage of the government's tolerance of contentious behavior as long as it did not directly target the state.

CHAPTER 8
Political Trust

An Experimental Study

(with Yang Zhang)

One of the key findings in this book is the high level of political trust in China. For example, chapters 2 and 5 show that political support of the Chinese government and the Communist Party rose steadily from the Tiananmen protests in 1989 to 2014. When the authoritarian China is compared to democratic Taiwan, China consistently demonstrated a much higher level of political support in public opinion surveys.

As elaborated in the previous chapters, the reasons for the high level of political support in China include the effective use of nationalism (chapter 3) and the strong feeling of external efficacy based on the government's responsiveness to public demand, in addition to economic growth and the cultural tradition of conformity (chapter 5).

However, some people still insist that they do not believe that survey respondents in China can truthfully answer questions about whether or not they can trust their government. They attribute the high level of political support in Chinese public opinion surveys to political fear. For example, some European scholars of public opinion and political behavior are convinced that survey respondents do not really have any opinion in a hierarchically structured Asian country like China:

> Asian communities are particularly hierarchically structured, which results in the elite having a much stronger influence on the attitudes and behavior of the average citizen than in the case of individualistic and egalitarian western communities. (Fuchs 2007, 173)

Others believe that people would never tell the truth in a repressive political system such as China:

> In a repressive regime behavior will reflect what the government wants rather than what individuals prefer and in a totalitarian regime opinions that subjects voice in public can be the opposite of what they think or say in private. (Rose 2007, 292)

In contrary, other researchers have shown that while people in China were politically intimidated in the past, they have become more outspoken in recent years following the country's global economic integration and the development of Internet communication. For example, Chinese Internet users regularly engage in heated debates on political issues, and some of them are highly critical of the regime but left untouched as long as they do not involve in organized political activities against the government (King, Pan, and Roberts 2013). If this view is true, political desirability may not be a serious problem as expected.

In the previous chapters (1, 2, and 5) of this book, we have attempted to address the question of political desirability in several ways. For example, we have shown that there are just as many people in China as in the United States who explicitly say that they would not support a bad government (figure 1.1), suggesting the openness of Chinese respondents. We also have proposed to deal with the problem of political sensitivity in China by treating "don't know" answers as a sign of hiding one's dissatisfaction so that these can be coded as political distrust (tables 5.1A, 5.1B, and 5.2).

Yet these measures are all indirect solutions to the problem of survey data reliability in China. In this chapter, we face this problem directly and provide a more systematic answer by relying on the technique of list experiment. Such a method can help us detect (1) the extent to which people hide their opinions, (2) the difference between social desirability and political desirability, and (3) who are more likely to hide their opinions. These three research questions can be stated as the following hypotheses.

First, we expect to see a low degree of hiding one's opinion about political trust. This is because of the increasingly open political environment and improved individual freedom. The high level of political trust is not likely due to political fear but more likely created by other reasons, such as nationalism and government responsiveness, as discussed in chapters 2, 3, and 5 of this book.

Second, while political sensitivity regarding regime trust may not be a problem, we do not want to argue that Chinese survey respondents are not afraid of revealing their attitudes and behavior on other issues.

In contrast, we expect that the Chinese public is likely to hide their responses if the survey questions are about certain behaviors and attitudes that are considered socially undesirable, particularly if the questions are about whether the respondents themselves are engaged in these behaviors. As we discuss below, many studies have shown that survey respondents in democratic societies hide their opinions if they are aware of the social undesirability of their opinions, such as racism in the United States (Kuklinski, Cobb, and Gilens 1997). For China, we use bribery as a socially undesirable behavior. Presenting gifts is a common practice in dealing with government officials, but not everyone wants to openly admit such behavior. Thus, survey respondents are expected to hide such behavior during interviews.

The third question is how individual characteristics affect political and social desirability. Specifically, we look into age, education, gender, urbanization, group membership, occupation, and social class. It is expected that individuals who have more vested interest in the political system, such as the middle-aged, men, and those holding managerial jobs and in higher social classes, are more likely to hide their political distrust than others, while others who are less embedded in the system, such as rural residents, women, non-Party members, less educated, and older respondents, and those in low social classes, are more likely to engage in and also hide their socially undesirable behavior such as bribery.

Before we can continue, it is necessary to discuss the methodological tool that is used to test the preceding hypotheses.

LIST EXPERIMENT

In the 1990s, scholars of public opinion research led by James Kuklinski invented list experiment in order to reveal hidden opinions among survey respondents (Sniderman 2011). Since then, this method has inspired a wave of studies aimed at detecting racial and religious prejudice in the United States (Kuklinski, Cobb, and Gilens 1997; Kuklinski, Sniderman, et al. 1997; Gilens, Sniderman, and Kuklinski 1998; Kane, Craig, and Wald 2004; Redlawsk, Tolbert, and Franko 2010).

The idea of the list experiment is to randomly divide the already randomly drawn survey sample into two subsamples, A and B.[1] Respondents in sample A (control) are given a list of several items and have to tell the researcher how many, but not which ones, make them feel upset or troubled. In sample B (treatment), the respondents are given the same list of items, plus one socially sensitive item such as being troubled by Obama as the first black president in the United States. The respondents feel comfortable to pick the socially sensitive item as troublesome that may reveal their racial prejudice, because they don't have to tell the interviewer which one troubles them but simply how many items on the list do.

Without the treatment item, the average number in sample B should be very similar to the average number in sample A, since both are random samples and the respondents should behave similarly. If the average number in sample B is greater than in sample A after adding the treatment item, the difference between the two average numbers (multiplied by 100) should be understood as the percentage of respondents who pick the sensitive item in sample B. This is a covert measure of racial prejudice.

Next, the researcher will use the treatment item in sample B as an overt measure and ask the respondents in both samples whether they are troubled by it. The percentage of troubled respondents in the overt measure will then be compared with the percentage in the covert measure. If the latter is greater than the former, that difference indicates the percentage of people who hide their true opinion in the overt measure. Using this method, for example, Redlawsk, Tolbert, and Franko (2010) found that about 33% of their Hawkeye poll respondents said they were not troubled by Obama being the first black president in the overt measure but actually felt so in the covert measure.

The list experiment method can only tell the portion of the prejudiced respondents in sample B; it cannot identify exactly which respondents are the prejudiced ones. Yet the researcher can still tell their individual characteristics, such as their party identification, geographic origin, education, age, and so on. For example, in their covert (unobtrusive) measures, Kuklinski, Cobb, and Gilens (1997) found much more anger toward the affirmative action policy among white respondents in the south than in other regions in the United States. Redlawsk, Tolbert, and Franko's list experiment during the Obama campaign showed a significantly stronger racial prejudice against Obama among the Republican and Independent voters than the Democratic voters (Redlawsk, Tolbert, and Franko 2010).

In short, list experiment is a simple, effective, and powerful technique to examine the social desirability effect. In this study, we use it to detect the political desirability effect among the Chinese survey respondents.

DATA AND METHODOLOGY

The data for this chapter are drawn from two sources. The first is the 6th Wave World Values Survey China, which was led by the University of Iowa and implemented by the Research Center for Contemporary China at Peking University from December 2012 to January 2013. The random sample of 2,300 respondents was selected from 40 county-level units distributed in the various geographic regions of the country. The demographic characteristics of the sample are similar to that of the 6th Population Census of China in 2010. The second source of data is the two waves of Urban Policy Satisfaction Survey of China conducted in October–November 2013 and May–July 2014. These telephone surveys are based on probability samples of 4,000 urban residents in 17 cities.[2] In the World Values Survey China and the Urban Policy Satisfaction Surveys, we embedded list experiments which can be used to test our hypotheses about political and social desirability.

In order to establish the benchmarks, it is necessary to create overt measures of the politically and socially sensitive questions. In the 2013 World Values Survey China, we asked every respondent in the entire sample of 2,300 to answer the following four questions:

A1.   Do you trust central government leaders?
1. Very much;   2. Somewhat;   3. Not very much;   4. Not at all.

A2.   Will you openly criticize the central government if you are unsatisfactorily treated?
1. Yes;   2. No;   3. Don't know;   4. No answer.

A3.   In the recent three years, did you, your family members, or acquaintances witness corruption by local cadres?
1. Yes;   2. No;   3. Don't know;   4. No answer.

A4.   Have you, your family members, or acquaintances bribed government officials?
1. Yes;   2. No;   3. Don't know;   4. No answer.

We then designed a list experiment which was embedded in the preceding survey. The purpose of this experiment was to test political and social desirability among Chinese respondents. We randomly split the sample into two subsamples, A and B. The two samples demonstrate very similar characteristics in age, education, gender ratios, urbanization, and party membership (table 8.1). It is essential that the two samples are similar so that the difference between them after the treatment is not due to some artificial effects. In other words, without the treatment, the two samples should have the same (or very similar) characteristics. Only by assuring that will we have the confidence that the difference between the two samples after the treatment is the true effect of the treatment, not some preexisting conditions.

Table 8.1. COMPARING THE CHARACTERISTICS OF THE TWO RANDOM SUBSAMPLES

Variable	Control group (A)				Treatment group (B)			
	Section 1.01 N	Mean	Std. Dev.	% Missing	Section 1.02 N	Mean	Std. Dev.	% Missing
Age	1,132	44.1	14.9	0%	1,168	43.7	15.0	0%
Female	1,132	0.51	0.50	0%	1,168	0.51	0.50	0%
Education Attainment	1,132	2.86	1.58	0%	1,168	2.86	1.58	0%
Household Income	1,010	4.34	1.89	10.8%	1,045	4.49	1.81	10.5%
City	1,132	0.54	0.50	0%	1,168	0.55	0.50	0%
Party Member	1,130	0.09	0.28	0.2%	1,167	0.08	0.27	0.1%

Source: World Values Survey China 2012–2013.

Sample A was the control group and sample B was the treatment group. The respondents in sample B were asked to respond to the following four items (see appendix 8.1 for these questions in Chinese):

B1. Please tell me how many types of the following people you don't trust. You don't need to tell me which ones. Just give me a number between 0 and 4.
   a. Drug users;
   b. Mafia heads;
   c. Policemen;
   d. Central government leaders.

B2. If possible, how many of the following things would you do? Just tell me how many, not which ones.
   a. Traveling around the world;
   b. Investing in the stock market;
   c. Running for American President;
   d. Openly criticizing the central government.

B3. Have you, your family members, or acquaintances experienced the following things? Just tell me how many, not which ones.
   a. Travel;
   b. Taking a train;
   c. Reading a novel;

  d. House renovation;
  e. Local cadres' corruption.

B4.   Have you, your family members, or acquaintances done the follow-
      ing things? Just tell me how many, not which ones.
      a. Moving;
      b. Buying a car;
      c. Traveling;
      d. Bribing government officials.

The last item in each of the preceding questions is the treatment item,
namely, trusting central government leaders (B1d), openly criticizing the
government (B2d), witnessing corruption by government officials (B3d),
and bribing government officials (B4d). In sample A, the respondents
were given the same four questions with the same lists of options except
for the last ones (B1d, B2d, B3d, and B4d). The mean score for each question in sample B is compared with the same question in sample A.

The first three questions about trusting central government leaders,
openly criticizing the government, and witnessing corruption by officials
are designed to test political sensitivity; the last question on the respondent's own corrupt behavior is to test social sensitivity. If there is no political desirability effect, the overt measures in A1, A2, and A3 and the covert
or unobtrusive measures in B1, B2, and B3 should be the same.[3] Similarly,
the overt and covert measures in A4 and B4 should have no significant
difference if there is no social desirability effect.

FINDINGS
Overt Measures

Table 8.2 shows the overt answers to the four politically and socially sensitive questions before the sample was split into two subsamples. Only 8% of
the respondents said they distrusted or distrusted a great deal the leaders
in the central government, and 92% of the valid answers indicated that they
trusted or trusted a great deal the central leaders. Only 14% of the respondents would openly criticize the government when they felt dissatisfied,
and the other 86% would not. When asked whether they had witnessed
local government corruption in the past three years, which was another potentially politically sensitive issue, and reporting such a problem may lead
to retribution by local officials, only 13% gave affirmative answers and 87%
said no. Finally, when asked whether the respondents or their family members or acquaintances were involved in bribing government officials, which

Table 8.2. NON-EXPERIMENTAL QUESTIONS RELATED TO SOCIAL
AND POLITICAL SENSITIVITY (WEIGHTED %)

	Entire sample (overt measures)	Section 1.03 N (not missing)
A1 distrust central leaders	7	2,091
A2 openly criticizing government.	12	1,980
A3 witnessed corruption	11	1,966
A4 bribed cadres	14	1,945

Source: World Values Survey China 2012–2013.

was a socially sensitive question because it is related to one's own misconduct (or knowledge thereof), only 16% responded yes, and the remaining 84% said they did not.

The obvious conclusion to draw from the overt measures in table 8.2 is that political support is very high in China because most people trusted the central government and would refrain from criticizing it even when they were dissatisfied. Further, the problem of corruption is not as rampant as expected, and most people followed the ethical standard of not bribing officials.

Many people, however, are not so eager to accept such conclusions. They are quick to point out the political and social desirability problem and suspect that the Chinese respondents were simply too fearful to express their distrust of the central government, to openly criticize the government, or to reveal the corruption scandals around them.

Unobtrusive (Covert) Measures

The next step is to measure the four questions in table 8.2 unobtrusively, or covertly. As discussed earlier, this is carried out by randomly splitting the entire sample into two subsamples, A and B. Respondents in sample B were given questions B1, B2, B3, and B4, and those in sample A received the same four questions but without the last item in each question. For each question, the mean numbers of items are compared in the two subsamples, and the difference indicates the percentage of respondents in sample B who picked the last item in B1, B2, B3, and B4.

In table 8.3 under the column labeled "(B–A)*100 (1%)," 12% of the respondents in sample B did not trust the central government leaders, 13% said they would openly criticize the government if dissatisfied, 26% witnessed local government corruption, and another 26% admitted that they actually bribed government officials in order to get things done.

Table 8.3. UNOBTRUSIVE MEASURES OF POLITICALLY AND SOCIALLY
SENSITIVE QUESTIONS

		Mean number of items	Section 1.04 N	(B–A)*100 (%)	Covert–Overt (from table 8.2), %
Distrust central leaders					
	A. control	2.06	1065		
	B. experiment	2.18	1083	12	12 – 8 = 4
Openly criticize government					
	A. control	1.11	1061		
	B. experiment	1.24	1077	13	13 – 14 = –1
Witnessed corruption					
	A. control	2.35	1061		
	B. experiment	2.61	1079	26	26 – 13 = 13
Bribed cadres					
	A. control	1.43	1066		
	B. experiment	1.69	1082	26	26 – 16 = 10

Source: World Values Survey China 2012–2013.
Notes: All differences between the control and the experiment groups are statistically significant at $p < = 0.001$; $r = 0.58$ for witnessing corruption and bribing officials.

Comparing with the overt measures in table 8.2, only 4% of additional respondents in the unobtrusive measures revealed their distrust of the central government officials. No one seemed to hide their opinion about openly criticizing the government, as there was no significant difference between overt and covert measures of that question (last column, table 8.3). Interestingly, these results suggest that there is very little political desirability effect. Even if the covert results are taken into consideration, political support is still very high in China, as 88% of the respondents indicated their trust of the central government officials and another 86% would not criticize their government even when they are dissatisfied.

Another interesting finding in the last column of table 8.3 is the desirability effect in the two questions about corruption. The percentage of people who witnessed local government corruption doubled from the overt measure (13%) to the unobtrusive measure (26%). On the surface, this increase looks like a political desirability effect due to the respondents' fear of retribution by local officials. However, the percentage of those who admitted their own misconduct of bribing government officials also increased significantly from the overt (16%) to the covert (26%) measures.

People lie about witnessing corruption not because they are afraid of retribution but because they don't want to admit their own wrongdoing. The two questions are closely related ($r = 0.58$); therefore, hiding one's knowledge about witnessing corruption is not a political but a social desirability effect.

Who Hide Their Opinions?

Finally, we examine the individual characteristics of the respondents who are more likely to hide their opinions in the overt measures but reveal their true opinion in the unobtrusive or covert measures. To simplify the analysis, we only use two items: distrusting central government leaders and bribing officials. Hiding opinion about political distrust reflects political desirability, while not revealing one's own bribery of government officials indicates social desirability. Witnessing corruption is similar to bribing officials, so only the latter is included. Open criticism of government is excluded because there is no difference between the overt and the covert measures, suggesting that there is little political desirability effect in that question.

For individual characteristics, we examine age, education, gender, urbanization, group membership, managerial job holders, and social class. Age includes five groups, 18–30, 31–40, 41–50, 51–60, and 61–75. Education has five levels: illiterate, elementary, junior high, senior high, and college and above. Social class has four levels: low, lower middle, middle, and upper middle and above. Group membership includes all political parties and not only the ruling Chinese Communist Party. Given the lack of political competition in China, one can expect that most group members are Communist Party members. Urbanization has three categories: urban residents, rural residents, and migrant workers. The results are presented in table 8.4.

Overall, the two youngest age groups (18–30 and 31–40) are less affected by political and social desirability. The middle age group (41–50) is more likely to hide their distrust of the central government leaders than both younger and older age groups. The two oldest groups (51–60 and 61–75) are under more social pressure to reveal their bribing behavior than the other three younger groups.

Education seems to have no effect on political desirability but enhances social desirability. The three more educated groups (junior high, senior high, and college) are more likely to hide their bribery of government officials. In particular, junior high graduates are affected by the social desirability effect most significantly.

Table 8.4. SOCIAL AND ECONOMIC CHARACTERISTICS OF SOCIAL
AND POLITICAL DESIRABILITY (% HIDDEN OPINION)

	Political desirability (distrust Beijing) covert–overt	Social desirability (bribing officials) covert–overt
Age		
18–30	18 – 12 = 5	25 – 17 = 8
31–40	7 – 7 = 0	22 – 20 = 2
41–50	19 – 8 = 11	28 –19 = 9
51–60	12 – 7 = 5	28 – 15 = 13
61–75	3 – 5 = –2*	25 – 10 = 15
Education		
Illiterate	11 – 10 = 1	17 – 16 = 1
Primary	20 – 13 = 7	21 – 29 = –8*
Junior High	7 – 5 = 2	41 – 11 = 30
Senior High	11 – 7 = 4	30 – 15 = 15
College	12 – 5 = 6	27 – 14 = 13
Gender		
Male	19 – 8 = 11	20 – 17 = 3
Female	5 – 8 = –3*	32 – 17 = 15
Residency		
Rural	11 – 6 = 5	26 – 13 = 13
Urban	11 – 10 = 1	28 – 21 = 7
Migrant	21 – 14 = 8	13 – 21 = –8*
Group membership		
Nonmember	11 – 8 = 3	26 – 15 = 11
Member	22 – 8 = 14	27 – 33 = –6*
Manager	8 – 15 = –7*	49 – 30 = 19
Social class		
Low	12 – 11 = 1	20 – 14 = 6
Lo-Middle	9 – 7 = 2	35 – 17 = 19
Middle	15 – 8 = 7	18 – 18 = 0
Upper-Middle	17 – 7 = 10	29 – 27 = 2

Source: World Values Survey China 2012–2013.
Notes: (1) The difference between covert and overt measures indicates the percentage of hidden opinion. (2) Overt measures are based on the entire sample, and covert measures are calculated from the difference of the mean numbers of items between samples A and B.
*Negative but not statistically significant (for details see Appendix 8.3).

Men and women show an interesting difference. Men are more likely to feel and hide their political distrust, while women are more likely to engage in but hide their bribery of government officials.

Urban residents are the least affected by both political and social desirability, though they bribed officials as much as the rural folks. Migrant workers are slightly more distrustful of central leaders, but they bribed the least comparing with rural and urban residents. Rural residents are more likely to be involved in but hide their bribery of government officials.

Interestingly, party members are less trusting of central government officials and also less likely to hide their feelings. Nonmembers are more likely to hide their bribing behavior.

Bribery seems to be widespread among those in managerial positions, as half of them reported such behavior. They are also more likely to hide it.

Finally, social class shows an interesting contrast. Higher social classes (middle and upper middle) are more likely to hide their distrust of the central government leaders, while the lower classes (low and lower middle) are more likely to bribe government officials but also lie about it. This is particularly noticeable in the lower middle class.

To summarize, those who show less political trust and the desire to hide it are more likely to be the middle-aged, male, migrants, and the respondents in higher social classes. The desire to hide bribery is found more commonly among the older age groups, middle-educated, women, rural residents, non-Party members, managers, and low social classes. These results provide some clues to who can produce more reliable responses to politically and socially sensitive questions in Chinese public opinion surveys. Relatively speaking, less desirability effect in both political and social categories is found among the young (under 40), college educated, and urban residents. These people are probably more difficult to get to agree to a survey interview, but they tend to provide more reliable responses once they agree to sit down with the interviewer.

ROBUSTNESS CHECK

The advantage of list experiment is its ability to identify the true attitudes toward sensitive social and political questions at the aggregate level while protecting the respondents' privacy. However, if a respondent selects all the control items *and* the sensitive item, his/her political position will be revealed. In this case, the respondent may hide his/her real attitudes by reducing an item or refusing to answer, resulting in the problem of ceiling effect. Ceiling effect will lower the treatment average. The estimate from a difference-of-means test therefore is biased downward, underestimating the proportion of people selecting the sensitive item. A longer list of control items can be used to avoid the ceiling effect, but the increased variance may dilute and hide the effect of the sensitive item (Fox and Tracy 1986). An efficient list experiment design should contain a short list of items (e.g., four or five) with a high level of variation[4] in responses, and it is better negatively correlated (Glynn 2013).

In our list experiments in the 6th Wave World Values Survey China, the question regarding the distrust in central government leaders (B1) has some signs of potential ceiling effect. For example, 20.5% of the respondents in the control group distrusted all the three control items (police officers, drug users, and gangsters). In the treatment group, similar respondents who distrust all three control items would not be able to hide their distrust of the central government leaders because they would have to tell the survey interviewer the number 4, which means that they distrust all of the three control items plus the treatment item (central government leaders). When the respondents sense this potential problem of not being able to hide their opinion of distrusting central government leaders, they would be motivated to give a smaller number than 4, thus creating the problem of ceiling effect (Redlawsk, Tolbert, and Franko 2010). Nevertheless, as we show in the following analysis, ceiling effect is unlikely to invalidate the conclusion from our list experiment.

The most effective way to check the robustness of the results on political trust is to conduct another list experiment with new control items but the same treatment item (trust central government leaders).[5] So we did. We embedded the new list experiment of political trust in the Wave I Urban Policy Satisfaction Survey of China conducted in October–November, 2013. The experiment contains four control items—family member, neighborhood committee director, policeman, and municipal official; central government leader is still the treatment item. These items make it very unlikely for people to distrust all of them, preventing the ceiling effect problem. Although "family member" may produce uniform positive answers, the proper selection of the other control items will provide enough variation among the respondents.

In the Wave I Urban Survey, when asked explicitly, 75% respondents trusted the central government leaders, 9% distrusted, and 16% answered "don't know" (weighted). Then, the sample was randomly split into two groups. The respondents in the first group (control group) were asked to pick a number of distrusted categories including family members, neighborhood committee directors, policemen, and municipal government officials. The respondents in the second group (treatment group) were asked to pick a number of distrusted categories among the same items as the control group *plus* the treatment item—central government leaders. The difference between the weighted averages of the treatment group and the control group is 1.48 – 1.32 = 0.16, suggesting that 16% of the respondents in the treatment group distrusted the central government leaders, which is 7% higher than the 9% in the entire sample of explicit answers. That is, about 7% of the respondents in the Wave I Urban Survey hid their distrust of the central government leaders in the overt measure but revealed their trust opinion in the covert measure. This is not very different from the World Values Survey China results, where 8% distrusted central government leaders in the entire sample, 12% did so in the list experiment, and 4% (12% –8%) hid their opinion in the overt question. Our second list experiment in the Wave I Urban Survey confirms that the ceiling effect in the first list experiment in the World Values Survey is minimal. The list experiment method can successfully detect about 4% to 7% non-truthful respondents.

Another common problem in experimental research is design effect, namely, that a subtle change in the experiment protocol may lead to inconsistent outcomes. List experiments are prone to two forms of design effects. One is the sequence of list experiment and overt question. Whether the overt question is presented before or after the list experiment question can make a difference in the respondents' answers (Sigelman 1981; McFarland 1981; Schuman, Pressor, and Ludwig 1981; Bishop, Oldendick, and Tuchfarber 1984). The other problem related to the design effects is the order of control and sensitive items in list experiment. For example, the respondents may be more alarmed and more likely to hide their distrust if the sensitive item is presented first than if it is listed as the last item (Redlawsk, Tolbert, and Franko 2010; Glynn 2013). To examine these two design effects, in Wave II of the Urban Survey conducted in May–July 2014, we embedded the third list experiment, following the previous two experiments in the World Values Survey China and the Wave I Urban Survey.

This time, the full list of items includes central media, family members, foreign media, democratic parties, and the Chinese Communist Party, among which the last one serves as the sensitive item. In the Wave I Urban Survey, the list experiment was placed after the overt question of political trust. In the Wave II Urban Survey, the list experiment was placed before the overt question of political trust. It turned out that this small change in experiment design did not contribute to a big difference in our list experiment estimates of political trust. As shown earlier in this section, the rate of lacking political trust is 0.16 in the Wave I Urban Survey, whereas in the Wave II Urban Survey it is 0.18, just two points higher. That is to say, switching the order between the overt question and the covert question makes little difference in political trust.

Our experiment in the Wave II Urban Survey also attempted to solve the second design effect problem—the order of the items in the list experiment. In three cities (Kashgar, Duyun, and Shanwei) in the Wave II Urban Survey, respondents were randomly assigned into three groups. Group 1 is the control group; group 2 and group 3 are treatment groups, between which the difference is that the sensitive item appeared as the last item in group 2 but as the first item in group 3. Changing the order of items did not cause substantial variation in responses: the treatment average is 1.27 in group 2, and 1.21 in group 3.[6] Since the control average is 1.19, the estimated proportion of those who distrust the Chinese Communist Party is 1.27 – 1.19 = 0.08 in group 2, and 1.21 – 1.19 = 0.02 in group 3. The difference, 0.08 – 0.02 = 0.06, is slight. In short, design effects in arranging the order of the items are not likely to create noticeable biases, at least not in political trust.

The inclusion of the Chinese Communist Party as a treatment item in the Wave II Urban Survey further expands the scope of our definition of political trust. In the World Values Survey China and the Wave I Urban Survey, political trust was based only on trusting central government officials. The low level of distrust of the CCP (about 8%) in the Wave II Urban Survey, together with the relatively low level of distrust of the central government officials (about 20%) found in the World Values Survey and the Wave I Urban Survey, provide more support for the validity and reliability in measuring political trust.

One remaining problem is "don't know" answers, which has captured the attention of many survey researchers (Shi 1996, Zhu 1996; Ren 2009). The question is whether our survey respondents hide their distrust in central government leaders through their "don't know" answers in the overt questions in both surveys. In attempting to answer this question, we only keep the observations that are coded missing ("don't know") in the overt measures of political trust, and then conduct the same list experiment analysis as in table 8.3.

In table 8.5, the "don't know" answers to the overt questions of trusting the central government leaders are 9% in the 2012–2013 World Values Survey China, 13% in the urban subsample of the same survey, and 16% in the Wave I Urban Survey (under the column of "% Don't know"). We then show the average numbers ("Mean" in table 8.5) of the "don't know" respondents' answers to the covert questions in the control group (A) and the experiment group (B). The differences between the two group means (B-A) suggest the percentages of the "don't know" respondents who hide their distrust in the overt questions, which are 13% in the World Values Survey, 17% in the urban subsample of the World Values Survey, and 31% in the Wave I Urban Survey. Finally, when we multiply the percentage of

Table 8.5. HIDING DISTRUST IN CENTRAL GOVERNMENT LEADERS BY GIVING "DON'T KNOW" ANSWERS

Survey and sample	% Don't know	Group	Mean	N	B–A	% DK* (B–A)
2012–2013 WVS	9%	A. control	2.23	97	13%	1%
Entire sample		B. experiment	2.36	89		
2012–2013 WVS	13%	A. control	2.29	70	17%	2%
Urban sample		B. experiment	2.46	74		
2013 10–City	16%	A. control	1.53	186	31%	5%
Policy Satisfaction Survey		B. experiment	1.83	164		
2014 10–City	4.5%	A. control	1.47	40	31%	1.4%
Policy Satisfaction Survey		B. experiment	1.78	48		

Notes: "% Don't know" is the percentage of "don't know" answers based on the overt question of political trust. In each sample, the covert measure of political distrust is the difference between group A's average and group B's average. The 2013 and 2014 Urban Policy Satisfaction Surveys are weighted on age, gender, and cities (ps_weight).

the overtly "don't know" but covertly distrusting respondents by the total percentage of the "don't know" answers in each survey (%DK*(B – A) in table 8.5), we find that only 1% out of the total 9% of the "don't know" answers to the overt question is actually hiding their distrust in the World Values Survey. Similarly, only 2% out of the 13% and 5% out of the 16% of the "don't know" respondents in the overt questions reveal their true distrust of the central leaders in the covert questions in the urban subsample of the World Values Survey and in the Wave I Urban Survey. In other words, only about 1% to 2% of respondents in the World Values Survey and only about 5% in the Wave I Urban Survey answered "don't know" in order to hide their distrust of the central government leaders, and the majority of the "don't know" answers were perhaps due to the lack of enough knowledge and information to judge the central government leaders who were far away from people's everyday lives. Additionally, in the Wave II Urban Survey, using the same method, we identified that only 1.4% of respondents did not offer an answer in an attempt to disguise their distrust of the Chinese Communist Party. Therefore, the "don't know" effect as a way of hiding one's political distrust is hardly noticeable.

In this section, we focused on the single most sensitive questions of not trusting the central government leaders and the Chinese Communist Party, and we analyzed the ceiling effect and the "don't know" answers in order to check the robustness of the findings about minimal political desirability. We successfully reduced the ceiling effect by conducting additional list experiments in the Wave I and Wave II Urban Surveys. With the ceiling effect under control, the list experiment detected about 7% of the respondents who did not reveal their distrust in the overt question. This is only slightly higher than the 4% in the World Values Survey when ceiling effect was not effectively controlled. Moreover, relying on the third list experiment in the Wave II Urban Survey, we demonstrate that altering the sequence of the overt question and list experiment or the order of control and sensitive items did not produce a big difference in the estimates. Further, our analysis of the "don't know" effect suggests that only about 1% of the respondents in the World Values Survey answered "don't know" in order to hide their political distrust. If one relies on the 7% with ceiling effect controlled and the 1% "don't know" problem found in the World Values Survey, the overtly reported amount of trust in central government leaders is only over-estimated by about 8% in the 2012–2013 World Values Survey China.

CONCLUSIONS AND DISCUSSION

This chapter has examined the political and social desirability effects in the Chinese public opinion surveys. It has used the list experiment technique that was originally invented in the 1990s to detect racial prejudice in public opinion surveys in the United States. Three hypotheses were developed and tested: (1) the political desirability effect is likely small; (2) the social desirability effect is more visible; (3) individuals with more institutional embedment are more likely to demonstrate political desirability effects, while the less embedded ones are more likely to show social desirability effects. We now return to these hypotheses, but in the reverse order.

First, our hypotheses about individual characteristics are partially supported by the findings. Those who are more embedded in the system are more likely to hide their political distrust, such as the middle-aged who are in the peak of their careers, male, Party members, and those in higher social classes. Those who are less embedded in the institutions are more likely to engage in and hide socially undesirable behaviors; these include the elderly, female, rural residents, non-Party members, and those in lower social classes. One interesting exception is that the more educated and those holding managerial jobs are also among the people who are involved in but also hide their socially undesirable behaviors. This finding may be a reflection of China's institutional deficiency that creates special opportunities for corruption only for those who have more information and higher level contacts.

Second, the available evidence from the list experiment supports the hypothesis of social desirability, as the respondents tried to hide their socially undesirable behavior such as bribing government officials in the overt responses. We also find a significant social desirability effect in another question about whether the respondents would keep money found on the street in the 6th wave of the World Values Survey China. While 19% of them said yes in the overt measure, 26% said yes in the covert measure. In other words, when the respondents sense that the behavior is seen as inappropriate by conventional social norms, they will hide their true answers in survey interviews.

Finally, the list experiment results also support the hypothesis of a limited amount of political desirability effect. We did not find any significant political effect in openly criticizing the government since there was no difference between the overt and covert measures. Through robustness check, we found only about 8% of the respondents who did not reveal their distrust of the central government leaders or the CCP in the overt measure, even when ceiling effect, design effects, and the "don't know" answers are taken into consideration. Therefore, even when political desirability is taken into consideration, the overall level of political trust in central government officials is still in the mid-70%, and trust in the Chinese Communist Party is even higher at around high-80%.

The high levels of political support in China have been repeatedly demonstrated in the previous chapters of this book and also by other scholars (Shi 2001; Chen 2004; Wang 2005; Tang 2005; Yang and Tang 2010; Lewis-Beck, Tang, and Martini 2014; Shi 2015). As mentioned earlier in this chapter, some have questioned the reliability of such strong political support and suggested that Chinese survey respondents are simply too nervous to report their true feelings toward the government and its leaders (Fuchs 2007; Rose 2007; Li 2013). While such concern of political desirability may have been a serious problem in the past, recent development in China's political environment seems to suggest that people are less afraid in openly expressing their dissatisfaction toward the government. Although our findings show some political desirability effect, even with our most conservative estimates the level of political trust in China is still significantly higher than in many other countries (Dalton 1999; Norris 2011). The findings in this study provide a little more confidence in judging survey results concerning political trust in China. Its high level of political trust has to be explained by the nature of China's populist authoritarian political culture, which is the focus of the next chapter.

CHAPTER 9

Populist Authoritarianism

A Preliminary Theoretical Discussion

KEY COMPONENTS OF THE PA MODEL

Following the political culture literature, this book emphasizes the importance of political socialization and its impact on people's political attitudes, values, and behavior. In the early years of the Communist rule, through the Mass Line-inspired political mobilization, collectivization, and provision of social services, China developed a political culture that can be described as populist authoritarianism. Such a political culture consists of several interrelated elements, including the wide acceptance of the Mass Line ideology, dense social capital and group solidarity, high political trust and regime support, strong national identity, direct public political involvement, particularly at the local level, a high level of government responsiveness, and the underdevelopment of intermediate institutions and procedures which are characteristic of a civil society. Together, these elements form the key components of the theoretical framework of Populist Authoritarianism, or the PA model, which is summarized herein from the findings in the previous chapters.

The Continuity of the Mass Line Ideology

Mass Line serves as the ideological foundation of the PA model. Since the 1940s when Mao Zedong first articulated the Mass Line, it became a widely accepted guiding principle of governance by the Chinese Communist Party (CCP). As discussed in chapter 1, the Mass Line became an effective instrument for political mobilization in rural China. The CCP relied on peasant support to defeat the Nationalist Party and eventually seized political power and founded the Communist regime in 1949. From 1949 to the late 1970s, the CCP continued to use mass political campaigns to mobilize political support and promote social and economic change.

Many people in and outside of China believed that such mass campaigns led to disastrous consequences due to the over-concentration of political power in the hands of Mao and his followers and their obsession with ideological purity. While the post-Mao leaders in the CCP showed some willingness to avoid the cult of personality and emphasized group leadership and adopted limited intra-party democracy, there was enough evidence that their populist orientation continued to dominate the CCP's governing style,[1] particularly in its effort to gain popular support through public campaigns (see chapter 1).

One example was the public campaign against prostitution in the early 2010s. Tens of thousands of police were dispatched in different cities, and many prostitutes and their customers were arrested on the spot. Their photos were widely publicized by the police, and some of them were chained and forced to walk in the streets as a way of public humiliation.[2]

Another example of public political campaign was anti-corruption. After the 18th Party Congress in 2012, the CCP was determined to clear up corruption among government officials and decided to launch a nationwide campaign under the leadership of the Central Commission for Disciplinary Inspection (CCDI). Such a campaign once again relied on mass movement. The CCDI encouraged the public to directly report the wrongdoings of government officials and then punished these officials publicly. On the CCDI's official website, 34 officials were exposed and dismissed within the first 15 days of July 2014, and there were 500 cases of dismissal of government officials from February 8, 2013, to July 15, 2014, averaging almost one dismissal every day.[3] Such mass campaigns remind people of the same techniques used during the Cultural Revolution in order to remove the unpopular Party and government officials through public humiliation. This tendency of continued mass movement and even the mob mentality in the post-Mao era were described in detail in chapter 6.

There is no clear sign that the Mass Line will be replaced by institutional measures in problem solving. Even though the CCP was talking about building institutional procedures such as the rule of law, such effort has easily given way to the direct interaction between the state and society every time there was an urgent problem.

The Mass Line mentality is not an invention by the CCP; it is deeply rooted in traditional Chinese political culture emerged in the dynastic history. The rulers served the Law of the Universe (*titian xingdao*) which meant the provision of public goods. The masses granted their loyalty and support only when the rulers fulfilled their responsibilities. As happened many times in Chinese history, the masses did not hesitate to overthrow the rulers when the latter failed to deliver. Such a direct relationship between the ruler and the ruled can be traced back to many dynasties and is still deeply rooted in the minds of the masses even though China is moving into a modern and industrial society.[4]

Social Capital and Interpersonal Trust

In addition to Mass Line as the ideological foundation, the social origin of the PA model is rooted in the continuous supply of strong interpersonal trust and rich social capital. As shown in chapter 4, China consistently ranked at the top among the countries and regions where data were available. The number of Chinese survey respondents who answered "most people can be trusted" ranged from 50% to 60%, while many other countries and regions were at the level of 30%, including industrial democracies such as the United States. When the meaning of interpersonal trust was dissected into traditional kinship trust, communal trust, and civic trust, communal trust stood out as the most significant contribution to China's high level of interpersonal trust. The existence of communal trust and its strong impact in interpersonal trust further provided the necessary social capital and more effectively facilitated regime support, national identity, political interest, political efficacy, and volunteerism than kinship trust and civic trust.

The origin of communal trust can be traced back to the Mass Line-based political mobilization and the primitive accumulation of social capital in the early days of the CCP's governing experiences, as elaborated in chapter 1. The rural and urban communities that were formed during the People's Commune Movement and around the urban work units in the 1950s generated a sense of community solidarity that continued to exist during China's economic marketization. While communal trust may decline as China further industrializes, it is likely to maintain its high level as long as the CCP stays on its course of the Mass Line.

The findings about high interpersonal trust in autocratic China question the relationship between democracy and social capital. It is possible that social capital is not necessarily a product of liberal democratic political culture. Historically, interpersonal trust as an important reflection of social capital also grew in other non-democratic societies. In a refreshing counterview of the traditional civic culture literature, Berman (1997) conducts a historical study of the collapse of the Weimer Republic and the rise of Nazi Germany. She contradicts the theory of civic culture and democracy advocated by what she calls the "neo-Tocquevillean" theorists such as Putnam, Leonardi, and Nanetti (1993) and Fukuyama (2000) and argues that social capital and citizen political activism emerged in the Weimar Republic as a reaction to the weakness of the Weimar political institutions. The National Socialist Party mobilized the social energy, network, and skills associated with German social capital and successfully established the Nazi regime. For Berman, civic culture and social capital led Germany to abandon democracy and adopt totalitarianism.

Both Berman's study of Germany and the findings about China in chapter 4 of this book suggest that social capital can be utilized for regime consolidation by democratic as well as autocratic governments.

Political Contention and Participation

As a result of the Mass Line style of political mobilization and the rich community-based social capital, the PA model further encourages political contention and high levels of mass political participation. Frequent mass political mobilization and public campaigns under the Mass Line ideology resulted in constant public involvement in local and national politics and increased direct public political exposure and awareness. Community-based social capital and interpersonal trust strengthened the sense of group solidarity among the members of communities that facilitated group action and open contention and confrontation against political authorities.

The findings in chapter 6 show that group protests were widespread in the contentious political cultural environment; the leaders of such protests were often social and political elites who experienced more political socialization in the Populist Authoritarian culture; collective protests were more likely to take place in the provinces with histories of factional fighting among the Red Guards during the Cultural Revolution.

The same tendency of contentious politics was also found in chapter 7 in the 2012 China Labor Dynamics Survey. In that survey, about 90% of the employees had at least one dispute in the past two years, and over 80% of the disputants took action to solve their problems through either individual or group negotiation, reflecting a high level of political activism and participation.

As mentioned previously, in addition to the Mass Line mentality, such political activism is partially a result of interpersonal trust, which formulates the strong personal ties that are necessary for high-risk collective action. For example, the participants of the Civil Rights Movement in the 1960s in the United States relied on such strong personal ties formulated in their church communities and successfully fought against racial discrimination (Gladwell 2010). In China, interpersonal trust that originated in local community networks helped the protest organizers to launch collective action against local authorities, and it also encouraged local residents to take the risk to participate in such activities.

Weak Institutions

As a consequence of direct mass political participation, another feature of the PA model is that it produces relatively weak political institutions, including the underdevelopment of the rule of law, intermediate social organizations, and the electoral system. This is a result of the CCP's obsession with the PA model that requires direct connection between the state and society in which both sides can reach each other quickly without the filtering of the often protracted institutional processes.

As discussed in the case studies in chapter 6, Chinese protestors frequently ignored institutional procedures and demanded intervention from the highest levels such as the provincial governments or even from Beijing. Similarly in chapter 7, in solving labor disputes, Chinese employees often resorted to direct negotiations with their employers, almost completely bypassing the intermediate institutions such as the court, trade unions, the media, the legislature, and the functional departments in the government.

The under-development of the intermediate institutions is both a cause and a result of the direct mass political participation. The weakness of institutions provides the justification for the public to ignore them and seek solutions directly from the authorities. The interference from above in the process of problem solving further weakens the role of the intermediate institutions and their procedures, and sometimes makes them irrelevant. One such example is the trade unions, which were almost completely excluded from the process of labor dispute resolution (see chapter 7).

On the surface, the slow development of democratic institutions seems to contradict the recent development of intra-party democracy that some scholars have noticed (Zheng 2010, 2014a, 2014b). Inside the CCP, elections are more competitive, leadership transition is more predictable, decision-making is more transparent, and there are more reliable mechanisms for checks and balances between party organizations.

While such new trends serve to consolidate the power and adaptability of the Party, so far there is no sign that the Party elites intend to loosen their grip of political monopoly and spread intra-Party democracy to Chinese society as a whole. In contrast, as shown in this book, there is ample evidence that the relationship between the state and society continues to rely on the Mass Line, and civil institutions remain weak and under-developed. Chinese leaders are more interested in seeking solutions in Chinese classics, rather than in building a Western-style liberal democracy (Buckley 2014). Even within the CCP, intra-Party democracy is by no means entirely consistent with the Western concept of the rule of law. One example is the anti-corruption campaign in the mid-2010s. Accused party officials were often "presumed guilty," humiliated publicly, and dismissed without due legal procedures (Jacobs and Buckley 2014).

The PA model does not exclude the study of political institutions. It serves as a reminder that institutions in China may not carry the exact features of the Weberian rational bureaucracy and that Chinese politics will have to be understood in both formal and informal contexts. Some scholars have already incorporated informal elements in the study of formal institutions in China. For example, Lily Tsai demonstrated the importance of kinship ties and informal folk religious organizations in village governance and public goods provision in rural China (Tsai 2007a, 2007b). Similarly, Shih, Adolph, and Liu (2012) reminded their readers that informal factional ties played a more significant role in party officials' career advancement than formal performance measures. One topic for future research is how the CCP's effort at institution building is shaped by its populist authoritarian style of governance.

The Hyper-Responsive Government

The Mass Line ideology, the contentious style of mass politics, and the high level of public political activism and participation in the PA model require a highly responsive government for it to maintain political power and stability. While the Populist Authoritarian state uses force without hesitation when its very survival is threatened, it also spends a lot of time and energy maintaining political power by responding to public demand. Consequently, people in a PA society are more likely to believe that their government responds to their needs than those in a democratic society. For example, in chapter 5, 77% of the Chinese survey respondents believed that their government were responsive to their demand, while only 36% of the respondents thought so in democratic Taiwan. Assuming that the survey samples were representative and the respondents were telling the truth, this was a huge gap.

But why do autocratic regimes respond to public demand more than democratic regimes? The answer partially lies in the institutional design of democracy, particularly in the electoral system. Democratic elections set the rules for different political interests to compete freely and to accept victories and losses. They provide the ultimate legitimacy for the winners as long as they receive majority votes. Therefore, majority rule is the cornerstone of democratic regime legitimacy.

One problem—or advantage, depending on how one views it—with majority rule in democratic societies is the lack of the need to satisfy everyone. Politicians only work to get elected regardless of the winning margin. In the case of Taiwan, Chen Shui-bian was elected in 2000 with only 39% of the votes, and the winning margin was only 0.028%. While it is true that the losing voters can wait until the next election (Przeworski 1991), such institutional arrangement can create a large number of disgruntled voters who show a weak support of the incumbent government.

The second problem of representative democracy is that it may make elected politicians less likely to respond to public opinion between elections. Once elected, their jobs are guaranteed until the next election. As a result, the public may become apathetic toward such a system (Dalton 1999).

In contrast, the single-party institutional design requires a PA regime to be more alert to public opinion in order to survive politically. In a formal model, Lorentzen (2013) shows that authoritarian regimes are compelled to allow and even encourage limited expression of discontent in order to target its response to public demand and to avoid potential political instability. Although they don't have to compete in elections, their legitimacy lies in the claim that they represent the interest of the majority. Lacking free elections, which provide a simple but effective yardstick for legitimacy, a PA regime can feel insecure even when it sees a single protestor on the street. Such institutional deficiency explains why the PA state tends to be hyper-responsive at times.

Some people may question the appropriateness of comparing government responsiveness in democracies and autocracies. For them, democratic citizens have higher expectations of their rights, and they make stronger demands with their governments that routinely respond to public requests. Consequently, they can become easily dissatisfied and underestimate their governments' responsiveness. The authoritarian citizens, on the other hand, live in a political system where government responsiveness is supposedly not required. They can be very happy and overestimate government responsiveness when their government does very little to satisfy their requests. In other words, perceived government responsiveness does not mean actual responsiveness.

Although this book examines Chinese citizens' perceived government responsiveness, some readers may argue that such perception can be manipulated by the officially controlled media; and perceived responsiveness is not the same as actual responsiveness. Yet there are reasons to believe that a PA regime does need to respond to public opinion in order to keep its legitimacy. It is not very difficult to find evidence of the PA state in China being sensitive to public opinion. In addition to censoring certain opinions and using force when necessary, it probably spends more time and resources in responding to public demands by policy adjustment. For example, the ethnic unrests in Tibet and Xinjiang not only resulted in Internet censorship and political control, they also brought huge amounts of economic aid to these regions. Similarly, the agricultural tax was abolished in 2006 in order to reduce public discontent and promote regime legitimacy in rural China (Whyte 2010). Some scholars even complain that the Chinese government is sometimes overly responsive to public nationalism in its foreign policy making (Shirk 2011).

Even if it is true that perceived government responsiveness is based on different realities in democracies and autocracies, perception itself is important because it is related to political trust and regime support. Ultimately, regime survival depends as much on the real action of the government as on people's *perceived* benefits of their government's action. In short, it makes sense to compare democracies and autocracies as long as government responsiveness explains political trust in both types of political systems.

Strong Political Support

The final component of the PA model is strong political support. This is a natural consequence of the Mass Line ideology, strong community solidarity, widespread public involvement and political participation, and a paranoidly responsive government.

Evidence of strong political support was found in chapters 2, 3, and 5. When political support was measured in different ways, including confidence in the key political institutions, national identity, satisfaction with government performance, support for one's own political system, or support for incumbent leaders, Chinese respondents consistently demonstrated one of the highest levels among the countries and regions where survey data were available. Chapter 8 further confirms that even taking into consideration a few percentage points of political desirability effect, the overall level of political support in China is still significantly higher than in many liberal democracies. Among the alternative explanations, such as political mobilization, economic development, Confucian cultural tradition, and internal efficacy explored in chapter 5, government responsiveness stood out as the most important reason for regime support.

In recent years, while the CCP suppressed any external challenge to its political monopoly, it took a number of measures to maintain political stability within the PA framework. It promoted within-system participation and expression of different opinions, encouraged the emergence of politically energized social groups such as migrant workers, co-opted private entrepreneurs, rural residents, certain ethnic minorities, and folk religious followers,[5] and tolerated ideological diversity within the Communist Party itself, while incorporating these new social forces into the framework of democratic centralism which is one of the key components of Mass Line (Salmenkari 2010). Lacking competitive elections, the CCP feels compelled to secure public trust by responding to public demand. The ability to maintain this Populist Authoritarian political culture is one reason for the CCP's sustainability.

Compared to liberal democracy, however, China's PA model is inherently unstable because it provides little institutional guarantee for personnel and policy changes and for conflict resolution. Regime legitimacy and political trust based on the government's hyper-responsiveness cannot be easily sustained. Satisfying everyone's demands is simply too costly and too exhausting. Without the institutional buffers such as elections and legal procedures, the public mood can swing violently and cause political earthquakes that can directly threaten the survival of the political system. Therefore, autocratic political trust, no matter how strong it may seem, is very costly to sustain. In liberal democracies that enjoy institutional stability, citizens can be distrustful of the incumbent government, but they can count on expressing their dissatisfaction in future elections and resolve their conflict in the legal system. Consequently, some people may argue that democratic distrust is healthy and authoritarian trust is unhealthy.

Some people may further argue that political trust may not be as important in liberal democracies as in authoritarian societies because democracies function through well-established institutions and do not rely on a particular party or group of leaders to sustain themselves. But if political trust is defined by the measures developed in chapter 5, namely, trust in the key institutions, trust in political leaders, national identity, and trust in the political system itself, then it seems that any government, authoritarian or not, can benefit from promoting these ideas. The question is at what cost and to what extent. With well-functioning political institutions, perhaps liberal democracies can afford to acquire less political trust and a larger number of politically unhappy citizens than authoritarian regimes that rely on political trust more heavily for their survival.

In sum, the PA model includes at least six key elements: (1) the Mass Line ideology, (2) rich social capital, (3) high degrees of public political activism and contention, (4) weak political institutions, (5) a highly responsive government, and (6) strong regime support. The preceding discussion showed the interrelationship between these elements. Future research may further examine their causal connections in a formal model.

THE PA MODEL AND CIVIC CULTURE

Scholars have shown a relationship between political culture and regime stability, but mostly in established democracies. For example, in the civic culture literature, the smooth functioning of democratic regimes depends on how well developed civic culture is. In their classic study, Almond and Verba (1963) define civic culture as the individual citizens' satisfaction with and support for their country's political institutions, national identity, involvement in political activities, a sense of political efficacy, social trust, and social tolerance (also see Kanvanagh 1989; Conradt 1989; Sani 1989; Putnam, Leonardi, and Nanetti 1993; Eberly 2000; Himmelfarb 2000; Fukuyama 2000; Sabetti 2007; Wnuk-Lipinski 2007).

Yet in the post–World War II era, the relationship between civic culture and democracy has experienced significant change (Pharr and Putnam 2000; Torcal and Montero 2006). While public support for the democratic system per se continues to be strong in Western democratic societies (Dalton 1999; Norris 2011), certain elements of the civic culture have declined, such as government support (Abramowitz 1989; Dalton 1999), political participation (Kavanagh 1989), and interpersonal trust (Putnam 1995; Newton 1999).

Instead, political culture has shifted in post-industrial democracies from survival to self-expressive values—or emancipative orientations (Inglehart and Welzel 2005; Welzel and Inglehart 2007; Inglehart 2007). These post-materialist emancipative values include individual freedom, civic action, life satisfaction, social tolerance, and interpersonal trust. Noticeably missing from the list are political support and national identity. Perhaps the most important difference between civic culture and the emancipative orientations is the shift from the group to the individual. The primary goal of the post-industrial politics is to benefit the individual, and the country as a whole becomes secondary.

While Western industrial democracies have shifted toward the emancipative values, empirical evidence shows that some elements of the classic civic culture can be found in an autocratic society like China, such as political support, national identity, social capital, and political involvement. These elements of the classic civic culture are likely the results of the regime's "primitive accumulation" of social and political capital in the early years, as well as the Mass Line doctrine.

THE PA MODEL AND THE BA STATE

Existing studies of authoritarian politics explain authoritarian regime re-siliency by emphasizing the top-down control by political elites and bu-reaucratic institutions. Such studies are often described as focusing on bureaucratic authoritarianism, or the BA state. For example, in South America from the 1960s to the 1980s, the bureaucratic authoritarian states such as Argentina, Brazil, Chile, and Uruguay successfully resisted democ-ratization not by relying on individual dictators but through bureaucratic military control by technocrats, while brutally suppressing the labor move-ments and other political parties (O'Donnell 1988; Dickovick and East-wood 2013).

The BA state finds its resemblance in China through many studies by China scholars, such as Oksenberg and Liberthal's book (1988) on the flattened, protracted, and fragmented bureaucratic rule in China, Liber-thal's comprehensive study on the Chinese bureaucratic authoritarian political system (2004), Landry's in-depth research on career advance-ment in Chinese local bureaucracies (2008), and Manion's works on deal-ing with bureaucratic corruption (2004) and the bureaucratic retirement system (1993).

In his comprehensive study of 138 countries with authoritarian po-litical experiences from 1946 to 2008, Svolik (2012) seems to think that China has solved the two key problems that make many authori-tarian regimes rely on dictatorship and repression: elite power sharing and mass political control. He shows that power sharing has been insti-tutionalized in China by term limit and collective leadership, thereby avoiding the dictatorship and cult of personality under Mao (also see Zheng 2010). Svolik is cautious, however, about future regime stability in China, as he points to the importance of power balance among the top ruling elites as a condition for successful power sharing and political stability.

For the second problem—mass political control, Svolik (2012) thinks that the CCP has effectively implemented the incentive structure that ties its members' political loyalty to their career development and material benefits. This mechanism is effective in producing the rank-and-file polit-ical activists (party members) who support the regime.

While the studies just discussed provide highly sophisticated and in-sightful discussion on authoritarian political sustainability in China and elsewhere in the world, they are studies about political elites and they mostly leave the masses out of the picture. One problem in China (and elsewhere) is that political elites only constitute a very small number. For example, the Communist Party members in China only comprise about

8% of the population. In Svoliks' study (2012), his reason to leave the more than 90% of the masses out of the discussion is that most authoritarian regime changes (68%) are the results of elite power struggles, and only 11% of such changes in his data set were caused by popular uprisings (figure 1.1, p. 5).

Authoritarian regimes may not fall due to popular uprisings, but the *fear* of such action often is a constraint to their rule, particularly when the masses are protesting in China almost on a daily basis. It is obvious that the authoritarian regime in China is using other means to keep political support in addition to recruiting the party loyalists.

In fact, top political elites often try to use the masses to achieve their political goals in their power struggle. In this sense, elites and the masses are often closely connected. Elite power struggle does not take place in isolation. It is sometimes more directly connected to public opinion precisely because of the absence of democratic institutions such as elections, independent social organizations, and the rule of law. As discussed earlier, the authoritarian leaders in China often attempted to connect directly to the masses in order to weaken their political opponents at the top, such as Mao's appeal to the Red Guards to overthrow his political opponents during the Cultural Revolution in the 1960s, Zhao Ziyang's attempt in Tiananmen Square, though failed, to connect to the student protestors in order to counterbalance the factional struggle within the CCP's Political Bureau in 1989, and Xi Jinping's effort at mobilizing mass political support by launching nationwide anti-corruption campaigns.

In sum, the PA model shares with bureaucratic authoritarianism the importance of the state, but it differs from the BA state in that mass mobilization, rather than demobilization, plays a decisive role in the political dynamic that propels policy making and regime sustainability.

THE PA MODEL AND EXISTING STUDIES OF MASS POLITICS

While the literature on bureaucratic authoritarianism rightly emphasizes the importance of the top, existing studies on mass politics provide detailed and rich information about the bottom of Chinese society. As discussed in the previous chapters, O'Brien and Li's (2005a) study on the "rightful resistance" tells the story of how the masses are able to successfully resist local governments' unpopular decisions and policies by quoting more general policy guidelines from higher level governments (also see Thireau and Hua 2007).

One question that needs to be further addressed from the aforementioned studies is whether the state and its political elites passively react to the pressure from below or proactively anticipate such bottom-up political energy in their design of the political system. The PA model shows that such a system of bypassing local authorities and reaching up to higher level governments may not be a random and passive act, and it is rooted in the idea of the Mass Line. While this book is mostly about individual citizens' attitudes and behavior, and not about government policy and organizations, there is enough evidence in the existing studies to show that scapegoating is a frequently used tactic by higher level authorities to blame those below and maintain mass political support at the center.

These studies include Manion's work on the central government's effort at exposing local officials' corruption in order to shift public attention from the top; Landry's book (2008) on promoting more capable cadres to higher level governments while leaving the less qualified officials at the local level; Lorentzen's (2013) research on implementing higher level policy initiatives locally in order to test public opinion and screen out unfeasible projects and unpopular officials; Perry's (2001) finding that localized protests are most likely tolerated; and others who also find that the PA state in China often relies on mass protests to maintain and consolidate its power (Saich 2007; Stockmann and Gallagher 2011; and Kennedy 2012). All these findings suggest that the PA state is not a passive reactor but an active participant in the process of mass politics.

Another group of existing studies on mass politics is the traditional political culture literature (Shi 2001; Shi and Lu 2010; Lu and Shi 2015; Shi 2015). This literature focuses on Confucian values and the kinship tradition in explaining mass support of the elite and the elite's effort at serving the masses. In this view, it is the paternalistic relationship between the state and the masses that explains the sustainability of the regime. In other words, it is the Confucian harmony that holds the state and society together.

While such a view makes a significant contribution to the comparative understanding of often misunderstood concepts such as democracy (Shi and Lu 2010; Lu and Shi 2015; Shi 2015) and the non-confrontational aspect of the state–society relationship, the PA model can contribute to the often confrontational style of the Chinese political culture. Further, while recognizing the role of Confucian paternalistic values, the PA model emphasizes the more recent political experience in the CCP's rule and its impact in regime sustainability. In short, the PA model and the paternalistic theory together form a more complete explanation of both the harmonious and contentious elements of Chinese political culture.

THE PA MODEL AND THE STUDY OF COMPARATIVE POLITICS

In comparative political studies, authoritarian regimes are typically seen as political systems in which political elites attempt to control and manipulate the masses (Svolik 2012). Such an approach assumes that in these authoritarian societies, there are minimum degrees of social and political rights, individual freedom, interpersonal trust, citizen political participation, regime responsiveness, and political trust of the regime.[6] Early studies showed that these traits were the exclusive products of civic culture and liberal democratic institutions (Almond and Verba 1963).

Comparative political studies have made many important advances since the early studies of civic culture and democracy. One such advance is the availability of large-scale cross-country public opinion survey data, such as the World Values Surveys, the World Barometer Surveys, and the International Social Surveys Programme (ISSP). The empirical evidence from these surveys provides only weak or no support for the relationship between democracy on one hand, and individual freedom, interpersonal trust, political participation, government responsiveness, and regime support and legitimacy on the other hand. In contrast, some of the authoritarian countries demonstrated the strongest regime support in these surveys (Norris 2011). These findings suggest that traditional understanding of authoritarianism needs to be further refined, and democracy alone cannot explain the existence of these concepts that are key phenomena in comparative political studies.

Based on the findings from more than 20 Chinese and cross-national public opinion surveys, the PA model developed in this book makes three contributions to comparative political research. First, it points out the universal nature of politics and governance by demonstrating that similar political outcomes can be generated by different governments, regardless of whether they are democratic or nondemocratic, rooted in different cultures, and operate in formal or informal institutions. The findings in this book caution the exclusive reliance on democratic institutions as the sole source of the political phenomena mentioned earlier and show that other types of political systems and political cultures can also produce similar results. In other words, liberal democracy may not be a very useful variable in explaining why people participate in politics, why they identify with their country, why the government responds to public demand, and why people trust their political system and each other.

Second, the cross-system nature of the preceding political phenomena calls for the expansion of these concepts. For example, political support does not only include supporting democracy but also any government.

Political participation means not only elections but also protest, informal group negotiations, and petitions. This conceptual enrichment is particularly necessary in comparative political studies. Of course, there is always the danger of *concept stretching*—a process whereby the same concept carries different meanings in different societies (Peters 1998). Such danger should not stop researchers from contextually defining abstract concepts in comparative political studies. Overly rigid definition leads to what can be called *concept freezing* that limits cross-country and cross-system comparisons. As long as the concrete definitions are consistent with the abstract concept, such comparative studies can often generate interesting findings, while avoiding concept stretching. For example, even if voting and protesting are different forms, they can be studied under the same label of political participation that is defined as bottom-up action aimed at influencing political outcomes.

Third, the PA model did not grow idiosyncratically in today's China. It can be applied to studying other authoritarian societies with similar characteristics. One group of such political systems to which the PA model is relevant is the totalist regimes (Tsou 1986) with strong populist orientations, such as China under Mao, Vietnam under Ho Chi Minh, and North Korea today. The other category of countries to which the PA model can be applied is the post-revolutionary societies such as Castro's Cuba, post-revolutionary Iran, Vietnam after Ho Chi Minh, and of course, China after Mao. Finally, the PA model is also applicable to some electoral democracies with a strong populist orientation, such as Argentina under Perón, Venezuela under Chávez, Russia under Putin, and the populist governments under Thaksin and Yingluck in Thailand. In addition to the populist orientation, these societies also share with varying degrees the traits of the PA model such as strong regime support (Norris 2011), responsive governments, social capital and interpersonal trust, strong public involvement and political participation, direct relationship between the state and society, the relative weakness of political institutions, and inherent political instability.

In conclusion, the PA model can serve to enrich comparative studies by broadening the key political concepts while avoiding concept stretching, by going beyond the traditional distinction of democracy versus non-democracy while emphasizing the universal experience of governance, and by refreshing the traditional definition of authoritarian regimes through the distinction between elite authoritarianism and populist authoritarianism.

Appendices

continued

Appendix 1.1. CONTINUED

	Organization/ privncipal investigator	Month/ year of survey	Number of observations	Sample sites
Semiannual Survey	ESRIC	10/1988	2,176	35 cities
Semiannual Survey	ESRIC	5/1988	2,577	39 cities
Semiannual Survey	ESRIC	10/1987	2,438	37 cities
Semiannual Survey	ESRIC	5/1987	2,576	40 cities

[a]Wenfang Tang and Yongnian Zheng.
[b]Mingming Shen, Wenfang Tang, Cheng-tian Kuo, Ronald Inglehart, Pierre Landry, and Mayling Berney.
[c]TAMU: Texas A&M University.
[d]ISR: Institute of Social Research, University of Michigan.
[e]AS/NTU: The Institute of Political Science, Academia Sinica, and the Institute for the Advanced Studies of Humanities and Social Sciences, National Taiwan University.
[f]Pierre Landry, Mingming Shen, Wenfang Tang, Yanqi Tong and Ming Yang.
[g]ISSP: International Social Survey Programme.
[h]Shanghai, Chongqing, Guangzhou, Shenyang, Wuhan, and Xian (see Tang 2005).
[i]ESRIC: Economic System Reform Institute of China.
[j]See Tang and Parish (2000), table B2.
[1]These four waves of telephone surveys were conducted in October 2013, May 2014, October 2014 and May 2015. The first survey contains a sample of 2,000 urban residents randomly selected by mobile phone numbers in Beijing, Shanghai, Guangzhou, Urumuqi, Xian, Shenyang, Wuhan, Shenzhen, Congqing, and Kunming. The May 2014 survey is based on a random sample of 2,000 respondents in Beijing, Deyang, Jinan, Jinzhou, Nantong, Duyun, Shanwei, Kashi, Guangzhou, and Congqing. The October 2014 random sample of 2000 was drawn in Beijing, Shanghai, Guangzhou, Chongqing, Wuhan, Shenyang, Kunming, Xian, Lhasa and Kashi. The May 2015 random sample of 2000 was drawn in Beijing, Guangzhou, Chengdu, Jinghong, Tongliao, Yanji, Yinchuan, Hetian, Yili and Rikeze. The surveys were supported by the Institute of Public Policy at the South China University of Technology.
[2]The 2012 World Values Survey China and the 2008 China Survey: In the multi-stage stratified random sample, 40 and 75 counties and county-level administrative districts (primary sampling units, or PSU) were selected from seven geographic regions which divide the entire country. The total population in each region is proportionate to the number of counties randomly drawn from that region. Two townships and township-level administrative districts (secondary sampling units, or SSU) were randomly drawn from each PSU. Two half-square minutes (HSM) of latitude and longitude were randomly selected within each SSU. Spatial square seconds (SSS, 90m × 90m) were selected based on the population density in each HSM. Twenty-five dwellings were randomly selected from each HSM based on the list of all dwellings from each SSS. For the 2012 World Values China, the response rate was about 66%. For the 2008 China Survey, a total of 5,525 target respondents were selected from the selected dwellings using the Kish Grid method. Among them, 3,989 completed the questionnaire, representing a response rate of 72.2%.
[3]The 2004 Institutionalization of Legal Reform Survey: The random sample covered 100 counties (PSU) in China's 31 provinces, autonomous regions, and provincial level cities. The survey researchers used population statistics to determine the number of counties from each provincial unit. At least one county or urban district was randomly selected in less populated units, including Beijing, Shanghai, Tianjin, Inner Mongolia, Xinjiang, Qinghai, Gansu, Xizang, Ningxia, and Hainan. Two townships or urban neighborhoods were randomly chosen from each county/district. Two half-degree geographic squares (village or urban residential communities) were selected using the GPS method. Within each half-degree square, two 80 × 80m squares were selected, again using the GPS method. All valid addresses were recorded, and 10,089 individuals ranging in age from 18 to 66 were included in the final list by using the Kish Table method. The response rate was 7,714/10,089 = 76.5%. The characteristics of the sample are fairly consistent with the 2000 population census (see appendices 5.2 and 5.4 for further details).
[4]See http://www.asianbarometer.org/newenglish/surveys/DataRelease.htm (accessed July 12, 2012).

Appendix 2.1. VARIABLES IN THE 2012 WORLD VALUES SURVEY CHINA
AND IN THE 2008 CHINA SURVEY

2012 WVS China	Obs.	Mean	Std. Dev.	Min.	Max.
Disat w. Beijing	2,069	2.492508	2.203296	0	10
Disat w. county	2,069	3.817303	2.388008	0	10
Disat w. village	2,041	4.492406	2.621567	0	10
Disatpolicy index	1,828	0.4624696	0.163534	0	1
Disat w. corruption & inefficiency	2,046	0.6072152	0.240901	0	1
Age	2,300	43.91826	14.94669	18	75
Education (educ5)	2,300	2.168696	1.183206	0	4
Rural	2,300	0.4956522	0.5000898	0	1
Female	2,300	0.5104348	0.4999998	0	1
Social class (myclass)	2,192	1.323449	0.8469546	0	4
Religiosity (burnpaper)	2,300	0.7295652	0.444281	0	1
Group membership	2,297	0.1010013	0.3581844	0	2

2008 China Survey	Obs.	Mean	Std. Dev.	Min.	Max.
Overall sat (single question)	3,737	0.4638293	0.1461742	0	1
Happiness	3,881	0.6815769	0.241074	0	1
Disatpolicy index (21 items)	3,737	0.5361707	0.1461742	0	1
Disat w. Beijing	3,848	0.1839127	0.2177745	0	1
Disat w. county	3,848	0.3461932	0.2619714	0	1
Disat w. village	3,848	0.4254345	0.2989838	0	1
May contact official	3,991	0.2440491	0.4295758	0	1
May contact media	3,991	0.2588324	0.4380482	0	1
May contact soc org	3,991	0.2385367	0.4262423	0	1
May join org	3,991	0.1623653	0.3688318	0	1
May petition	3,991	0.1713856	0.3768928	0	1
May protest	3,991	0.0957154	0.2942374	0	1
Contacted official	3,991	0.15109	0.3581814	0	1
Contacted media	3,991	0.0285643	0.1665992	0	1
Contacted soc org	3,991	0.0536206	0.2252958	0	1
Joined org	3,991	0.0684039	0.2524694	0	1
Petitioned	3,991	0.0516161	0.2212785	0	1
Protested	3,991	0.0230519	0.150087	0	1
Prodemocracy	3,438	0.3418296	0.1788097	0	1
Civil disobedience	3,646	0.1873978	0.1698858	0	1
Nationalism	3,829	0.7755863	0.1505746	0	1

continued

Appendix 2.1. CONTINUED

2008 China Survey	Obs.	Mean	Std. Dev.	Min.	Max.
Age/10	3,989	4.598646	1.563274	1.8	9.2
Age10^2	3,989	23.59076	15.38065	3.24	84.64
Educ (yr)	3,946	6.390015	4.24929	0	18
Group membership	3,991	0.0265754	0.0757909	0	1
Female	3,991	0.5174142	0.4997593	0	1
Fam inc 2007(imputed, logged)	3,981	0.7399627	0.1532233	0	1
Welfare benefits	3,991	0.2251315	0.2426717	0	1
Rural	3,991	0.6945628	0.4606501	0	1
Migrant	3,991	0.1162616	0.3205785	0	1
Urban	3,991	0.1836632	0.3872578	0	1
Han	3,991	0.8539213	0.3532293	0	1
Farmer	3,991	0.4317214	0.4953782	0	1
Sales/service (saleserv)	3,991	0.021799	0.1460452	0	1
Geti (private entrepreneur)	3,991	0.0651466	0.2468152	0	1
Firmowner	3,991	0.0070158	0.0834764	0	1
Blue collar	3,991	0.0764219	0.2657053	0	1
Pubemployee	3,991	0.0125282	0.11124	0	1
Manager	3,991	0.009772	0.0983815	0	1
Professional/technical (pro_tech)	3,991	0.0263092	0.1600732	0	1
Clerk	3,991	0.0461037	0.209736	0	1
Retired	3,991	0.1443247	0.3514627	0	1
Unemployed	3,991	0.078677	0.2692677	0	1
Neverworked	3,991	0.0653971	0.2472563	0	1
Occ_oth	3,991	0.0147833	0.1206995	0	1
3rd party presence	3,991	0.1571035	0.3639439	0	1

Notes: Missing values can be calculated by the difference between the total number of respondents in the survey and the valid cases. For example, the number of valid cases for happiness is 3,881, the total number of respondents is 3,991, and the missing value is 110, which is 2.7%.

Appendix 2.2. LIFE SATISFACTION IN URBAN CHINA: 1987–2014 (WEIGHTED%, FIGURE 2.2)

Satisfaction 1987–2014 (weighted%)

	May '87	Oct '87	May '88	Oct '88	May '89	Oct '89	Oct '91	May '99	May '08	Dec '12	Oct '13	May '14
Price	16	11	6	4	6	14	30		13		38	41
Anti-corruption	33	29	21	13	9	18	18		24	22	42	60
Income	55	48	37	34	28	35	43	37	31	46	42	41
Equality	48	47	44	41	8	10	15		34	42	40	47
Free say	76	77	76	71	52	53	64	66	62	65	68	75
Env'ment	56	50	43	38	35	41	44	30	32	56	44	49
Job oppt	37	30	29	27	15	17	17	23	32	46	64	57
Housing	47	42	43	43	37	39	43	51	35	57	42	52
Medicare	56	53	43	37	29	32	40		36	66	52	51
Pension	65	59	49	49	41	51	55		36	59	52	49
Crime	65	62	42	36	43	53	54	36	39	66	70	69
N of observations	2576	2534	2569	2173	2126	2003	2499	1820	3989	2300	2000	2000

Sources: 1987–1991 Economic System Reforms Institute of China Urban Surveys; 1999 6-City survey; 2008 China Survey; 2012 World Values Survey China; 2013 and 2014 Urban Surveys.
Notes: (1) For 1987–1999, 2012, and 2013, "don't know" is not excluded from calculating the percentages. (2) The 1987–1992 surveys are weighted by the urban education data from the 1990 population census. (3) For 2008, (a) the rates are the averages based on a 0–10 scale, (b) urban subsample only, (c) missing values are not included, (d) "job" is satisfaction with unemployment benefit, (e) weighted by sampling probability *wt_psbfc* (other years by education in 1990 and 2000 population censuses). (4) 2012 values are weighted by sampling probability (*wt_base*). (5) 2013–2014 values are weighted by ps_weight (sample city age and gender weights). (6) Some surveys only have satisfaction and dissatisfaction, others have four categories, including "very satisfied," "satisfied," "dissatisfied," and "very dissatisfied." For the latter surveys, "very satisfied" and "satisfied" are combined.

Appendix 2.3. GOVERNMENT DISSATISFACTION BY LIFE DISSATISFACTION OLS (FIGURE 2.4)

	(1)	(2)	(3)
VARIABLES	disatbeijing	disatcounty	disatvillage
disatpolicy index	2.824***	4.817***	5.146***
Age	−0.012***	−0.007	−0.009*
Educ5	0.041	−0.061	−0.158**
Rural	−0.427***	−0.320**	−0.211
Female	0.001	−0.120	−0.218*
Myclass	0.119*	−0.029	−0.126
Religiosity	−0.412***	−0.255*	−0.122
Groupmem	−0.144	0.087	0.018
Statejob	−0.486***	−0.026	0.038
Privatejob	−0.120	−0.016	−0.090
Constant	2.141***	2.468***	3.329***
Observations	1,676	1,676	1,657
R^2	0.086	0.127	0.118

Source: 2012 World Values Survey China.
Notes: (1) "Disatbeijing," "disatcounty," and "disatvillage" are the reversed 0–10 scales of the respondents' satisfaction with the central, county/city, and village/residential governments. (2) "Disatpolicy" is a reversed 0–1 scale of a factor index of the respondents' satisfaction with 12 policy items, including environment, employment, social stability, social equality, democracy, health care, clean government, effective governance, income level, crime control, housing, and pension/welfare. (3) If the policy dissatisfaction index only includes clean government and effective governance, the gap between the OLS regression coefficients for "disatbj," "disatcty," and "disatvil" are even wider (1.174, 3.069, and 3.676). (4) "Educ5" has five levels: 0 = no education, 1 = primary, 2 = junior high, 3 = senior high, and 4 = college and postgraduate. (5) "Myclass" is the respondent's self-assessed social status: 0 = low, 1 = lower middle, 2 = middle, 3 = upper middle, and 4 = upper. (6) "Religiosity" is measured by the respondent's ancestral worship by burning paper money (1 = yes, 0 = no). (7) "Groupmem" represents the respondents' organizational membership: 0 = nonmember, 1 = member, 2 = active member. (8) For all variables, missing values are excluded.
*$p < 0.1$, **$p < 0.05$, ***$p < 0.01$

Appendix 2.4. POLITICAL ACTION BY GOVERNMENT DISSATISFACTION (FIGURE 2.5)

	Contact official	Contact media	Contact social org	Join advocacy group	Petition	Protest
Disatbeijing	−0.344	−0.759***	−0.470*	−0.478*	0.195	−0.291
Disatcounty	−0.281	0.208	0.765*	0.211	1.153***	0.678**
Disatvillage	0.156	−1.064**	−0.807**	−0.168	−0.683*	−0.395
Life disat index	0.863***	0.215	0.634*	0.707*	0.46	0.601
Age10	−0.460***	−0.209	−0.067	−0.388**	−0.231	−0.277
Age10^2	0.030*	0.009	−0.008	0.024	0.015	0.031
Educ (yr)	0.032**	0.050***	0.051***	0.052***	0.060***	0.068***
Groupmem	−0.893	1.018*	0.619	0.848	0.488	0.165
Female	−0.214**	−0.183**	−0.275***	−0.179*	−0.308***	−0.04
Faminc07 (logged)	0.705**	0.339	0.483	0.177	0.649*	0.12
Welfare	−0.029	0.23	−0.195	−0.204	−0.048	−0.598**
Rural	−0.078	−0.101	−0.211	−0.014	−0.155	−0.278
Migrant	−0.133	−0.179	−0.370**	−0.095	0.111	−0.475*
Han	0.128	0.222	0.194	0.399*	0.025	0.211
Farmer	−0.121	−0.188	0.035	0.138	0.057	0.051
Geti	0.206	0.149	0.27	−0.169	0.166	0.545*
Neverworked	0.322	0.085	0.707***	0.553**	0.554**	0.740**
Firmowner	0.388	−0.172	0.17	0.222	0.054	0.861
Saleserv	0.732**	0.636**	0.827***	1.007***	0.749**	1.120***
Blue	0.197	0.033	0.387*	0.242	0.161	0.18
Pro_tech	−0.121	0.082	0.156	0.094	0.066	0.15
Clerk	0.171	0.034	0.319	0.267	0.255	0.106
Retired	−0.16	−0.104	−0.065	−0.402	−0.318	−0.351
Manager	0.206	0.251	0.287	−0.25	−0.162	0.673
Pubemployee	−0.761*	−0.005	−0.352	−0.018	−0.031	0.319
Occ_oth	0.836**	0.655*	0.781**	0.316	0.582	0.73
3rd party	−0.195	−0.103	−0.094	−0.096	−0.249*	0.044
Constant	−0.195	−0.103	−0.094	−0.096	−0.249*	0.044
Observations	−19.137***	−19.228***	−19.921***	−19.622***	−20.125***	−19.406***
R^2	1,613	3,613	3,580	3,541	3,613	3,271

Source: 2008 China Survey.
Notes: For dissatisfaction with village and dissatisfaction with county, coefficients for "contact media," "contact social organization," and "petition" are based on actions already taken; other coefficients are actions the respondents may take. See appendix 2.1 and the notes in appendix 2.3 for the descriptions of the variables in this table.
*p < 0.1; **p < 0.05; ***p < 0.01.

Appendix 2.5. PRO-DEMOCRACY AND CIVIL OBEDIENCE BY GOVERNMENT
DISSATISFACTION (FIGURE 2.6)

	Pro-democracy	Pro-democracy	disobedience	disobedience
Disatbeijing	0.091***	0.061***	0.172***	0.151***
Disatcounty	−0.001	−0.001	0.007	0.008
Disatvillage	0.009	0.005	−0.004	−0.005
Life disat index	0.107***	0.070***	0.004	−0.02
Nationalism		−0.286***		−0.186***
Age10	−0.019*	−0.013	−0.004	0.001
Age10^2	0.001	0.001	0.000	0.000
Education yr	−0.001	0.000	−0.002**	−0.002**
Groupmem	−0.104***	−0.096**	−0.026	−0.023
Female	−0.006	−0.007	−0.003	−0.004
Finc07log	0.042**	0.029	0.050***	0.043**
Welfare	0.012	0.016	−0.018	−0.018
Rural	−0.031***	−0.027**	0.003	0.004
Migrant	−0.021*	−0.02	0.004	0.006
Urban (cf.)				
Han	0.011	0.012	−0.01	−0.011
Farmer	0.009	0.014	0.003	0.006
Geti	−0.019	−0.016	0.015	0.018
Neverworked	0.02	0.027*	0.028*	0.028*
Firmowner	0.009	0.014	−0.004	−0.003
Saleserv	0.033	0.038*	0.004	0.006
Blue	0.016	0.021	0.016	0.019
Pro_tech	0.014	0.01	−0.005	−0.006
Clerk	0.045***	0.042**	−0.007	−0.007
Retired	0.009	0.01	0.003	0.008
Manager	0.088***	0.091***	0.047*	0.050*
Pubemployee	0.015	0.009	0.006	0.009
Occ_oth	−0.026	−0.025	0.021	0.021
Unemployed (cf.)				
3rd party	0.011	0.01	−0.001	−0.002
Constant	0.351***	0.575***	0.225***	0.368***
Observations	3273	3241	3442	3395
R^2	0.189	0.231	0.191	0.209

Source: 2008 China Survey.
Note: County dummies are controlled. See appendix 2.1 and the notes in appendix 2.3 for further details of the variables in this table.
*p < 0.1; **p < 0.05; ***p < 0.01.

Appendix 3.1. SUMMARY STATISTICS

Variable	Obs.	Mean	Std. Dev.	Min.	Max.
Nationalism	3,076	0.81	0.16	0	1
Pro-democracy (prodemo)	3,991	0.34	0.17	0	1
Civic disobedience (civdisobey)	3,991	0.19	0.16	0	1
Trustbeijing (trustbj)	3,782	0.76	0.24	0	1
Pro-market (profcap)	3,102	0.53	0.24	0	1
Tolerance	3,316	0.56	0.19	0	1
Age 35 & younger	3,991	0.27	0.44	0	1
Age 36–46	3,991	0.29	0.45	0	1
Age 47–58	3,991	0.22	0.41	0	1
Age 59 & older	3,991	0.23	0.42	0	1
CCP	3,991	0.08	0.28	0	1
Ed_no	3,946	0.16	0.37	0	1
Ed_primary	3,946	0.35	0.48	0	1
Ed_jrhi	3,946	0.30	0.46	0	1
Ed_srhi	3,946	0.12	0.32	0	1
Ed_college	3,946	0.07	0.25	0	1
Faminc2007 (imputed, Finc07imp)	3,981	0.19	0.19	0	1
Finc07imp^2	3,981	0.08	0.13	0	1
Urban	3,991	0.18	0.39	0	1
Rural	3,991	0.69	0.46	0	1
Migrant	3,991	0.12	0.32	0	1
Han	3,991	0.85	0.35	0	1
Hui	3,991	0.01	0.12	0	1
Wei	3,991	0.02	0.14	0	1
Man	3,991	0.02	0.13	0	1
Meng	3,991	0.00	0.04	0	1
Eth_south	3,991	0.05	0.22	0	1
Eth_oth	3,991	0.04	0.20	0	1
Female	3,991	0.52	0.50	0	1

Source: 2008 China Survey.

Appendix 3.2. FULL MODELS FOR FIGURES 3A–3 F AND FOR TABLE 3.2

	nationalism	prodemo	civdisobey	trustbj	procap	tolerance
Nationalism		−0.357***	−0.258***	0.437***	−0.119***	−0.203***
age 35 & younger	−0.050***	0.026***	0.025***	−0.076***	0.015	−0.018
age 36–46	−0.027***	0.024***	0.018**	−0.061***	0.02	−0.029**
age 47–58	−0.019***	0.01	0.013	−0.016	−0.02	−0.015
59 & older						
CCP	0.030***	−0.020*	−0.012	−0.019	0.024	−0.050***
Ed = 0						
Ed_primary	0.023***	−0.021**	−0.031***	0.009	0	−0.015
Ed_jrhi	0.028***	−0.030***	−0.031***	−0.01	0.016	−0.023*
Ed_srhi	0.01	−0.019	−0.036***	0.017	0.053**	−0.006
Ed_college	−0.024***	0.049***	−0.041***	0.02	0.066***	0.041**
Finc07imp	−0.232***	0.067	0.180***	−0.108*	−0.025	0.098*
Finc07imp^2	0.273***	−0.079	−0.220***	0.182**	0.117	−0.144*
Rural	0.014***	−0.017**	0.041***	0.016	−0.02	0
Migrant	0.020***	−0.032***	0.025**	0.009	−0.030*	−0.017
Urban						
Han	0.183***	−0.027*	−0.049***	−0.110***	0.042*	0.047**
Hui	0.224***	−0.029	−0.063**	−0.054	0.138***	−0.002
Wei	0.161***	−0.017	−0.037	0.047	0.070*	−0.044
Man	0.175***	−0.039	−0.094***	−0.100***	0.076*	−0.015
Meng	0.202***	−0.008	−0.085	−0.079	−0.073	0.126
Eth_oth	0.150***	−0.032	−0.022	−0.107***	0.064*	0.037
Eth_south						
Female	0.002	−0.012*	−0.006	−0.003	−0.018*	−0.003
Constant	0.653***	0.674***	0.414***	0.537***	0.579***	0.702***
Observations	12,012	3,042	3,042	2,958	2,631	2,643
R^2	0.116	0.151	0.113	0.107	0.037	0.051

Source: 2008 China Survey.
*$p < 0.1$; **$p < 0.05$; ***$p < 0.01$.

Appendix 4.1. FACTOR ANALYSIS OF TRUST TYPES

Variable	Factor1	Factor2	Factor3	Uniqueness
Family	0.0625	−0.0241	*0.8383*	0.2928
Relative	0.3582	0.0469	*0.7535*	0.3017
Neighbor	*0.6726*	0.0932	0.3793	0.3951
Schoolmate	*0.8035*	0.0944	0.1139	0.3325
Villager	*0.5524*	0.0975	−0.0938	0.6765
Coworker	*0.8041*	0.1371	0.2328	0.2805
Hometowner	*0.8383*	0.1079	0.0481	0.2833
Urbanite	0.2289	*0.6759*	0.0057	0.4908
Businessman	0.2232	*0.7202*	0.0499	0.4290
Out-of-towner	0.1094	*0.8128*	0.0033	0.3273
Foreigner	0.0131	*0.7851*	0.0449	0.3815
Stranger	0.0365	*0.7592*	0.0547	0.4193

Source: The 2008 China Survey.
Notes: (1) Number of observations = 3,849; (2) method: principal-component factors; (3) retained factors = 3; (4) the numbers are varimax-rotated factor loadings (pattern matrix) and unique variances.

Appendix 4.2. POLITICAL VALUES AND BEHAVIOR BY TRUST TYPE AND OTHER SOCIO-ECONOMIC CHARACTERISTICS, OLS REGRESSION COEFFICIENTS (SEE TABLE 4.3)

	Interpersonal trust	System support	Nationalism	Political interest	Social activism	Efficacy	Donation	Tolerance
Parochial trust	0.126**	0.144**	0.103**	0.027	0.143**	0.023	-0.013	-0.030**
Communal trust	0.549**	0.437**	0.247**	0.273**	0.121**	0.269**	0.044**	-0.007
Civic trust	0.310**	0.017	-0.039**	0.034	-0.148**	0.020	0.015	0.053**
Age/10	0.019**	0.007**	0.011**	0.014**	-0.002	0.002	-0.012**	-0.012**
Female	-0.024**	-0.007**	-0.001	-0.060**	0.008	0.013**	-0.003	-0.024**
Educ yr/10	0.028	0.011**	0.015**	0.083**	-0.046**	-0.003	0.088**	0.047**
Faminc03/10k	0.002	0.001	0.001	0.004**	0.001	0.002**	0.003**	0.001**
Han	0.000	0.004	0.020**	-0.005	0.030*	-0.007	-0.006	0.013*
Party	0.005	0.016**	0.013*	0.089**	-0.018	0.031**	0.082**	0.019**
Urban	0.043**	-0.006	-0.018**	0.006	-0.025**	-0.011	0.108**	0.021**
Migrant	0.097**	0.006	0.005	-0.028	-0.029	0.003	0.008	0.018
Constant	-0.195	0.265**	0.578**	0.265**	0.127	0.320**	0.175	0.701**
Adj. R^2	0.111	0.293	0.210	0.127	0.173	0.156	0.325	0.203
Section 1.01 N	7594	7528	7304	7563	7614	7356	7614	7614

Source: 2004 Legal Reform Survey.

Notes: Township is controlled but not shown. Highlights are displayed in table 4.3.

Appendix 4.3. VARIABLES USED IN OLS REGRESSION ANALYSES IN TABLE 4.3
AND IN APPENDIX 4.2

Variable	Section 1.02 Observations	Mean	Std. Dev.	Minimum	Maximum
Parochial trust	7,689	0.7867918	0.1097155	0	1
Communal trust	7,689	0.5972819	0.1341444	0	1
Civic trust	7,689	0.3565435	0.1494222	0	1
Interpersonal trust	7,688	0.5066149	0.4822574	0	1
Age/10	7,714	4.100104	1.182189	1.8	6.6
Female	7,714	0.5002593	0.5000323	0	1
Education year/10	7,639	0.6755858	0.3996262	0	2.3
2003 fam inc/10 k	7,714	1.025075	1.89914	0	94.9
Han	7,714	0.9312938	0.2529703	0	1
Party member	7,714	0.0693544	0.2540723	0	1
Urban	7,714	0.2071558	0.4052944	0	1
Migrant	7,714	0.044335	0.2058516	0	1
Rural	7,714	0.7485092	0.4338981	0	1
Social tolerance	7,714	0.6585386	0.1355451	0	1
Regime support	7,605	0.725077	0.1635761	0	1
Efficacy	7,432	0.5669212	0.1811469	0	1
Nationalism	7,379	0.7908974	0.170858	0	1
Donation	7,714	0.1623023	0.2291967	0	1
Political interest	7,659	0.6053445	0.2708418	0	1
Social activism	7,714	0.1842037	0.265705	0	1
Beijing	7,714	0.0025927	0.0508557	0	1
Tianjin	7,714	0.008167	0.0900073	0	1
Shanghai	7,714	0.0102411	0.1006854	0	1
Guangzhou	7,714	0.0080373	0.089296	0	1
Chongqing	7,714	0.0213897	0.1446889	0	1
North	7,714	0.0986518	0.2982133	0	1
South	7,714	0.0928183	0.2901964	0	1
Central	7,714	0.266658	0.4422407	0	1
Northeast	7,714	0.085818	0.2801133	0	1
East	7,714	0.1616541	0.3681571	0	1
Southwest	7,714	0.1742287	0.3793306	0	1
North	7,714	0.0986518	0.2982133	0	1

Source: 2004 Legal Reform Survey.
Notes: Missing values in "social tolerance," "regime support," and "political efficacy" were imputed by the variables used to construct each index.

Appendix 5.1. FACTOR ANALYSIS OF POLITICAL TRUST (PRINCIPAL-COMPONENT) (SOURCE: ABSII)

(A) Entire sample (n = 5,071):

Variable	Factor1	Uniqueness
Goodsys (trust system)	0.6900	0.5239
Trustinst (trust institutions)	0.7699	0.4072
Goodlead (trust leaders)	0.6652	0.5575
Nationalism	0.6546	0.5715

(B) Mainland China (n = 3,666):

Variable	Factor1	Uniqueness
Goodsys (trust system)	0.5812	0.6623
Trustinst (trust institutions)	0.7106	0.4951
Goodlead (trust leaders)	0.4831	0.7666
Nationalism	0.6784	0.5398

(C) Taiwan (n = 1,405):

Variable	Factor1	Uniqueness
Goodsys (trust system)	0.6410	0.5891
Trustinst (trust institutions)	0.6339	0.5982
Goodlead (trust leaders)	0.7444	0.4458
Nationalism	0.6763	0.5427

Appendix 5.2. CHARACTERISTICS OF VARIABLES IN TABLES 5.3A
AND 5.3B (SOURCE: ABSII)

A. China	Obs.	Weight	Mean	Std. Dev.	Min.	Max.
Trustinst	5,098	5,098.28036	0.6113225	0.2879993	0	1
Goodlead	4,323	4,297.34202	0.5415549	0.1954166	0	1
Nationalism	5,017	5,016.77942	0.7120046	0.1284712	0.22	1
Goodsys	3,934	3,885.23238	0.6885021	0.1262482	0	1
Psupport index	3,666	3,614.55021	0.6596152	0.1037482	0.22	1
Age 32 & younger	5,042	5,044.42853	0.1759702	0.3808326	0	1
Age 33–45	5,042	5,044.42853	0.3313944	0.4707612	0	1
Age 46–58	5,042	5,044.42853	0.2604465	0.4389218	0	1
Age 59–75	5,042	5,044.42853	0.1970831	0.3978351	0	1
Age 76 & older	5,042	5,044.42853	0.0351058	0.1840655	0	1
Female	5,075	5,076.08636	0.4919918	0.4999851	0	1
Primary	4,813	4,825.76025	0.4511317	0.4976579	0	1
Hischool	4,813	4,825.76025	0.5018607	0.5000485	0	1
College	4,813	4,825.76025	0.0470076	0.211677	0	1
Urban	5,098	5,098.28036	0.337306	0.4728367	0	1
Buddhist	5,098	5,098.28036	0.1226813	0.3281032	0	1
Tradition	4,895	4,876.34489	0.5437409	0.1383031	0	1
Incnowimp	5,062	5,058.37265	0.5765691	0.2356934	0	1
Incfimp	5,062	5,058.37265	0.7527069	0.1753559	0	1
Group	5,098	5,098.28036	0.0258025	0.1585613	0	1
TV	5,098	5,098.28036	0.819913	0.3842976	0	1
Voted	5,098	5,098.28036	0.5577929	0.4966975	0	1
Contact	5,098	5,098.28036	0.0741323	0.1501182	0	1
Petition	5,098	5,098.28036	0.006098	0.0668252	0	1
Fairvote	5,098	5,098.28036	0.6078694	0.2515366	0	1
Sayorg	5,098	5,098.28036	0.6173464	0.1325588	0	1
Respond	5,098	5,098.28036	0.7062714	0.2059242	0	1
Inteff	5,030	5,031.16703	0.4170038	0.1309683	0	1
Trust	5,098	5,098.28036	0.5553843	0.4969719	0	1
Exteff	4,488	4,437.18085	71.49312	21.9421	0	100

continued

B. Taiwan

Trustinst	1,587	1,586.87663	0.2012596	0.1793216	0	1
Goodlead	1,483	1,488.79437	0.3822471	0.19149	0	1
Nationalism	1,582	1,582.28203	0.654794	0.1495967	0	1
Goodsys	1,441	1,443.56956	0.5613767	0.1825514	0	1
Psupport index	1,405	1,410.77657	0.4789917	0.1180538	0	0.96
Age 32 & younger	1,587	1,586.87663	0.2893084	0.4535843	0	1
Age 33–45	1,587	1,586.87663	0.2723893	0.4453294	0	1
Age 46–58	1,587	1,586.87663	0.2421888	0.428543	0	1
Age 59–75	1,587	1,586.87663	0.151248	0.3584034	0	1
Age 76 & older	1,587	1,586.87663	0.0448656	0.2070741	0	1
Female	1,587	1,586.87663	0.4972371	0.50015	0	1
Primary	1,584	1,584.20419	0.2157296	0.4114574	0	1
Hischool	1,584	1,584.20419	0.5581725	0.4967613	0	1
College	1,584	1,584.20419	0.226098	0.4184354	0	1
Urban	1,587	1,586.87663	0.8029568	0.3978906	0	1
Buddhist	1,587	1,586.87663	0.2843905	0.4512659	0	1
Tradition	1,574	1,574.10736	0.4292394	0.1520354	0	1
Incnowimp	1,582	1,581.55955	0.5462658	0.2077801	0	1
Incfimp	1,582	1,581.55955	0.5645177	0.2161106	0	1
Group	1,587	1,586.87663	0.2851516	0.4516289	0	1
TV	1,587	1,586.87663	0.5446394	0.4981603	0	1
Voted	1,587	1,586.87663	0.8149497	0.3884608	0	1
Contact	1,587	1,586.87663	0.0756534	0.169686	0	1
Petition	1,587	1,586.87663	0.0430667	0.1777279	0	1
Fairvote	1,587	1,586.87663	0.487983	0.3427964	0	1
Sayorg	1,587	1,586.87663	0.6198651	0.1741466	0	1
Respond	1,587	1,586.87663	0.441354	0.2279258	0	1
Inteff	1,578	1,576.6258	0.3985953	0.165059	0	1
Trust	1,587	1,586.87663	0.3283402	0.4697573	0	1
Exteff	1,506	1,512.0753	43.1124	22.86926	0	100

Appendix 5.3. POLITICAL SUPPORT IN CHINA AND TAIWAN
(OLS COEFFICIENTS) (SOURCE: ABSII)

A. China	Trustinst	Goodlead	Nationalism	Goodsys	Psupport (factor index)
BIOLOGICAL & SOCIOECONOMIC TRAITS:					
(Age 32 & younger as comparison)					
Age 33–45	0.021*	−0.005	0.014***	0.014**	0.014***
Age 46–58	0.034***	0.028***	0.031***	0.016**	0.028***
Age 59–75	0.045***	0.048***	0.048***	0.023***	0.040***
Age 76 & older	0.021	0.038*	0.063***	−0.008	0.023*
Female	−0.001	0.016***	0.008**	−0.003	0.005
Edyr10	0.012	−0.068*	0.108***	0.014	0.024
Edyr10^2	−0.059**	0.002	−0.048***	−0.01	−0.029***
Urban	0.012	0.015*	−0.012**	0.005	0.004
Buddhist	−0.055***	0.002	−0.004	0.024***	0
CONFUCIAN VALUES:					
Tradition	0.276***	0.329***	−0.002	0.015	0.120***
ECONOMIC SATISFACTION:					
Incnowimp	0.044**	0.006	0.040***	0.001	0.024***
Incfimp	0.103***	0.02	0.071***	0.035***	0.056***
POLITICAL MOBILIZATION:					
Group	0.01	−0.012	0.031***	−0.002	0.008
TV	0.046***	0.007	0.013**	0.012**	0.017***
POLITICAL PARTICIPATION:					
Voted	−0.002	−0.003	−0.005	0.001	−0.002
Contact	−0.028	−0.019	−0.025**	0.035***	−0.015
Petition	−0.059	−0.026	−0.001	−0.039	−0.025
INTERNAL EFFICACY:					
Inteff	0.135***	0.026	0.075***	0.013	0.048***
Trust	0.027***	0.016***	−0.001	0.020***	0.012***
EXTERNAL EFFICACY:					
Fairvote	0.089***	0.083***	0.022***	0.034***	0.054***
Sayorg	0.223***	0.138***	0.074***	0.080***	0.115***
Respond	0.377***	0.064***	0.113***	0.083***	0.141***
Constant	−0.181***	0.161***	0.388***	0.469***	0.269***
Observations	4,534	4,018	4,507	3,688	3,459
R^2	0.212	0.146	0.12	0.068	0.265

*$p < 0.1$, **$p < 0.05$, ***$p < 0.01$.

Appendix 5.3. *CONTINUED*

B. Taiwan	Trustinst	Goodlead	Nationalism	Goodsys	Psupport
BIOLOGICAL & SOCIOECONOMIC TRAITS:					
(age 32 & younger as comparison)					
age 33–45	0.002	0.012	0.039***	0.034***	0.023***
age 46–58	−0.002	0.006	0.081***	0.025*	0.032***
age 59–75	−0.002	0.051***	0.090***	0.040**	0.051***
age 76 & older	0.02	0.029	0.079***	0.019	0.039**
Female	−0.008	−0.013	−0.015**	−0.008	−0.011**
Edyr10	−0.014	0.032	0.050*	0.035	0.009
Edyr10^2	−0.009	−0.029	−0.032**	−0.016	−0.014
Urban	−0.009	0.038***	−0.007	−0.004	0.003
Buddhist	0.016*	0.012	0.007	0.006	0.010*
CONFUCIAN VALUES:					
Tradition	0.101***	0.190***	0.069***	0.099***	0.116***
ECONOMIC SATISFACTION:					
Incnowimp	0.070***	−0.036	−0.012	0	0.003
Incfimp	0.040*	0.024	0.029*	0.014	0.032**
POLITICAL MOBILIZATION:					
Group	0.002	0.009	0.006	−0.018*	−0.003
TV	0	0.002	0.014*	0.002	0.003
POLITICAL PARTICIPATION:					
Voted	0	−0.007	0.004	−0.014	−0.003
Contact	0.032	−0.015	0.01	0.001	0.002
Petition	−0.058**	−0.071***	−0.014	−0.033	−0.042***
INTERNAL EFFICACY:					
Inteff	0.054*	0.015	−0.090***	−0.037	−0.02
Trust	0.037***	0.001	0.020***	0.005	0.014***
EXTERNAL EFFICACY:					
Fairvote	0.072***	0.084***	0.052***	0.048***	0.062***
Sayorg	0.103***	0.024	0.087***	0.117***	0.084***
Respond	0.147***	0.228***	0.095***	0.139***	0.151***
Constant	−0.064*	0.118***	0.464***	0.353***	0.257***
Observations	1,560	1,473	1,556	1,433	1,398
R^2	0.168	0.216	0.21	0.106	0.339

*$p < 0.1$; **$p < 0.05$; ***$p < 0.01$.

Appendix 6.1. CHARACTERISTICS OF VARIABLES IN TABLE 6.2
(SOURCE: 2010 CGSS)

Variable	Obs.	Mean	Std. Dev.	Min.	Max.
Group action	1,313	0.2261995	0.3902574	0	1
Trust_Beijing	1,310	0.8032443	0.2371184	0	1
Trust_local gov.	1,307	0.5485845	0.2980795	0	1
Against_Firm	1,307	0.3366488	0.4727445	0	1
Against_Org	1,307	0.1009946	0.301437	0	1
Against_Cadre	1,307	0.1277735	0.3339652	0	1
Againstbureau	1,307	0.5416985	0.4984489	0	1
Againstpolicy	1,307	0.061974	0.2412006	0	1
Unfair treatment	1,313	0.2048743	0.4037635	0	1
Age 35–48	1,313	0.3564356	0.4791285	0	1
Age 49–60	1,313	0.1980198	0.398659	0	1
Age 61–77	1,313	0.126428	0.3324578	0	1
Age 78–96	1,313	0.0083778	0.0911806	0	1
Primary	1,313	0.1477532	0.3549904	0	1
Jr. hi	1,313	0.282559	0.4504153	0	1
Sr. hi	1,313	0.262757	0.4402992	0	1
Collegedu	1,313	0.2414318	0.4281146	0	1
Female	1,313	0.4653465	0.4989877	0	1
Ind. inc. 10k	1,284	2.504064	8.383999	0	200
Urban	1,313	0.5491241	0.4977706	0	1
CCP	1,313	0.1766946	0.3815554	0	1
Non_Han	1,308	0.0458716	0.2092865	0	1

Appendix 7.1. CHARACTERISTICS OF VARIABLES IN TABLE 7.1
(SOURCE: 2004 LEGAL SURVEY)

Variable	Obs.	Mean	Std. Dev.	Min.	Max.
Actnone	2,671	0.1382753	0.1845435	0	1
Official	2,671	0.1355298	0.3423526	0	1
Newofficial	2,671	0.3129914	0.4637977	0	1
Private Talk	2,671	0.4140771	0.4926542	0	1
Fight	2,671	0.0396855	0.1952558	0	1
Age/10	2,671	4.228379	1.1563	1.8	6.6
Female	2,671	0.3867465	0.487096	0	1
Educ In Year	2,654	7.064054	3.658279	0	20
Party member	2,671	0.064021	0.2448361	0	1
Indinc03/10k	2,462	0.2757778	1.05498	0	40
Migrant	2,671	0.087982	0.2833218	0	1
Urban	2,671	0.2231374	0.4164277	0	1
Rural	2,671	0.6888806	0.4630382	0	1
Legalinfo	2,671	0.5382191	0.1418949	0.17	1
Faith in state	2,636	0.6912497	0.1665048	0	1
Efficacy	2,583	0.5211326	0.1537944	0	1
Risk taking	2,671	0.1843165	0.327191	0	1
Paytax	2,465	0.4273158	0.3023363	0	1
No result	2,671	0.1176838	0.1849602	0	1
Compromise	2,671	0.1091976	0.1856657	0	1
Win	2,671	0.0776239	0.1547088	0	1
Lose	2,671	0.0935979	0.2044455	0	1

Appendix 7.2. CHARACTERISTICS OF VARIABLES IN TABLE 7.3

Variable	Obs.	Weight	Mean	Std. Dev.	Min.	Max.
Solvedpct	3,743	230,139,762	0.1682903	0.1883759	0	1
Unfairpay	3,743	230,139,762	0.6475287	0.4778036	0	1
Paydelay	3,743	230,139,762	0.3175001	0.465566	0	1
Badenv	3,743	230,139,762	0.4769294	0.4995342	0	1
Overwork	3,743	230,139,762	0.6463955	0.4781521	0	1
Injury	3,743	230,139,762	0.1898355	0.3922233	0	1
Groupfirm	3,743	230,139,762	0.2611295	0.6610839	0	5
Indfirm	3,743	230,139,762	0.5961211	0.8618048	0	4
Govinst	3,743	230,139,762	0.0564763	0.2596365	0	3
Protest	3,743	230,139,762	0.0786029	0.3732751	0	4
Dangzheng	3,743	230,139,762	0.0505801	0.2191679	0	1
Shiye	3,743	230,139,762	0.1096445	0.3124879	0	1
Waizi	3,743	230,139,762	0.0373759	0.1897066	0	1
Minying	3,743	230,139,762	0.4245816	0.4943454	0	1
Guoying	3,743	230,139,762	0.1592789	0.3659848	0	1
Geti	3,743	230,139,762	0.1618622	0.3683736	0	1
Nongfuye	3,743	230,139,762	0.0040144	0.0632406	0	1
Typeoth	3,743	230,139,762	0.0225957	0.1486305	0	1
Age	3,743	230,139,762	33.52115	10.11366	15	60
Female	3,743	230,139,762	0.2838605	0.4509302	0	1
Degree	3,743	230,139,762	2.533048	1.568801	0	6
CCP	3,743	230,139,762	0.1448992	0.3520462	0	1
Local Hukou	3,743	230,139,762	0.8295875	0.3760451	0	1
Loginc11	3,606	221,226,840	0.8425672	0.8773818	−3.218876	9.10498

Source: 2012 CLDS.

Appendix 8.1. LIST EXPERIMENT QUESTIONS IN CHINESE
(2012–2013 WORLD VALUES SURVEY CHINA)

B1. 请告诉我对下面四类人您不信任的有几类，您不必说具体
哪种人，只要告诉我0到4之间的一个数字就可以了。
   a. 吸毒的人
   b. 黑社会老大
   c. 警察
   d. 中央政府的领导

B2. 如有可能，您会做下面几件事情？只说几件，不要说具体
哪件事。
   a. 周游世界
   b. 投资股市
   c. 竞选美国总统
   d. 公开场合批评中央政府

B3. 您自己和家人或熟人是否经历过下面的事情？只要告诉我
有几件有可以了，不要说具体哪件事。
   a. 旅游
   b. 坐火车
   c. 看小说
   d. 装修房子
   e. 本地干部的腐败

B4. 您自己和家人或熟人是否做过下面的事情？只要告诉我有
几件有可以了，不要说具体哪件事。
   a. ．搬家
   b. 买汽车
   c. 旅游
   d. 为了办事向政府官员送礼

Appendix 8.2. LIST EXPERIMENT QUESTIONS EXCLUDED

We decided to exclude the following two questions in the list experiment of the 2012–2013 World Values Survey China from the analysis due to the problems related to question wording:

A5. Do you think the Chinese Communist Party can represent your interest? (Q126 on the questionnaire.)
1. Yes;   2. No;   3. No answer.

B5. Among all the following people, how many types can represent your interest? Just tell me a number between 0 and 4. (B3 on the questionnaire.)
a. Family members;
b. Consumers' association;
c. Media;
d. Chinese Communist Party.

A6. Do you agree or not that the people should directly elect our national leaders? (Q132 on the questionnaire.)
1. Agree;   2. Don't agree;   3. Don't know;   4. No answer.

B6. Do you agree with the following arguments? Just tell me how many, not which ones. (B8 on the questionnaire.)
a. TV shows are of low quality;
b. Wild animals are poorly protected;
c. College education should be free;
d. The head of a village committee should be directly elected;
e. National leaders should be directly elected.

On the surface, the results about whether CCP represents the interests of the people seem to show desirability effect, as the covert measure shows less respondents (52%) agreeing with such a statement than the overt measure (73%).

However, the low percentage in the covert measure is likely to be the problem related to the lack of saliency of the issue, rather than people hiding their opinions. The respondents had to take a pick when the question was presented as a standalone question (yes or no). They were likely to miss it when it was presented together with other issues such as family, consumer association, and media (B5).

A more effective list experiment question should create some kind of emotional reaction from the respondent, such as "openly criticizing the government" (B7) or "distrusting central government officials" (B2).

Other studies that generated effective results also used questions that caused the respondents to feel emotionally "upset" (Kuklinski, Cobb, and Gilens 1997; Kuklinski et al. 1997; Gilens, Sniderman, and Kuklinski 1998; Kane, Craig, and Wald 2004; Redlawsk, Tolbert, and Franko 2010).

This problem of the lack of saliency is further reflected in the question about direct election of the Chinese president. In the overt question, when the respondents were forced to take a pick of yes or no, 45% said yes. In the covert question, when the respondents did not have to pick it, only 29% said the country's president should be directly elected by popular vote. In both of these examples, the survey design failed to frame the questions in a way that would stir up an emotional reaction from the respondents. As a result, they simply did not care enough to pick the supposedly sensitive items. This is a lesson to be learned for future research.

Appendix 8.3. CONFIDENCE INTERVALS OF NEGATIVE SOCIAL DESIRABILITY EFFECTS

Distrusting Beijing

	mean	confidence interval
61–75	–2	(–13, 10)
Female	–3	(–11, 5)
Manager	–7	(–29, 14)

Bribing

	mean	confidence interval
Primary	–8	(–27, 10)
Migrant	–7	(–32, 20)
Member	–6	(–37, 22)

Source: 2012–2013 World Values Survey China.
Note: Confidence intervals are at the 95% level and generated by 1,000 bootstrap simulations. Zero is included in each confidence interval, thus the negative desirability effect is all statistically insignificant.

NOTES

CHAPTER 1

1. See http://news.xinhuanet.com/yuqing/2013–06/25/c_124907918.htm (accessed May 16, 2015).
2. For example, Womack describes the state–society relationship as sheep and shepherd. The sheep's interests control the shepherd's behavior (Womack 1990, 17).
3. See http://qzlx.people.com.cn/n/2013/0620/c364565-21911800.html (accessed July 6, 2014).
4. See http://qzlx.people.com.cn/n/2014/0828/c364565-25553975.html (accessed November 29, 2014).
5. See the 2000 China Population Census, table 3–1, http://www.stats.gov.cn/tjsj/pcsj/rkpc/5rp/index.htm (accessed November 29, 2014).
6. See Lewis-Beck, Tang, and Martini (2014) for further discussion on treating "don't knows" as random missing values.

CHAPTER 2

1. In the 2012 World Values Survey, the level remains very similar at 64 out of 100 (weighted by education, 65 if not weighted).
2. The earlier urban surveys between 1987 and 1992 were conducted by the Economic System Reform Institute of China. They were based on probability samples in more than 40 cities of varying sizes. These earlier surveys can be compared to the more recent surveys which are also based on random samples. See appendix 1.1 for further details of these surveys.
3. The methods of conversion are (trust score)/3*100 for government trust, and (satisfaction score)*100 for government satisfaction.

CHAPTER 3

1. An earlier version of this chapter was published in Wenfang Tang and Benjamin Darr, "Chinese Nationalism and Its Political and Social Origins," in *Journal of Contemporary China* 21, No. 77 (September 2012): 811–26.
2. This seems to be the majority view among scholars, although disagreement still exists. For example, Anderson (1991) instead argues that nationalism first arose in the Americas before manifesting in Europe.
3. For the culturalist school, also see Hall (1996), Smith (1996, 2000), Connerton (1998), Keating and McGarry (2001), Fishman (2002), and Horowitz (2002).
4. Although Smith is possibly the most well-known premodernist, many authors make stronger claims than him against modernists. See van den Berghe (1978) and Hastings (1997) for other examples of premodernist arguments for earlier origins of the nation.

5. Cornell (1996) develops a synthesis of the three different theories by arguing that group identity varies along three dimensions: shared interests, shared institutions, and shared culture. Also see Scott (1990) for a synthesis between the primordial and the circumstantial approaches.

6. For a similar finding on the effect of education on authoritarian regime support, see Barbara Geddes and John Zaller, "Sources of Popular Support for Authoritarian Regimes," *American Journal of Political Science* 33, No. 2 (1989): 319–47.

7. Other recent examples include protests over the U.S. bombing of the Chinese embassy in Belgrade in 1999 and the collision of the U.S. spy plane with a Chinese fighter jet in 2001 (Zhao 2004).

8. In Reilly's experimental study (Reilly 2013), anti-democratic sentiment intensifies when the Chinese experimental subjects are shown with pro-Tibetan symbols and photos.

CHAPTER 4

1. See https://freedomhouse.org/report-types/freedom-world#.Vce4DEo8KrV, accessed August 9, 2015.

2. For example, Tang's earlier study was based on an urban survey of the six largest cities (Tang 2005).

3. Since interpersonal trust is a dichotomous variable, logit repression is the appropriate method. However, I use OLS regression because it produces coefficients that are more intuitive and easier to interpret. For example, the coefficient of 0.549 can be interpreted as a 54.9% increase in interpersonal trust when communal trust increases from 0 (minimum) to 1 (maximum). The other advantage of the OLS method is that the coefficients in table 4.2 can be easily compared with other coefficients that are also based on OLS methods in appendix 4.2. A comparison between the two methods shows that both produce the same results without any change in the sign (+ or –) and the significance level for each coefficient. The coefficients of the logit regression based on the 2008 China Survey data are 4.16, 2.80, and 2.15 for communal trust, civic trust, and parochial trust, respectively ($p < 0.000$).

4. Measuring the change of the adjusted R^2 value is another way to evaluate the relative importance of the three types of trust on interpersonal trust (Lewis-Beck 1990). In the 2008 China Survey, adding parochial trust to the equation with interpersonal trust as the dependent variable only results in an increase of the adjusted R^2 value from 0.034 to 0.048. Adding civic trust and communal trust results in the adjusted R^2 values of 0.062 and 0.089, respectively. Clearly, communal trust demonstrates the most importance among the three types of trust in predicting the overall interpersonal trust.

5. See Shi (2001) for a further discussion on cultural values and political trust in China and Taiwan.

CHAPTER 5

1. This number seems a bit low, since the official number of the Communist Party members is around 8% of the population.

2. For example, one study finds that supporting individual leaders is strong when political institutions are weak in 14 countries (Manzetti and Wilson 2007).

3. Appendix 5.3 shows the results of the OLS regression analysis for each of the four trust items and for the combined factor index of political trust without imputing the missing values. The results are very similar with and without imputation. The advantage of

imputing missing values is that it can keep more observations in the analysis and make use of more information in the survey.

4. Missing values are coded as the mean for government responsiveness, fairness of elections, freedom of speech, and freedom of organization.

5. The coefficients in tables 5.3A and 5.3B are further compared, using the Seemingly Unrelated Estimation (suest) method, and the results show that the coefficients in China and Taiwan are significantly different ($p< = 0.05$) for female, high school education, Buddhist, future income expectation, TV as a source of political news, and internal political efficacy.

CHAPTER 6

1. See *Tigao Jianshe Shehuizhuyi Hexie Shehui Nengli—Improving the Capacity to Construct the Socialist Harmonious Society*, Beijing: Central Party School Press, 2006.

2. For the PEW survey results, see James Areddy, "Chinese Concern on Inequality Rises: A Survey Shows Rising Concerns, But Indicates Most See China Going in Right Direction," *Wall Street Journal*, October 17, 2012.

3. See O'Brien and Stern 2008, p. 12, for an excellent overview of the studies on contentious politics in China.

4. Xinhua News Agency, " Rebiya Kadeer's Separatist Stories Challenged by EU Lawmakers," China View, September 2, 2009.http://www.zonaeuropa.com/20090902_1.htm (accessed November 3, 2014).

5. Observer, "The Wukan Incident," http://www.guancha.cn/WuKanShiJian/ (accessed August 17, 2015).

6. The urban intellectuals during the 1989 Tiananmen protests also demonstrated similar behavior when they sought support from their political patrons at the very top (Perry 1994).

7. Xinhua Public Opinion (Xinhua Yuqing), "An Analysis of Public Opinion During the Sichuan Shifang Incident," http://news.xinhuanet.com/yuqing/2013–10/23/c_125585811.htm October 23, 2013 (accessed August 17, 2015).

8. The author wishes to thank Professor Wang Weidong at Renmin University for providing the 2010 CGSS dataset for this study.

9. In the 2010 6th Population Census, the total population above age 15 is 1.1 billion (table A0107a), which can be roughly compared to the 2010 CGSS sample drawn from age 17 and above.

10. See Sina News Center (Xinlang Xinwen Zhongxin), "The Violence in Guizhou Wengan," various articles at http://news.ifeng.com/mainland/special/wengan628 (accessed August 17, 2015).

11. See Zhang, Hanying, "Neglecting Public Opinion on the Internet Led to the Qidong Mass Protest in Jiangsu" (Wushi Wangluo Minyi Daozhi Jiangsu Qidong Qunti Shijian, Shanxi Public Opinion Net (Shanxi Minyi Wang), July 30, 2012, http://www.hxmyw.org/show.aspx?id=6611&cid=10 (accessed August 17, 2015).

12. See Epoch News, "Thousands of Tibetan Students Protest Against Chinese Language Education," October 20, 2010, http://www.epochtimes.com/gb/10/10/21/n3060774.htm (accessed August 17, 2015).

13. See Lu, Xia, "People's Daily on the Shishou Incident," June 24, 2009, news.163.com, http://news.163.com/09/0624/10/5CIM8T3100012Q9L.html (accessed August 17, 2015).

14. See news.163.com, "Hubei Shishou Mass Incident," various articles at news.163.com, http://news.163.com/special/00013FJU/shishou.html (accessed August 17, 2015).

15. See BBC Chinese News, " Female Police Led to Mass Protest in a Beating Incident," BBC Chinese News Net, August 19, 2011, http://www.bbc.co.uk/zhongwen/simp/chinese_news/2011/08/110819_china_policewoman.shtml (accessed August 17, 2015).

CHAPTER 7

1. Hainan, Tibet, Macau, and Hong Kong are not included in the sample.
2. Co-principal investigators include Mingming Shen and Ming Yang, Yanqi Tong, Pierre Landry, and Wenfang Tang.
3. The population figure in China in 1995 was 12.24 billion (http://www.cpirc.org.cn/tjsj/tjsj_cy_detail.asp?id=304; accessed March 25, 2006), and the 1995 total number of court-filed disputes in China was 4.55 million (National Bureau of Statistics of China 2004). The method for calculating China's number of disputes per 100,000 population is total court-filed disputes divided by total population multiplied by 100,000 (4.55/1,224*100,000 = 371). This number would only increase slightly to about 400 if the base were the total working population age 18 and above (about 1.1 billion).
4. See Xi Chen (2008, 2011) for examples of in-depth qualitative studies of the Letters and Visits system.
5. See State Council Decree #185 in *Zhongguo gaige, nongcunban* (*Chinese Reform, rural edition*) (August, 2003): 7.
6. See "The Supreme People's Court's interpretations of the implementation of the Administrative Litigation Law of the People's Republic of China," *The Law Library*, March 10, 2000. http://www.law-lib.com/law/law_view1.asp?id=33 (accessed August 20, 2015).
7. National Bureau of Statistics of China (2004).
8. *New York Times* (8 March, 2005).
9. Party membership is treated as a modernization effect here because it represents organizational resources and political sophistication.
10. One exception was the older respondents, who were more likely to take action than the younger ones, perhaps as a result of possessing more knowledge and social resources. Income is not significant.

CHAPTER 8

1. Randomization in experiments solves the problem of selection bias, which is difficult to deal with in observational research (Drukman et al., 2011).
2. The Urban Policy Satisfaction Surveys were sponsored by the Institute of Public Policy at the South China University of Technology, and fielded by the Research Center for Contemporary China at the Pecking University. The co-principal investigators were Wenfang Tang at the University of Iowa and Yongnian Zheng at National University of Singapore. The first wave included 2,000 urban respondents in Beijing, Guangzhou, Kunming, Shanghai, Shenzhen, Shenyang, Urumqi, Wuhan, Xian, and Chongqing, and the second wave contained 2,000 urban residents in Beijing, Guangzhou, Chongqing, Jinan, Kashgar, Jingzhou, Deyang, Duyun, Shanwei, and Nantong. Both samples were randomly drawn from mobile phone numbers and then screened by the 2010 census results based on age, gender, and education of the urban population.
3. See appendix 8.2 for a discussion of our decision to exclude other questions from the analysis.
4. An item should be excluded from the list if it is unanimously agreed or disagreed. Although adding an innocuous item can significantly decrease the likelihood that all items are selected, the privacy of an individual might be broken by near-ceiling effects (Glynn 2013). In the treatment group, choosing all but one item indicates that the sensitive item is probably chosen because the one item left is very likely to be the innocuous one.
5. Another way to check the robustness is by pairwise tabulation in order to find the distribution of latent respondent types (Imai 2011; Blair and Imai, 2012). We use (m, n)

to indicate respondents who distrust m control items (0, 1, 2, or 3) and n sensitive items (0 or 1). When $p(3, 1)^{\text{ceiling effect}} = 0$, namely zero ceiling effect, the overall rate of political distrust is $p(0, 1) + p(1, 1) + p(2, 1) + p(3, 1)^{\text{ceiling effect}} + p(3, 1)^{\text{no ceiling effect}} = 0.7 + 4.9 + 2.6 + 0 + 4.1 = 12\%$. And when $p(3, 1)^{\text{ceiling effect}} = 16.4$, namely the maximal ceiling effect, the overall rate of political distrust is $p(0, 1) + p(1, 1) + p(2, 1) + p(3, 1)^{\text{ceiling effect}} + p(3, 1)^{\text{no ceiling effect}} = 0.7 + 4.9 + 2.6 + 16.4 + 4.1 = 29\%$. Therefore, in China, trust in central government leaders should fall within the range between 71% and 88%. Even by our most conservative estimation (71%), trust in political leaders is still considerably higher in China compared to most industrial democracies (Dalton 1999; Norris 2011).

6. The 2014 Wave II Urban Survey was weighted on ps_weight.

CHAPTER 9

1. For examples, the Mass Line Net (Qunzhong Luxian Wang) published speeches about upholding the Mass Line by Party leaders such as Deng Xiaoping, Jiang Zemin, Hu Jintao, and Xi Jinping (http://qzlx.people.com.cn/GB/364566/index.html). Accessed August 20, 2015.

2. For example, in a video clip posted online, two handcuffed prostitutes were paraded in public in Shenzhen. See http://news.sohu.com/20100717/n273571611.shtml (accessed July 15, 2014)

3. See www.ccdi.gov.cn/jlsc (accessed August 20, 2015).

4. Several people made this comment to me in person, including Elizabeth Perry and Stephen Angle.

5. See Landry (2009), Tong (2009), and Diamant, Lubman, and O'Brian (2010) for within-system participation; Tang and Yang (2008) for cooption of migrant workers; Tsai (2007) and Chen and Dickson (2008) for private entrepreneurs; Tsai (2007a, 2007b) and Whyte (2010) for rural residents; Tang and He (2010), and Tang (2014) for ethnic minorities and religious followers.

6. See, for example, the Freedom House Reports (http://www.freedomhouse.org/ (accessed July 22, 2014).

REFERENCES

Abramowitz, Alan I. 1989. "The United States: Political Culture under Stress," in Gabriel A. Almond and Sidney Verba, eds., *The Civic Culture Revisited*, 177–211. Newbury Park, CA: Sage Publications.

Abramson, Paul. R. 1983. *Political Attitudes in America: Formation and Change*. San Francisco: W. H. Freeman and Company Press.

Almond, Gabriel A. 1989. "The Intellectual History of the Civic Culture Concept," in Gabriel A. Almond and Sidney Verba, eds., *The Civic Culture Revisited*, 1–36. Newbury Park, CA: Sage Publications.

Almond, Gabriel A. 1990. "The Study of Political Culture," in Gabriel A. Almond, ed., *A Discipline Divided: Schools and Sects in Political Science*, 138–156. Beverly Hills, CA: Sage.

Almond, Gabriel A., and Verba, Sidney. 1963. *The Civic Culture: Political Attitudes and Democracy in Five Nations*. Princeton, NJ: Princeton University Press.

Anderson, Benedict. 1991. *Imagined Communities*. New York: Verso.

Angle, Stephen C. 2005. "Decent Democratic Centralism." *Political Theory* 33, no. 4 (August): 518–546.

Balch, George I. 1974. "Multiple Indicators in Survey Research: The Concept Sense of Political Efficacy." *Political Methodology* 1, no. 2: 1–43.

Berman, Sheri. 1997. "Civil Society and the Collapse of the Weimar Republic." *World Politics* 49, no. 3 (Apr.): 401–429.

Bernhard, Michael. 1993. "Civil Society and Democratic Transition in East Central Europe." *Political Science Quarterly* 108, no. 2 (Summer): 307–326.

Bishop, George F., Robert W. Oldendick, and Alfred J. Tuchfarber. 1984. "Interest in Political Campaigns: The Influence of Question Order and Electoral Context." *Political Behavior* 6, no. 2: 159–169.

Blair, Graeme, and Kosuke Imai. 2012. "Statistical Analysis of List Experiments." *Political Analysis* 20, no. 1: 47–77.

Blecher, Marc. 1979. "Consensual Politics in Rural Chinese Communities: The Mass Line in Theory and Practice." *Modern China* 5, no. 1 (January): 105–126.

Booth, John A., and Patricia Bayer Richard. 1998. "Civil Society and Political Context in Central America." *American Behavioral Scientist* 42, no. 1 (September): 33–46.

Bovens, Mark, and Anchrit Wille. 2008. "Deciphering the Dutch Drop: Ten Explanations for Decreasing Political Trust in The Netherlands." *International Review of Administrative Sciences* 74:283–305.

Brady, Anne-Marie. 2007. *Marketing Dictatorship: Propaganda and Thought Work in Contemporary China*. Lanham, MD: Rowman & Littlefield.

Brass, Paul R. 1991. *Ethnicity and Nationalism: Theory and Comparison*. New Delhi: Sage Publications.

Braverman, Harry. 1974. *Labor and Monopoly Capitalism*. New York: Monthly Review Press.

Brehm, John, and Wendy Rahn. 1997. "Individual-Level Evidence for the Causes and Consequences of Social Capital." *American Journal of Political Science* 41, no. 3: 999–1023.

Breuilly, John. 1982. *Nationalism and the State*. Manchester: Manchester University Press.

Bryant, Lee Ouyang. 2005. *Songs of the Battlefield*. Ph.D. dissertation, University of Pittsburgh.

Buckley, Chris.2014. "Leader Taps Into Chinese Classics in Seeking to Cement Power." *New
York Times*, October 11.

Burawoy, Michael. 1979. *Manufacturing Consent*. Chicago: University of Chicago Press.

Burawoy, Michael, and Janos Lucas. 1985. "Mythologies of Work: A Comparison of Firms in
State Socialism and Advanced Capitalism." *American Sociological Review* 50:723–737.

Campbell, Angus, Gerald Gurin, and Warren E. Miller. 1954. *The Voter Decides*. Westport, CT:
Greenwood Press.

Central Committee of the Chinese Communist Party. 1994. *Aiguo Zhuyi Jiaoyu Shishi Gangyao*
[Guidelines for Patriotic Education]. http://news.xinhuanet.com/ziliao/2005–2003/16/
content_2705546.htm (accessed May 5, 2011).

Chan, Anita. 2001. *China's Workers Under Assault: The Exploitation of Labor in a Globalizing
Economy*. Armonk, NY: M. E. Sharpe.

Chang, Gordon G. 2001. *The Coming Collapse of China*. New York: Random House.

Chen, Feng. 2008. "Worker Leaders and Framing Factory-Based Resistance," in Kevin O'Brien,
ed., *Popular Protest in China*, 88–108. Cambridge, MA: Harvard University Press.

Chen, Jie. 2004. *Popular Political Support in Urban China*. Stanford University Press.

Chen, Jie, and Bruce Dickson. 2008. "Allies of the State: Democratic Support and Regime
Support among China's Private Entrepreneurs." *The China Quarterly* 196:780–804.

Chen, Jie, and Bruce Dickson. 2010. *Allies of the State: China's Private Entrepreneurs and Democratic Change*. Cambridge, MA: Harvard University Press.

Chen, Jie, and Chunlong Lu. 2007. "Social Capital in Urban China: Attitudinal and Behavioral
Effects on Grassroots Self-Government." *Social Science Quarterly* 88:422–442.

Chen, Xi. 2008. "Collective Petitioning and Institutional Conversion," in Kevin O'Brien, ed.,
Popular Protest in China. Cambridge, MA: Harvard University Press.

Chen, Xi. 2011. *Social Protest and Contentious Authoritarianism in China*. New York: Cambridge University Press.

Chen, Yung-fa. 1986. *Making Revolution: The Communist Movement in Eastern and Central China, 1937–1945*. Berkeley: University of California Press.

Cheng, Andria. 2014. "Nike, Adidas Warily Eye Latest Round of Labor Protests in China."
Wall Street Journal, April 16.

Chu, Yun-han. 2012. "China and East Asian Democracy: The Taiwan factor." *Journal of Democracy* 23, no. 1 (January): 42–56.

Chu, Yun-han, Andrew Nathan, and Doh Chull Shin, eds. 2010. *How East Asians View Democracy*. New York: Columbia University Press.

Clark Donald C. 1991. "Dispute Resolution in China," *Journal of Chinese Law* 5, no. 2 (Fall):
245–296.

Cohen, Jean L., and Andrew Arato. 1992. *Civil Society and Political Theory*. Cambridge, MA:
MIT Press.

Collier, David, and James E. Mahon. 1993. "Conceptual 'Stretching' Revisited: Adapting Categories in Comparative Analysis." *American Political Science Review* 87:845–855.

Conradt, David P. 1989. "Changing German Political Culture," in Gabriel A. Almond and
Sidney Verba, eds., *The Civic Culture Revisited*, 212–272. Newbury Park, CA: Sage
Publications.

Cornell, Stephen. 1996. "The variable ties that bind: content and circumstance in ethnic
processes." *Ethnic and Racial Studies* 19, no. 2 (April): 265–289.

Craig, Stephen C., Richard G. Niemi, and Glenn E. Silver. 1990. "Political Efficacy and Trust:
A Report on the NES Pilot Study Items." *Political Behavior* 12, no. 3: 289–314.

Dahl, Robert A. 1966. *Political Oppositions in Western Democracies*. New Haven, CT: Yale University Press.

Dahl, Robert A. 1985. *A Preface to Economic Democracy*. Berkeley: University of California Press.

Dalton, Russell. 1999. "Political Support in Advanced Industrial Democracies," in Pippa Norris, ed., *Critical Citizens, Global Support for Democratic Government*, 57–77. New York: Oxford University Press.

Dalton, Russell J., and Doh Chull Shin. 2007. "Democratic Aspirations and Social Modernization," in Russell J. Dalton and Doh Chull Shin, eds., *Citizens, Democracy and Markets around the Pacific Rim: Congruence Theory and Political Culture*, 75–96. Oxford: Oxford University Press.

Denters, Bas, Oscar Gabriel, and Mariano Torcal. 2007. "Political Confidence in Representative Democracies, in Citizenship and Involvement in European Democracies: A Comparative Analysis," in Jan van Deth, Jose Montero, and Anders Westholm, eds., *Citizenship and Involvement in European Democracies*, 66–87. New York: Routledge.

Deutsch, Karl W. 1953. *Nationalism and Social Communication: An Inquiry into the Foundations of Nationality*. Cambridge, MA: MIT Press.

Diamant, Neil, Stanley Lubman, and Kevin O'Brien, eds. 2010. *Engaging the Law in China: State, Society, and Possibilities for Justice*. Stanford, CA: Stanford University Press.

Diamond, Larry. 2010. "The Meanings of Democracy: Introduction." *Journal of Democracy* 21, no. 4 (October): 102–105.

Diamond, Larry. 2012. "China and East Asian Democracy: The Coming Wave." *Journal of Democracy* 23, no. 1 (January): 5–13.

Diamond, Larry Jay. 2008. *The Spirit of Democracy: The Struggle to Build Free Societies throughout the World*. New York: Henry Holt and Company.

Dickovick, J. Tyler, and Jonathan Eastwood. 2013. *Comparative Politics: Integrating Theories, Methods, and Cases*. New York: Oxford University Press.

Di Palma, G. 1991. "Legitimation from the Top to Civil Society: Politico-Cultural Change in Eastern Europe." *World Politics* 44, no. 1 (October): 49–80.

Downey, Tom. 2010. "China's Cyberposse." *New York Times Sunday Magazine*, March 7.

Druckman, James N., Donald P. Green, James H. Kuklinski, and Arthur Lupia. 2011. "Experiments: An Introduction to Core Concepts," in *Cambridge Handbook of Experimental Political Science*, 15–26. Cambridge: Cambridge University Press.

Easton, David. 1965. *A Systems Analysis of Political Life*. New York: Wiley.

Easton, David. 1975. "A Reassessment of the Concept of Political Support," *British Journal of Political Science* 5 (October): 435–457.

Eberly, Don E. 2000. "The Meaning, Origins, and Applications of Civil Society," in Don E. Eberly, ed., *The Essential Civil Society Reader*, 3–32. Lanham, MD: Rowman & Littlefield Publishers, Inc.

Eckstein, Harry. 1988. "A Culturalist Theory of Political Change." *American Political Science Review* 82, no. 3 (September): 789–804.

Edwards, Richard. 1979. *Contested Terrain: The Transformation of the Workplace in the Twentieth Century*. New York: Basic Books.

Elster, Jon. 1983. *Sour Grapes: Studies in the Subversion of Rationality*. Cambridge: Cambridge University Press.

Fell, Dafydd. 2005. *Party Politics in Taiwan: Party Change and the Democratic Evolution of Taiwan, 1991–2004*. New York: Routledge.

Fell, Dafydd. 2008. "Party Competition in Taiwan: Toward a New Party System?" in Steven M. Goldstein and Julian Chang, eds., *Presidential Politics in Taiwan: The Administration of Chen Shui-bian*, 49–84. Norwalk, CT: EastBridge.

Ferejohn, John A., and Kuklinski, James H., eds. 1990. *Information and Democratic Processes*. Urbana, IL: University of Illinois Press.

Fewsmith, Joseph, and Stanley Rosen. 2001. "The Domestic Context of Chinese Foreign Policy: Does 'Public Opinion' Matter?" in David M. Lampton, ed., *The Making of Chinese Foreign and Security Policy in the Era of Reform 1978–2000*. Stanford, CA: Stanford University Press (copy).

Finkel, Steven E. 1987. "The Effects of Participation on Political Efficacy and Political Support: Evidence from a West German Panel." *Journal of Politics* 49, no. 2: 441–464.

Fishman, Joshua A. 2002. "The Primordialist–Constructivist Debate Today," in Daniele Conversi, ed., *Ethnonationalism in the Contemporary World*, 83–91. New York: Routledge.

Fox, James Alan, and Paul E. Tracy. 1986. *Randomized Response: A Method for Sensitive Surveys*. Beverly Hills, CA: Sage Publications.

Friedman, Milton. 1962. *Capitalism and Freedom*. Chicago: University of Chicago Press.

Fu, Hualing, and Richard Cullen. 2011. "From Mediatory to Adjudicatory Justice: The Limits of Civil Justice Reform in China," in Margaret Y. K. Woo and Mary E. Gallagher, eds., *Chinese Justice: Civil Dispute Resolution in Contemporary China*. New York: Cambridge University Press.

Fuchs, Dieter. 2007. "The Political Culture Paradigm," in Russell J. Dalton and Hans-Dieter Klingemann, eds., *Oxford Handbook of Political Behavior*, 161–184. Oxford Handbooks Online.

Fukuyama, Francis. 1996. *Trust: The Social Virtues and the Creation of Prosperity*. New York: Free Press.

Fukuyama, Francis. 2000. "Trust: The Social Virtues and the Creation of Prosperity," in Don E. Eberly, ed., *The Essential Civil Society Reader*. Lanham, MD: Rowman & Littlefield.

Gallagher, Mary Elizabeth. 2002. "'Reform and Openness': Why China's Economic Reforms Have Delayed Democracy." *World Politics* 54, no. 3 (April): 338–372.

Gallagher, Mary Elizabeth. 2005. *Contagious Capitalism: Globalization and the Politics of Labor in China*. Princeton, NJ: Princeton University Press.

Gallagher, Mary Elizabeth, and Wang, Yuhua. 2011. "Users and Nonusers: Legal Experience and Its Effect on Legal Consciousness," in Margaret Y. K. Woo and Mary E. Gallagher, eds., *Chinese Justice: Civil Dispute Resolution in Contemporary China*. Cambridge: Cambridge University Press.

Gamson, William A. 1968. *Power and Discontent*. Homewood, IL: Dorsey Press.

Ge, Jianxiong. 1996. "Minzu zhuyi shi jiuguo lingdan?" [Is Nationalism a Panacea to Save the National?] *Yazhou Zhoukan* [Asia Weekly], April 26:14.

Geddes, Barbara, and John Zaller. 1989. "Sources of Popular Support for Authoritarian Regimes." *American Journal of Political Science* 33, no. 2: 319–347.

Geertz, Clifford. 1973. *The Interpretation of Cultures*. New York: Basic Books.

Gellner, Ernest. 1983. *Nations and Nationalism*. Oxford, England: Basil Blackwell.

Gilens, Martin, Paul M. Sniderman, and James H. Kuklinski. 1998. "Affirmative Action and the Politics of Realignment." *British Journal of Political Science* 28, no. 1: 159–183.

Gilley, Bruce. 2006. "The Determinants of State Legitimacy: Results for 72 Countries." *International Political Science Review* 27, no. 1: 47–71.

Gilley, Bruce, and Heike Holbig. 2009. "The Debate on Party Legitimacy in China: A Mixed Quantitative/Qualitative Analysis," *Journal of Contemporary China* 18, no. 59 (March): 339–358.

Gladwell, Malcolm. 2010. "Small Change: Why the Revolution Will Not Be Tweeted." *The New Yorker*, October 4.

Glynn, Adam N. 2013. "What Can We Learn with Statistical Truth Serum? Design and Analysis of the List Experiment." *Public Opinion Quarterly* 77 (Special Issue): 159–172.

Gries, Peter Hays. 2004a. *China's New Nationalism: Pride, Politics and Diplomacy*. Berkeley: University of California Press.

Gries, Peter Hays. 2004b. "Popular Nationalism and State Legitimation in China," in Peter Hays Gries and Stanley Rosen, eds., *State and Society in 21st Century China*. London: RoutledgeCurzon.

Gries, Peter Hays, Qingmin Zhang, H. Michael Crowson, and Huajian Cai. 2011. "Patriotism, Nationalism, and China's US Policy: Structures and Consequences of Chinese National Identity." *The China Quarterly* 205:1–17.

Guo, Yingjie. 2004. "Barking Up the Wrong Tree: The Liberal–Nationalist Debate on Democracy and Identity," in Leong H. Liew and Shaoguang Wang, eds., *Nationalism, Democracy and National Integration in China*. 23–43, London: RoutledgeCurzon.

Gurr, Ted. 1970. *Why Men Rebel*. Princeton, NJ: Princeton University Press.

Gyimah-Boadi, E. 1996. "Civil Society in Africa." *Journal of Democracy* 7:118–132.

Hall, Stuart. 1996. "Ethnicity: Identity and Differences," in Geoff Eley and Ronald Grigor Suny, eds., *Becoming National: A Reader*, 339–350. New York: Oxford University Press.

Han, Chunping and Martin King Whyte. 2009. "The Social Contours of Distributive Injustice Feelings in Contemporary China," in Deborah S. Davis and Wang Feng, eds., *Creating Wealth and Poverty in Postsocialist China*, 193–212. Stanford, CA: Stanford University Press.

Han, Zhenfeng, and Ji Shuyun. 2013. "The Origin and Development of the Party's Mass Line." *Guangming Daily*, July 3. http://qzlx.people.com.cn/n/2013/0703/c364565-22059661.html (accessed June 18, 2014).

Hastings, Adrian. 1997. *The Construction of Nationhood: Ethnicity, Religion, and Nationalism*. Cambridge: Cambridge University Press.

He, Baogang. 2004. "China's National Identity: A Source of Conflict between Democracy and State Nationalism," in Leong H. Liew and Shaoguang Wang, eds., *Nationalism, Democracy and National Integration in China*. RoutledgeCurzon.

Heath, Anthony, Stephen Fisher, and Shawna Smith. 2005. "The Globalization of Public Research." *Annual Review of Political Science* 8:297–333.

Hesli, Vicki L. 2007. *Governments and Politics in Russia and the Post-Soviet Region*. New York: Houghton Mifflin.

Himmelfarb, Gertrude. 2000. "The Demoralization of Society: What's Wrong with the Civil Society," in Don E. Eberly, ed., *The Essential Civil Society Reader*, 95–100. Lanham, MD: Rowman & Littlefield.

Hong, Jinhao. 2012. "From the World's Largest Propaganda Machine to a Multipurposed Global News Agency: Factors in and Implications of Xinhua's Transformation Since 1978," in Wenfang Tang and Shanto Iyengar, eds., *Political Communication in China: Convergence or Divergence between the Media and Political System?*, 117–134. New York: Routledge.

Horowitz, Donald L. 2002. "The Primordialists," in Daniele Conversi, ed., *Ethnonationalism in the Contemporary World*, 72–82. New York: Routledge.

Hsieh, John Fuh-Sheng. 2010. "Is the Kuomingtang Invincible?" in Wei-Chin Lee, ed., *Taiwan's Politics in the 21st Century: Changes and Challenges*, 25–40. Singapore: World Scientific Publishing Co.

Hu, Jintao. 2006. *Zhonggong Zhongyang Guanyu Goujian Shehui Zhuyi Hexie Shehui Ruogan Zhongda Wenti de Jueding* [Party Central Committee's Decisions on the Important Issues Regarding the Construction of Socialist Harmonious Society], http://politics.people.com.cn/GB/1026/4932440.html (accessed August 22, 2015).

Hu, Lianhe, Hu, Angang and Wang, Lei. 2006. "Yingxiang Shehui Wending de Shehui Maodun Taishi de Shizheng Fenxi" [An Empirical Analysis of Social Conflict and Social Stability], *Shehui Kexue Zhanxian* [Social Scientific Front], 4: 175–185.

Huntington, Samuel P. 1968. *Political Order in Changing Societies*. New Haven, CT: Yale University Press.

Huntington, Samuel P. 1993a. "The Clash of Civilizations?" *Foreign Affairs* 72, no. 3 (Summer): 22–49.

Huntington, Samuel P. 1993b. *The Third Wave: Democratization in the Late 20th Century*. Norman: University of Oklahoma Press.

Hutchison, Marc L., and Kristin Johnson. 2011. "Capacity to Trust? Institutional Capacity, Conflict, and Political Trust in Africa, 2000–2005." *Journal of Peace Research* 48, no. 6: 737–752.

Imai, Kosuke. 2011. "Multivariate Regression Analysis for the Item Count Technique." *Journal of the American Statistical Association* 106, no. 494: 407–416.

Inglehart, Ronald. 1999. "Trust, Well-Being and Democracy," in Mark E. Warren, ed., *Democracy and Trust*, 88–120. Cambridge: Cambridge University Press.

Inglehart, Ronald. 2007. "Postmaterialist Values and the Shift from Survival to Self-Expression Values," in Russell J. Dalton and Hans-Dieter Klingemann, eds., *Oxford Handbook of Political Behavior*, 223–239. New York: Oxford University Press.

Inglehart, Ronald, and Christian Welzel. 2005. *Modernization, Cultural Change, and Democracy: The Human Development Sequence*. New York: Cambridge University Press.

Inglehart, Ronald, and Christian Welzel. 2009. "How Development Leads to Democracy." *Foreign Affairs*, March/April:33–48.

Inkeles, Alex. 1974. *Becoming Modern: Individual Change in Six Developing Countries*. Cambridge, MA: Harvard University Press.

Inkeles, Alex. 1978. "National Differences in Individual Modernity." *Comparative Studies in Sociology* 1:47–72.

Jackman, Robert W. 1987. "Political Institutions and Voter Turnout in the Industrial Democracies." *American Political Science Review* 81, no. 2 (June) 405–423.

Jackman, Robert W., and Ross A. Miller. 1996a. "The Poverty of Political Culture." *American Journal of Political Science* 40 (3): 697–716.

Jackman, Robert W., and Ross A. Miller. 1996b. "A Renaissance of Political Culture?" *American Journal of Political Science* 40, no. 3: 632–659.

Jacobs, Andrew. 2009. "Seeking Justice, Chinese Land in Secret Jails." *New York Times*, March 9.

Jacobs, Andrew. 2011a. "Village Revolts Over Inequities of Chinese Life." *New York Times*, December 14.

Jacobs, Andrew. 2011b. "Harassment and Evictions Bedevil Even China's Well-Off." *New York Times*, December 27.

Jacobs, Andrew, and Chris Buckley. 2014. "Presumed Guilty in China War on Corruption, Targets Suffer Abuses." *New York Times*, October 19.

Jennings, M. Kent. 1997. "Political Participation in the Chinese Countryside." *American Political Science Review* 91 (June): 361–372.

Jennings, M. Kent. 2007. "Political Socialization," in Russell J. Dalton and Hans-Dieter Klingemann, eds., *Oxford Handbook of Political Behavior*, 29–44. New York: Oxford University Press.

Kahn, Joseph. 2005. "China to Drop Urbanite–Peasant Legal Differences." *New York Times*, November 3.

Kavanagh, Dennis. 1989. "Political Culture in Great Britain: The Decline of the Civic Culture," in Gabriel A. Almond and Sidney Verba, eds., *The Civic Culture Revisited*, 124–176. Newbury Park, CA: Sage Publications.

Keele, Luke. 2007. "Social Capital and the Dynamics of Trust in Government." *American Journal of Political Science* 51, no. 2: 241–254.

Kennedy, John James. 2008. "Maintaining Popular Support for the Chinese Communist Party: The Influence of Education and the State-Controlled Media." *Political Studies* (June): 1–20.

Kennedy, John James. 2009. "Legitimacy with Chinese Characteristics: 'Two Increases, One Reduction.'" *Journal of Contemporary China* 18, no. 60: 391–395.

Kennedy, John James. 2012. "What Is the Color of a Non-Revolution? Why the Jasmine Revolution and Arab Spring Did Not Spread to China." *The Whitehead Journal of Diplomacy and International Relations* 13, no. 1 (Winter): 63–74.

Kim, Ji-Young. 2005. "'Bowling Together' Isn't a Cure-All: The Relationship between Social Capital and Political Trust in South Korea." *International Political Science Review* 26, no. 2: 193–213.

King, Gary, Jennifer Pan, and Margaret E. Roberts. 2013. "How Censorship in China Allows Government Criticism but Silences Collective Expression." *American Political Science Review* 107, no. 2 (May): 1–18.

Kornhauser, William. 1959. *The Politics of Mass Society.* Glencoe, IL: Free Press.

Kubba, Laith. 2000. "Arabs and Democracy: The Awakening of Civil Society," *Journal of Democracy* 11, no. 3: 84–90.

Kuklinski, James H., Michael D. Cobb, and Martin Gilens. 1997. "Racial Attitudes and the 'New South.'" *Journal of Politics* 59, no. 2: 323–349.

Kuklinski, James H., Paul M. Sniderman, Kathleen Knight, Thomas Piazza, Philip E. Tetlock, Gordon R. Lawrence, and Barbara Mellers. 1997. "Racial Prejudice and Attitudes toward Affirmative Action." *American Journal of Political Science* 41, no. 2: 402–419.

Laitin, David, and Aaron Wildavsky. 1988. "Controversy: Political Culture and Political Preferences." *American Political Science Review* 82, no.2: 589–596.

Landry, Pierre F. 2008. *Decentralized Authoritarianism in China the Communist Party's Control of Local Elites in the Post-Mao Era.* New York: Cambridge University Press.

Landry, Pierre F. 2009. "Does the Communist Party Help Strengthen China's Legal Reforms?" in Pierre F. Landry, Yanqi Tong, and Mingming Shen, eds., *Markets, Courts and Leninism*, Special issue, *The China Review* 9, no.1 (Spring): 45–72.

Lane, Robert E. 1959. *Political Life: Why and How People Get Involved in Politics.* New York: Free Press.

Lane, Ruth. 1992. "Political Culture: Residual Category or General Theory?" *Comparative Political Studies* 25, no.3 (October): 362–387.

Lau, Richard R., and Redlawsk, David P. 2006. *How Voters Decide: Information Processing in Election Campaigns.* New York: Cambridge University Press.

Law Yearbook Editorial Committee. 2004. *Zhongguo Falü Nianjian 2004* [Law Yearbook of China 2004]. Beijing: Zhongguo Falü Nianjian She [China Law Yearbook Publishing House].

Lei, Ya-Wen. 2012. "The Political Consequences of the Rise of the Internet: Political Beliefs and Practices of Chinese Netizens," in Wenfang Tang and Shanto Iyengar, eds., *Political Communication in China: Convergence or Divergence between the Media and Political System?* 31–62. New York: Routledge.

Lemos, Gerard. 2012. *The End of the Chinese Dream: Why Chinese People Fear the Future.* New Haven, CT: Yale University Press.

Lewis-Beck, Michael S., Helmut Norpoth, William G. Jacoby, and Hebert Weisberg. 2008. *The American Voter Revisited.* Ann Arbor: University of Michigan Press.

Lewis-Beck, Michael S., and Andrew Skalaban. 1990. "The R-Squared: Some Straight Talk." *Political Analysis* 2:153–171.

Lewis-Beck, Michael S., Wenfang Tang, and Nicholas F. Martini. 2014. "A Chinese Popularity Function: Sources of Government Support." *Political Research Quarterly* 67, no. 1 (March):16–25.

Li, Cheng. 2007. "China's Leadership, Fifth Generation." *Brookings.* http://www.brookings.edu/research/articles/2007/12/china-li (accessed August 22, 2015).

Li, Lianjiang. 2004. "Political Trust in Rural China." *Modern China* 30, No. 2 (April): 228–258.

Li, Lianjiang. 2013. Hierarchical Trust in China. Paper presented at the Iowa Conference on the Rise of Public Opinion in China, October 18–19.

Li, Peilin. 2005. *Ling Yizhi Kan bu Jian de Shou: Shehui Jiegou Zhuanxing [The Other Invisible Hand: The Transformation of Social Structure]*. Beijing: Social Science Academic Press.

Li, Peilin, Guangjin Chen, Yi Zhang, and Wei Li. 2008. *Zhongguo Shehui Hexie Wending Baogao* [Social Harmony and Stability in China Today]. Beijing: Shehui Kexue Wenxian Chunbanshe.

Lieberthal, Kenneth. 2004. *Governing China: From Revolution Through Reform*, 2nd ed. New York: W. W. Norton.

Lieberthal, Kenneth, and Oksenberg, Michel.1988. *Policy Making in China: Leaders, Structures, and Processes*. Princeton, NJ: Princeton University Press.

Liebman, Benjamin. 2011. "A Populist Threat to China's Courts?" in Margaret Y. K. Woo and Mary E. Gallagher, eds., *Chinese Justice: Civil Dispute Resolution in Contemporary China*, 269–313. New York: Cambridge University Press.

Lipset, Seymour Martin. 1960. *Political Man: The Social Basis of Politics*. New York: Doubleday.

Lodge, Milton, and Charles S. Taber. 2005. "Implicit Affect for Candidates, Parties, and Issues: An Experimental Test of the Hot Cognition Hypothesis." *Political Psychology* 26, no. 3: 455–482.

Lorentzen, Peter L. 2013. "Regularizing Rioting: Permitting Public Protest in an Authoritarian Regime." *Quarterly Journal of Political Science* 8(2): 127–158.

Lu, Jie, and Tianjian Shi. 2015. "The Battle of Ideas and Discourses before Democratic Transition: Different Democratic Conceptions in Authoritarian China." *International Political Science Review*, January, 36: 20–41.

Lubman, Stanley B. 1999. *Bird in a Cage: Legal Reform in China after Mao*. Stanford, CA: Stanford University Press.

Lubman, Stanley B. 2000. "Bird in a Cage: Chinese Law Reform after Twenty Years." *Northwestern Journal of International Law and Business* 20, no. 3 (Spring): 383.

Lupia, Arthur, Mathew D. McCubbins, and Samuel L. Popkin, eds. 2000. *Elements of Reason: Cognition, Choice, and the Bounds of Rationality*. New York: Cambridge University Press.

Ma, Deyong. 2007. "Zhengzhi Xinren jiqi Qiyuan: Dui Yazhou Bage Guojia he Diqu de Bijiao Yanjiu" [Political Trust and Its Origins]. *Jingji Shehui Tizhi Bijiao* [Comparative Economic and Social Systems] 5: 79–86.

Mackerras, Colin. 2004. "China's Minorities and National Integration," in Leong H. Liew and Shaoguang Wang, eds., *Nationalism, Democracy and National Integration in China*. London and New York: Routledge Curzon.

Manion, Melanie. 1993. *Retirement of Revolutionaries in China: Public Policies, Social Norms, Private Interests*. Princeton, NJ: Princeton University Press.

Manion, Melanie. 1994. "Survey Research in the Study of Contemporary China: Learning from Local Samples." *China Quarterly* 139 (September): 741–765.

Manion, Melanie. 2004. *Corruption by Design: Building Clean Government in Mainland China and Hong Kong*. Cambridge, MA: Harvard University Press.

Manion, Melanie. 2006. "Democracy, Community, Trust: The Impact of Chinese Village Elections in Context." *Comparative Political Studies* 39, no. 3 (April): 301–324.

Manion, Melanie. 2010. "A Survey of Survey Research on Chinese Politics: What Have We Learned?" in Allen Carlson, Mary Gallagher, Kenneth Lieberthal, and Melanie Manion, eds., *Chinese Politics: New Sources, Methods, and Field Strategies*. 181–199. New York: Cambridge University Press.

Mann, James. 2000. *About Face: A History of America's Curious Relationship with China, from Nixon to Clinton*. New York: Vintage.

Manzetti, Luigi, and Carole Wilson. 2007. "Why Do Corrupt Governments Maintain Public Support?" *Comparative Political Studies* 40, no. 8 (August): 949–970.

Mao, Zedong. 1967. "Some Questions Concerning Methods of Leadership." *Selected Works of Mao Tse-tunq*, Vol. 3. Beijing: Foreign Languages Press.

Marx, Karl. 1867. "Expropriation of the Agricultural Population from the Land." *Capital*, Vol. 1, chapter 27, transcribed by Zodiac; html Markup by Stephen Baird (1999). http://www.marxists.org/archive/marx/works/1867-c1/ (accessed May 1, 2011).

McFarland, Sam G. 1981. "Effects of Question Order on Survey Responses." *Public Opinion Quarterly* 45, no. 2: 208–215.

McFauquer, Roderick. 2006, October 5. "Debate #1: Is Communist Party Rule Sustainable in China?" Reframing China Policy: The Carnegie Debates, Library of Congress, Washington, DC.

Meisner, Mitch. 1978. "Dazhai: The Mass Line in Practice." *Modern China* 4, no. 1 (January): 27–62.

Michelson, Ethan. 2008. "Justice from Above or Below? Popular Strategies for Resolving Grievances in Rural China." *China Quarterly* 193:43–64.

Miller, Arthur H., Vicki L. Hesli, and William M. Reisinger. 1994. "Reassessing Mass Support for Political and Economic Change in the Former USSR." *American Political Science Review* 88, no. 2 (June): 399–411.

Miller, Arthur H, William M. Reisinger, and Vicki L. Hesli. 1996. "Understanding Political Change in Post-Soviet Societies: A Further Commentary on Finifter and Mickiewicz." *American Political Science Review* 90, no. 1 (March):153–166.

Minzner, Carl. 2006. "Xinfang: An Alternative to the Formal Chinese Legal System." *Stanford Journal of International Law* 42:103–179.

Mishler, William, and Richard Rose. 2001. "What Are the Origins of Political Trust? Testing Institutional and Cultural Theories in Post-Communist Societies." *Comparative Political Studies* 34, no. 1 (February): 30–62.

Mishler, William, and Richard Rose. 2005. "What Are the Political Consequences of Trust? A Test of Cultural and Institutional Theories in Russia." *Comparative Political Studies* 38 (November): 1050–1078.

Nathan, Andrew. 2006. "Debate #2: Is Communist Party Rule Sustainable in China?" Reframing China Policy: The Carnegie Debates, Library of Congress, Washington, DC, October 5.

National Bureau of Statistics of China. 2004. *China Statistical Yearbook*. Beijing: China Statistics Press.

Newton, Kenneth. 1999. "Social and Political Trust in Established Democracies," in Pippa Norris, ed., *Critical Citizens: Global Support for Democratic Government*, 169–187. Oxford: Oxford University Press.

Newton, Kenneth, and Pippa Norris. 2000. "Confidence in Public Institutions: Faith, Culture, or Performance?" in Joseph Nye, Philip Zelikow, and David King, eds., *Why People Don't Trust Government?*, 52–73. Cambridge, MA: Harvard University Press.

Norris, Pippa, ed. 1999. *Critical Citizens: Global Support for Democratic Government*. New York: Oxford University Press.

Norris, Pippa. 2011. *Democratic Deficit: Critical Citizens Revisited*. Cambridge: Cambridge University Press.

O'Brien, Kevin J., and Lianjiang Li. 2005a. "Popular Contention and Its Impact in Rural China." *Comparative Political Studies* 38, no. 3 (April): 235–259.

O'Brien, Kevin J., and Lianjiang Li. 2005b. "Suing the Local State: Administrative Litigation in Rural China," in Neil J. Diament, Stanley B. Lubman, and Kevin J. O'Brien, eds., *Engaging the Law in China: State, Society, and Possibilities for Justice*. Stanford, CA: Stanford University Press.

O'Brien, Kevin J., and Lianjiang Li. 2006. *Rightful Resistance in Rural China*. Cambridge: Cambridge University Press.

O'Brien, Kevin J., and Rachel E. Stern. 2008. "Introduction: Studying Contention in Contemporary China," in Kevin J. O'Brien, ed., *Popular Protest in China*. Cambridge: Cambridge University Press, pp. 11–25.

O'Donnell, Guillermo. 1988. *Bureaucratic Authoritarianism: Argentina, 1966–1973, in Comparative Perspective*. Berkeley: University of California Press.

Olson, Mancur. 1971. *The Logic of Collective Action: Public Goods and the Theory of Groups*, rev. ed. Cambridge, MA: Harvard University Press.

Orlik, Tom. 2011. "Unrest Grows as Economy Booms." *Wall Street Journal*, September 26.

Page, Benjamin I., and Shapiro, Robert Y. 1992. *The Rational Public: Fifty Years of Trends in Americans' Policy Preferences*. Chicago: University of Chicago Press.

Parish, William L., and Martin King Whyte. 1978. *Village and Family in Contemporary China*. Chicago: University of Chicago Press.

Pearce, J. 1997. "Civil Society, the Market and Democracy in Latin America." *Democratization* 4, no. 2: 57–83.

Pei, Minxin. 2002. "China's Governance Crisis." *Foreign Affairs* 81, no. 5: 96–119.

Pei, Minxin. 2006. *China's Trapped Transition: The Limits of Developmental Autocracy*. Cambridge, MA: Harvard University Press.

Pei, Minxin. 2012. "China and East Asian Democracy: Is CCP Rule Fragile or Resilient?" *Journal of Democracy* 23, no. 1 (January): 27–41.

Perez-Diaz, V. 1994. *The Return of Civil Society*. Cambridge, MA: Harvard University Press.

Perkovich, Robert. 1996. "A Comparative Analysis of Community Mediation in the United States and the People's Republic of China." *Temple International and Comparative Law Journal* 10, no. 2: 313–328.

Perry, Elizabeth J. 1994. "Casting a Chinese 'Democracy' Movement: The Roles of Students, Workers, and Entrepreneurs," in Jeffrey N. Wasserstrom and Elizabeth J. Perry, eds., *Popular Protest & Political Culture in Modern China*, second edition, 74-92. Boulder, Co: Westview.

Perry, Elizabeth. 2001. "Challenging the Mandate of Heaven: Popular Protest in Modern China." *Critical Asian Studies* 33, no. 2: 163–180.

Peters, B. Guy. 1998. *Comparative Politics: Theory and Method*. New York: New York University Press.

Pharr, Susan, and Robert Putnam, eds. 2000. *Disaffected Democracies: What's Troubling the Trilateral Countries?* Princeton, NJ: Princeton University Press.

Pollock, Philip H., III. 1983. "The Participatory Consequences of Internal and External Political Efficacy: A Research Note." *Western Political Quarterly* 36, no. 3: 400–409.

Popkin, Samuel L. 1991. *The Reasoning Voter: Communication and Persuasion in Presidential Campaigns*. Chicago: University of Chicago Press.

Przeworski, Adam. 1991. *Democracy and the Market: Political and Economic Reforms in Eastern Europe and Latin America*. New York: Cambridge University Press.

Przeworski, Adam, and Fernando Limongi. 1997. "Modernization: Theories and Facts." *World Politics* 49, no. 2 (January): 155–183.

Przeworski, Adam, and Henry Teune. 1970. *The Logic of Comparative Social Inquiry*. New York: Wiley-Interscience.

Putnam, Robert D. 1995. "Bowling Alone: America's Declining Social Capital." *Journal of Democracy* 6:65–78.

Putnam, Robert D., with Robert Leonardi and Raffaella Y. Nanetti. 1993. *Making Democracy Work: Civic Tradition in Modern Italy*. Princeton, NJ: Princeton University Press.

Pye, Lucian W. 1996. "How China's Nationalism Was Shanghaied," in Jonathan Unger, ed., *Chinese Nationalism*, 86–112. Armonk, NY: M. E. Sharpe.

Rawls, John. 1999. *The Law of Peoples*. Cambridge, MA: Harvard University Press.

Read, Benjamin L. 2003. "Democratizing the Neighbourhood? New Private Housing and Home-Owner Self-Organization in Urban China." *The China Journal* 49 (January): 31–59.

Redlawsk, David P., Caroline J. Tolbert, and William Franko. 2010. "Voters, Emotions, and

Race in 2008: Obama as the First Black President." *Political Research Quarterly* 63, no. 4: 875–889.

Reilly, Jonathan. 2013. "No Postmaterialists in Foxholes: Modernization, Nationalism and National Threat in the People's Republic of China." Paper presented at the University of Iowa's International Conference on the Rise of Public Opinion in China, Iowa City, IA.

Reisinger, William M. 1993. "Conclusions: Mass Public Opinion and the Study of Post-Soviet Societies," in Arthur H. Miller, William M. Reisinger, and Vicki L. Hesli, eds., *Public Opinion and Regime Change*, 271–277. Boulder, CO: Westview Press.

Reisinger, William M. 1995. "The Renaissance of a Rubric: Political Culture as Concept and Theory." *International Journal of Public Opinion Research* 7, no. 4: 328–352.

Reisinger, William M., Arthur H. Miller, and Vicki L. Hesli. 1995. "Public Behavior and Political Change in Post-Soviet States." *Journal of Politics* 57, no. 4 (November): 941–970.

Reisinger, William M., Arthur H. Miller, Vicki L. Hesli, and Kristen Maher. 1994. "Political Values in Russia, Ukraine and Lithuania: Sources and Implications for Democracy." *British Journal of Political Science* 24 (April): 183–223.

Ren, Jiantao. 2010. "Zai Zuzhi Lilun de Shiyezhong – Lun Dangnei Minzhu yu Renmin Minzhu de Guanxi" [The Organization Theory in Perspective: On the Relationship between Intra-Party Democracy and People's Democracy], *Scientific Socialism*, Vol. 1: 24–30.

Ren, Liying. 2009. *Surveying Public Opinion in Transitional China: An Examination of Survey Response*. Ph.D. dissertation, University of Pittsburgh.

Ren Zhongping. 2010. "Renda Shidu zai Shixian Dangnei Minzhu Daidong Renmin Minzhu Zhongde Zuoyong" [The Role of the People's Congress in the Promotion of People's Democracy from Intra-Party Democracy] *Social Sciences in Yunnan* 2:25–29.

Research Group, Organization Department of the Chinese Communist Party, ed. 2001. *Zhongguo Diaocha Baogao (2000–2001): Xinxingshi Xia Renmin Neibu Maodun Yanjiu* [China Investigative Report 2000–2001]. Beijing: Central Compilation & Translation Press.

Rhodes, R. A. W., Sarah A. Binder, and Bert A. Rockman, eds. 2008. *Oxford Handbook of Political Institutions*. New York: Oxford University Press.

Rice, Tom W. 2001. "Social Capital and Government Performance in Iowa Communities." *Journal of Urban Affairs* 23, nos. 3–4: 375–389.

Rigger, Shelley. 2010. "The Democratic Progressive Party: From Opposition to Power, and Back Again," in Wei-Chin Lee, ed., *Taiwan's Politics in the 21st Century: Changes and Challenges*. 41–68. Singapore: World Scientific Publishing Co.

Rogowski, Rondal. 1976. *A Rational Theory of Legitimacy*. Princeton, NJ: Princeton University Press.

Rose, Richard. 2007. "Perspectives on Political Behavior in Time and Space," in Russell J. Dalton and Hans-Dieter Klingemann, eds., *Oxford Handbook of Political Behavior*, 283–304. Oxford Handbooks Online.

Rousseau, Jean Jacques. 1762. *The Social Contract, or Principles of Political Rights*. Translated 1782 by G. D. H. Cole. http://www.constitution.org/jjr/socon.htm (accessed May 10, 2012).

Rowen, Henry S. 1996. "The Short March: China's Road to Democracy." *National Interest* 45 (Fall): 61–70.

Rucht, Dieter. 2007. "The Spread of Protest Politics," in Russell J. Dalton and Hans-Dieter Klingemann, eds., *Oxford Handbook of Political Behavior*, 708–723. New York: Oxford University Press.

Sabetti, Filippo. 2007. "Democracy and Civic Culture," in Carles Boix and Susan C. Stokes, eds., *Oxford Handbook of Comparative Politics*, 340–362. New York: Oxford University Press.

Saich, Anthony. 2007. "Citizens' Perception on Governance in Rural and Urban China." *Journal of Chinese Political Science* 12, no. 1 (Spring): 1–28.

Said, Edward. 1995. *Orientalism*. New York: Penguin Books. (Orig. pub. 1978.)

Salmenkari, Taru. 2010. "Searching for a Chinese Civil Society Model." *China Information* 22, no. 3: 397–421.

Sani, Giacomo. 1989. "The Political Culture of Italy: Continuity and Change," in Gabriel A. Almond and Sidney Verba, eds., *The Civic Culture Revisited*, 273–324. Newbury Park, CA: Sage Publications.

Sartori, Giovanni. 1970. "Concept Misinformation in Comparative Politics." *American Political Science Review* 64, no. 4 (December): 1033–1053.

Schmetzer, Uli. 1993. "Chinese Dissident Optimistic." *Chicago Tribune*, October 10.

Schuman, Howard, Stanley Presser, and Jacob Ludwig. 1981. "Context Effects on Survey Responses to Questions about Abortion." *Public Opinion Quarterly* 45, no. 2: 216–223.

Scott, James. 1979. *The Moral Economy of the Peasant: Rebellion and Subsistence in Southeast Asia*. New Haven, CT: Yale University Press.

Seligson, Mitchell. 2002. "The Renaissance of Political Culture or the Renaissance of the Ecological Fallacy." *Comparative Politics* 34, no. 3 (April): 273–292.

Shambaugh, David. 2015. "The Coming Chinese Crackup." *Wall Street Journal*, March 7.

Shen, Jie. 2007. *Labor Disputes and Their Resolution in China*. Oxford: Chandos Publishing.

Shi, Fayong, and Yongshun Cai. 2006. "Disaggregating the State: Networks and Collective Resistance in Shanghai." *The China Quarterly* 186 (June): 314–332.

Shi, Tianjian. 1996. "Survey Research in China," in Michael X. Delli-Carpini, Leonie Huddy, & Robert Y. Shapiro, eds., *Research in Micropolitics*, vol. 5: *Rethinking Rationality* (pp. 213–250). Greenwich, CT: JAI Press.

Shi, Tianjian. 1997. *Political Participation in Beijing*. Cambridge, MA: Harvard University Press.

Shi, Tianjian. 2001. "Cultural Impact on Political Trust: A Comparison of the People's Republic of China and Taiwan." *Comparative Politics* 33, no. 4 (July):401–419.

Shi, Tianjian. 2009. "The Gap between Distrust towards Officials and Distrust towards Regime in the PRC: A Cultural Explanation." Unpublished manuscript.

Shi, Tianjian. 2015. *The Cultural Logic of Politics in Mainland China and Taiwan*. Cambridge: Cambridge University Press.

Shi, Tianjian, and Jie Lu. 2010. "The Meanings of Democracy: The Shadow of Confucianism." *Journal of Democracy* 21, no. 4 (October): 123–130.

Shih, Victor, Christopher Adolph, and Mingxing Liu. 2012. "Getting Ahead in the Communist Party: Explaining the Advancement of Central Committee Members in China." *American Political Science Review* 106, no. 1 (February): 166–187.

Shirk, Susan. 2002. "The Delayed Institutionalization of Leadership Politics," in Jonathan Unger, ed., *The Nature of Chinese Politics, From Mao to Jiang*. 297–311, Armonk, NY: M. E. Sharpe.

Shirk, Susan. 2007. *China: Fragile Superpower*. New York: Oxford University Press.

Shirk, Susan, ed. 2011. *Changing Media, Changing China*. New York: Oxford University Press.

Shyu, Huo-yan. 2010. "Trust in Institutions and the Democratic Consolidation in Taiwan," in Wei-Chin Lee, ed., *Taiwan's Politics in the 21st Century: Changes and Challenges*, 69–99. Singapore: World Scientific Publishing Co.

Sigelman, Lee. 1981. "Question-Order Effects on Presidential Popularity." *Public Opinion Quarterly* 45, no. 2 (1981): 199–207.

Simon, Herbert. 1991. "Bounded Rationality and Organizational Learning." *Organization Science* 2, no. 1: 125–134.

Smith, Anthony D. 1983. *Theories of Nationalism*, 2nd ed. New York: Holmes & Meier Publisher.

Smith, Anthony D. 1995. *Nations and Nationalism in a Global Era*. Cambridge: Polity Press.

Smith, Anthony D. 1996. "The Nation: Real or Imagined?: The Warwick Debates on Nationalism." *Nations and Nationalism* 2, no. 3: 357–370.

Smith, Anthony D. 1998. *Nationalism and Modernism: A Critical Survey of Recent Theories of Nations and Nationalism.* London: Routledge.

Smith, Anthony. 2000. *The Nation in History: Historiographical Debates about Ethnicity and Nationalism.* Hanover, NH: University Press of New England.

Sniderman, Paul M. 2011. "The Logic and Design of the Survey Experiment," in James N. Druckman, Donald P. Green, James H. Kuklinski, and Arthur Lupia, eds., *Cambridge Handbook of Experimental Political Science*, 102–114. Cambridge: Cambridge University Press.

Sniderman, Paul M., Richard A. Brody, and Phillip E.Tetlock, eds. 1991. *Reasoning and Choice: Explorations in Political Psychology.* Cambridge: Cambridge University Press.

Song, Huichang. 2011. "Minzhu Zhengzhi yu Shehui Xinren" [Democratic Politics and Social Trust].*Xuexi Shibao* [Study Times], January 24. Published by the Communist Party of China Central Party School. http://www.studytimes.com.cn:9999/epaper/xxsb/html/2011/01/24/03/03_30.htm (accessed January 28, 2011).

Stockmann. Daniela. 2012. "Race to the Bottom: Media Marketization and Increasing Negativity Toward the United States in China," in Wenfang Tang and Shanto Iyengar, eds., *Political Communication in China: Convergence or Divergence between the Media and Political System?* New York: Routledge.

Stockmann, Daniela, and Mary E. Gallagher. 2011. "Remote Control: How the Media Sustain Authoritarian Rule in China." *Comparative Political Studies* 44, no.4 (April): 436–467.

Stokes, Donald E. 1962. "Popular Evaluations of Government: An Empirical Assessment," in Harlan Cleveland and Harold D. Lasswell, eds., *Ethics and Bigness: Scientific, Academic, Religious, Political, and Military*, 61–72. New York: Kraus Reprint Company.

Stolle, Dietlind, and Thomas R. Rochon. 1998. "Are All Associations Alike? Member Diversity, Associational Type, and the Creation of Social Capital." *American Behavioral Scientist* 42, no. 1 (September): 47–65.

Sun, Liping. 2011. "Chinese Society Speeds Up to Collapse" [Zhongguo Shehui Zhengzai Jiasu Zouxiang Bengkui], *Tengxun Pinglun* [Tencent Review] http://view.news.qq.com/a/20110215/000054.htm (accessed August 22, 2015).

Svolik, Milan W. 2012. *The Politics of Authoritarian Rule.* Cambridge: Cambridge University Press.

Taber, Charles S., Milton Lodge, and Jill Glatha. 2001. "The Motivated Construction of Political Judgments," in James H. Kuklinski, ed., *Citizens and Politics: Perspectives from Political Psychology.* Cambridge: Cambridge University Press.

Tang, Wenfang, 1993. "Workplace Participation in Chinese Local Industrial Enterprises," *American Journal of Political Science*, Vol. 37, No. 3, August: 920–940.

Tang, Wenfang, 1996. *Shui Lai Zuo Zhu? Dangdai Zhongguo de Qiye Juece* [Who Should Rule? Workplace Decision Making in Chinese Local Industries]. Hong Kong: Oxford University Press.

Tang, Wenfang. 2005. *Public Opinion and Political Change in China.* Stanford, CA: Stanford University Press.

Tang, Wenfang, 2009. "Dispute Resolution and Legal Reform in China." *China Review* 9, no. 1 (Spring): 73–96.

Tang, Wenfang. 2014. "The Worshiping Atheist: Diffused and Systematic Religiosities in China." *China: An International Journal* 12, no. 3 (December): 1–26.

Tang, Wenfang, and Benjamin Darr. 2012. "Nationalism in China." *Journal of Contemporary China* 21, no. 77 (September): 811–826..

Tang, Wenfang, and Gaochao He. 2010. *Separate and Loyal: Ethnicity and Nationalism in China.* Washington, DC: The East-West Center.

Tang, Wenfang, and William L. Parish. 2000. *Chinese Urban Life under Market Reform: The Changing Social Contract.* New York: Cambridge University Press.

Tang, Wenfang, and Qing Yang. 2008. "The Chinese Urban Caste System in Transition." *China Quarterly* 196 (December): 759–779.

Tarrow, Sidney. 2011. *Power in Movement: Social Movements and Contentious Politics,* 3rd ed. New York: Cambridge University Press.

Thireau, Isabelle, and Linshan Hua. 2007. "New Institutions in Practice: Migrant Workers and Their Mobilization of the Labor Law," in Wenfang Tang and Burkart Holzner, eds., *Social Transformation in Contemporary China: C. K. Yang and the Concept of Institutional Diffusion,* 65–88. Pittsburgh, PA: University of Pittsburgh Press.

Tilly, Charles. 1986. *The Contentious French.* Cambridge, MA: Harvard University Press.

Tilly, Charles. 1995. *Popular Contention in Great Britain, 1758–1834.* Boulder, CO: Paradigm Publishers.

Tilly, Charles. (2004). *Social Movements, 1768–2004.* Boulder, CO: Paradigm Publishers.

Tilly, Charles, and Sidney Tarrow. 2007. *Contentious Politics.* Boulder, CO: Paradigm Publishers.

Tocqueville, Alexis de. 2000. *Democracy in America.* Indianapolis, IN: Hackett Publishing.

Tong, Yanqi. 2009. "Dispute Resolution Strategies in a Hybrid System," in Pierre F. Landry, Yanqi Tong, and Mingming Shen, eds., *Markets, Courts and Leninism.* Special Issue, *The China Review* 9, no. 1 (Spring).

Tong, Yanqi, and Lei, Shaohua. 2014. *Social Protest in Contemporary China, 2003–2010: Transitional Pains and Regime Legitimacy.* New York: Routledge.

Torcal, Mariano, and Jose R. Montero, eds. 2006. *Political Disaffection in Contemporary Democracies: Social Capital, Institutions, and Politics.* New York: Routledge.

Tsai, Kellee S. 2007. *Capitalism without Democracy: The Private Sector in Contemporary China.* Ithaca, NY: Cornell University Press.

Tsai, Lily. 2007a. *Accountability Without Democracy: Solidarity Groups and Public Goods Provision in Rural China* (Cambridge Studies in Comparative Politics). New York: Cambridge University Press.

Tsai, Lily. 2007b. "Solidary Groups, Informal Accountability, and Local Public Goods Provision in Rural China." *American Political Science Review* 101, no. 2 (May): 355–372.

Tsebelis, George. 2002. *Veto Players: How Political Institutions Work.* Princeton, NJ: Princeton University Press.

Tsfati, Yariv, Riva Tukachinsky, and Yoram Peri. 2009. "Exposure to News, Political Comedy, and Entertainment Talk Shows: Concern about Security and Political Mistrust." *International Journal of Public Opinion Research* 21, no. 4: 399–423.

Tsou, Tang. 1986. "Reflections on the Formation and Foundations of the Communist Party-State in China," in Tang Tsou, ed., *The Cultural Revolution and the Post-Mao Reforms,* 259–334. Chicago: University of Chicago Press.

van den Berghe, Pierre. 1978. "Race and Ethnicity: A Sociobiological Perspective." *Ethnic and Racial Studies* 1, no. 4: 402–411.

Verba, Sidney, Norman H. Nie, and Jae-on Kim. 1978. *Participation and Political Equality.* Chicago: University of Chicago Press.

Wan, Jun. 2003. "Xin Shiji Zhongguo Gongchandang Chuantong Hefaxing Ziyuan Mianlin de Tiaozhan" [Challenges for the Traditional Resources of Legitimacy of the CCP in the New Century]. *Kexue Shehuizhuyi* [Scientific Socialism] 3:30–33.

Wang, Feng, and Tianfu Wang. 2007. "Categorical Sources of Income Inequality: The Case of Urban China," in Wenfang Tang and Burkart Holzner, eds., *Social Transformation in Contemporary China: C. K. Yang and the Concept of Institutional Diffusion,* 125–152. Pittsburgh, PA: University of Pittsburgh Press.

Wang, Shaoguang. 2009. "Minzuzhuyi yu Minzhu" [Nationalism and Democracy]. *Renwen yu Shehui* [Humanity and Society]. wen.org.cn (accessed March 22, 2009).

Wang, Weidong. 2012. "Chinese General Social Survey 2003–2011," unpublished paper, Renming University.

Wang, Zhengxu. 2005. "Before the Emergence of Critical Citizens: Economic Development and Political Trust in China." *International Review of Sociology* 15, no. 1: 155–171.

Wang, Zhengxu. 2006. "Explaining Regime Strength in China." *China: An International Journal* 4, no. 2 (September): 217–237.

Whyte, Martin King. 2010. *Myth of the Social Volcano: Perceptions of Inequality and Distributive Injustice in Contemporary China.* Stanford, CA: Stanford University Press.

Whyte, Martin King, and William L. Parish. 1984. *Urban Life in Contemporary China.* Chicago: University of Chicago Press.

Wines, Michael. 2011. "A Village in Revolt Could Be a Harbinger for China." *New York Times,* December 25.

Wnuk-Lipinski, Edmund. 2007. "Civil Society and Democratization," in Russell J. Dalton and Hans-Dieter Klingemann, eds., *Oxford Handbook of Political Behavior.* New York: Oxford University Press.

Womack, Brantly. 1990. "Party-State Democracy: A Theoretical Exploration," in King Yuh Chang, ed., *Mainland China after the Thirteenth Party Congress,* 11–29. Boulder, CO: Westview.

Womack, Brantly. 1991. "Review Essay: Transfigured Community: Neo-Traditionalism and Work Unit Socialism in China." *The China Quarterly* 126 (June): 313–332.

Womack, Brantly, and James Townsend. 1996. "Politics in China," in Gabriel A. Almond and G. Bingham Powell, Jr., eds., *Comparative Politics Today: A World View,* 6th ed., 438–491. New York: HarperCollinsCollege Publishers.

Wong, Timothy Ka-ying, Po-san Wan, and Hsin-Huang Michael Hsiao. 2011. "The Bases of Political Trust in Six Asian Societies: Institutional and Cultural Explanations Compared." *International Political Science Review* 32, no. 3: 263–281.

Woo, Margaret Y. K. 1997. "Adjudication Supervision and Judicial Independence in the P.R.C.," in Tahirih V. Lee, ed., *Contract, Guanxi, and Dispute Resolution in China.* New York & London: Garland Publishing, Inc.

Woo, Margaret Y. K. 1999. "Law and Discretion in the Contemporary Chinese Courts." *Pacific Rim Law & Policy Journal* 8, no. 3 (September): 581–616.

Wooldridge, Jeffrey M. 2010. *Econometric Analysis of Cross Section and Panel Data.* Cambridge, MA: MIT Press.

World Bank. 2002. *World Development Report.* New York: Oxford University Press.

Wright, Teresa. 2010. *Accepting Authoritarianism: State–Society Relations in China's Reform Era.* Stanford, CA: Stanford University Press.

Xi, Jinping. 2013. Speech at the 80th Anniversary Celebration of the Central Party School. 在中央党校建校80周年庆祝大会上的讲话, March 3. http://news.12371. cn/2013/03/03/ARTI1362258936670364.shtml (accessed November 29, 2014).

Xi, Jinping. 2014. *Tan Zhiguo Lizheng* [On Governance]. Beijing: Foreign Language Publishing House (Waiwen Chubanshe).

Yang, Dali. 2006a. *Remaking the Chinese Leviathan: Market Transition and the Politics of Governance in China.* Stanford, CA: Stanford University Press.

Yang, Dali. 2006b. "Economic Transformation and Its Political Discontents in China: Authoritarianism, Unequal Growth, and the Dilemmas of Political Development." *Annual Review of Political Science* 9:143–164.

Yang, Dali. 2007. "China's Long March to Freedom." *Journal of Democracy* 18, no. 3 (July): 58–64.

Yang, Mayfair Mei-Hui. 1994. *Gifts, Favors, and Banquets: The Art of Social Relationships in China.* Ithaca, NY: Cornell University Press.

Yang, Qing, and Wenfang Tang.2010. "Exploring the Sources of Institutional Trust in China: Culture, Mobilization, or Performance?" *Asian Politics & Policy* 2, no. 3: 415–436.

Zhao, Suisheng. 2004. *A Nation-State by Construction: Dynamics of Modern Chinese Nationalism.* Stanford, CA: Stanford University Press.

Zhao, Ziyang. 1944. "How Were the Masses Mobilized in Hua County?" *Issues and Studies* 19, nos. 6–7 (June and July 1983): 76–114.

Zheng, Yongnian. 1999. *Discovering Chinese Nationalism in China: Modernization, Identity, and International Relations*. Cambridge: Cambridge University Press.

Zheng, Yongnian. 2004. *Will China Become Democratic? Elite, Class, and Regime Transition*, Singapore, London, and New York: Eastern Universities Press.

Zheng, Yongnian. 2010. *The Chinese Communist Party as Organizational Emperor*. Routledge.

Zheng, Yongnian. 2014a. *Da Ge Ju: Zhongguo Jueqi Yinggai Chaoyue Qinggan he Yishi Xingtai* [Big Structure: China's Rise Should Go beyond Emotion and Ideology]. Beijing: Dongfang Chubanshe [Eastern Publishing House].

Zheng, Yongnian. 2014b. *Guanjian Shike: Zhongguo Gaige Hechuqu* [Crucial Moment: Where Is China's Reform Heading to?] Beijing: Dongfang Chubanshe [Eastern Publishing House].

Zhu, Jianhua. 1996. "'I Don't Know' in Public Opinion Surveys in China: Individual and Contextual Causes of Item Non-Response." *Journal of Contemporary China* 5, no. 12: 223–244.

Zweig, David, and Chung Siu Fung. 2007. "Elections, Democratic Values, and Economic Development in Rural China." *Journal of Contemporary China* 16, no. 50 (February): 25–45.

INDEX

Letters in *italics* following a page number indicate a figure (*f*) or table (*t*).